national WRITERS union

SECOND EDITION
COMPLETELY UPDATED AND REVISED

Freelance Writers' Guide

Edited by
JAMES WALLER

NATIONAL WRITERS UNION
National Offices: New York and Oakland

National Writers' Union
Freelance Writers' Guide
Second Edition

First edition published in 1995 as *National Writers Union Guide to Freelance Rates & Standard Practice*

Publisher:
National Writers Union
113 University Place
Sixth Floor
New York, NY 10003
tel: (212) 254-0279
fax: (212) 254-0673
www.nwu.org

Distributors to the trade in the United States and Canada:
Writer's Digest Books
An imprint of F&W Publications, Inc.
1507 Dana Avenue
Cincinnati, OH 45207
tel: (800) 289-0963
www.writersdigest.com

Editor:
James Waller, Thumb Print New York, Inc.

Editorial consulting/assistance:
Denell Downum, Amy K. Hughes

Cover and text design:
Jay Anning, Thumb Print New York, Inc.

ISBN 0-9644208-1-3

Library of Congress Control Number 00-092771

Printed and bound in the United States of America

10 9 8 7 6 5 4 3 2 1

Contents

Acknowledgments

"This book is a true product of collective labor": so wrote the editors of this *Guide* in the acknowledgments section of the first edition, published in 1995. The sentiment applies equally well to this second edition.

Many, many people participated in the second edition's creation. Foremost among them are those who contributed their writing talents: Joan E. Bertin, Mike Bradley, Cate T. Corcoran, Denell Downum, Alec Dubro, Betsy Feist, Bruce Hartford, JoAnn Kawell, Susan Lee, Judith Levine, David Lida, Yleana Martinez, Philip Mattera, Tommye-K. Mayer, Emma Morgan, Todd Pitock, Catherine Revland, Marcia Savin, Marie Shear, Jonathan Tasini, Ray Tennenbaum, Ken Wachsberger, and Keith Watson. It should be mentioned up front that the authors of bylined essays and credited sections generously donated their labor to this work. All the contributors did a superb job; they're owed the appreciation of the National Writers Union and all the users of this book.

The second edition of the *Guide* is built on the very solid foundation provided by the first. Much of what appears in these pages is the work of the first *Guide*'s project director, Judith Levine, and its writer/editor, Alex Kopelman. The text design of the present edition, though new, relies in important respects on the work of the first edition's designer, Kathryn Shagas.

Several people gave essential assistance by proposing names of writers who could lend their experienced, insightful voices to the *Guide.* For this help, Barbara Beckwith, Bob Chatelle, Ann Lewinson, and Emma Morgan have my thanks. Attorney Patsy Felch reviewed and updated the copyright sections of Chapter 1. Myrna Watanabe organized the creation of the *Guide*'s new chapter on NWU grievance procedures. Chris Wilson graciously consented to be interviewed for the "Writing for Performance" chapter. Bill Lynch helped me prepare the material on grant writing in Chapter 6 by sharing his experience as a development consultant.

Critical contributions to the *Guide*'s content were provided by Cate T. Corcoran (Chapter 3); Bruce Hartford, Andreas Ramos, Amy Rothman, and Elizabeth Chesla (Chapter 5); Betsy Feist (Chapter 7); Dean Paton (Chapter 8); and Ken Wachsberger (Chapter 10).

In the book's editorial production, I was assisted by Amy K. Hughes and Denell Downum. Both lent their substantial publishing-industry expertise, sizable research skills, and editorial and writing talent to the job; it couldn't have been done without them. Marie Shear also provided essential editorial help (and a shoulder to cry on). Amy Rothman, who helped out in many other ways, assisted in the preparation of the *Guide*'s index.

Putting together lists of prospective respondents to the targeted surveys conducted for this *Guide* was a tall order. Wanda Phipps, Rob Ramer, Andreas Ramos, and Ken Wachsberger provided me with essential contacts; Betsy Feist did the lion's share of work of lining up book-author and academic participants. I also thank the scores of writers who gave their time to complete the (in some cases) long and complicated survey forms.

National Writers Union officers and staff provided critical help throughout the book's production. NWU president Jonathan Tasini and secretary-treasurer Bruce Hartford were constant supporters of the project and lent assistance in countless ways. Kenya Briggs, director of the NWU's Job Hotline, generously provided the results of the Hotline's 1999 survey for use in this *Guide*. NWU staff deserving special mention are former operations manager Corrina Marshall, current operations manager Karen Ford, former BITE Division organizer Alice Sunshine, and Arlene Lopez and Marilynn J. Johnson. Members of the NWU's National Executive Board participated in the review of the manuscript; NEB reviewers not mentioned above in other capacities are Sarah Bewley, Dennis Demaio, Charlotte Dennett, Frank H. Free, and Susan Heinlein. Longtime NWU activist and book grievance head Phil Mattera was instrumental in getting this *Guide* published. Liz Koffel of F&W Publications, Inc., was a steady source of information and support. All these people have my sincere thanks.

An enormous debt of gratitude is owed my colleagues at Thumb Print New York, Inc.—Jay Anning and Areta Buk. Jay's superb design work is, of course, evidenced in the book you hold. Marian Appellof contributed essential advice during the job's early stages.

Finally, words can't express the degree to which I've relied, throughout this process, on the unflagging support of my life-partner, Jim O'Connor. I used to wonder why book authors and editors always credit their mates in the acknowledgments. Now I know.

—JAMES WALLER, Editor

Introduction

by Jonathan Tasini, President
National Writers Union

In the five short years since we published the first edition of this *Guide*, the world of working writers has changed dramatically. Almost every day, unparalleled opportunities and new dangers are unfolding before us. The overall trends? On the one hand, the explosion in electronic media is providing writers with uncountable new venues for putting their work before the public, as well as many new ways of earning a living from their writing. On the other, a handful of companies is exerting ever-growing influence over what creative works are written and published and how they are distributed and sold.

The *National Writers Union Freelance Writers' Guide* has two goals. First, it describes the rules being set by the people who define and control our work. Whether we like it or not, the rule makers are our adversaries, by which I mean simply that they have a different agenda than we do. Second, the *Guide* seeks to show that, if we understand the rules, we can shape them. The rules of our working lives are not inevitable or unchangeable. The *Guide* not only lets you know what the rules are, but it also lays out a path by which, working together, we can bend the rules in our favor.

So who are the rule makers and what are the rules? Well, by trying to tell you who the rule makers are months before you will see these words in print, I run a big risk, since the power centers are changing at a staggering pace. It's hard to keep track of who is doing what. But the "why" is easy enough to figure out. The fewer and fewer companies that control a larger and larger share of information and entertainment media worldwide are acting on two imperatives: (1) to own, control, and profit from what they are selling—in other words, content—and (2) to own, control, and profit from the means by which content reaches people, whether the pathways (like cable) for transmitting content or the tools for viewing or interacting with content (like your computer's operating system). In many cases, single companies are trying to accomplish both goals. The people who dictate our economic lives lead a neoteric industry that melds the once-separate corporate powers of publishing, cable, telephone, computing, consumer electronics, broadcast, and entertainment.

New Yorker media correspondent Ken Auletta has termed this combination of linked enterprises a global version of the Japanese *keiretsu*—a web of companies that invest in each other, do business with each other, and divide up the world to the exclusion of all other players. This is not a secret plot but a drama enacted right out in the open on the business pages. When these folks look at you, they don't see a "writer"; they see a lowly "content provider."

In the very first moments of the new century, we were greeted with a stunning representation of how the rule makers operate: the huge merger between America Online and Time Warner. This one deal, which some argued was ill-thought-out, perfectly illustrates how the worlds of content creation and content transmission are coming together. The new company's holdings cover an enormous territory: film production, music, publishing, cable and broadcast television, satellite communications, and the Internet.

Oiling the corporate transformation are national and international governmental and quasi-governmental rule makers. Here at home, bipartisan government policy is making sure that the information superhighway doesn't have a single stoplight that might slow the businesses hurtling toward the next IPO pot of gold. The nadir of this policy was the Telecommunications Act of 1996, whose ardent apostles pledged would usher in a new era of competition, giving consumers more choice and lower prices. Instead, of course, the law has given us less competition, higher prices (particularly for cable TV), and a rapidly consolidating industry.

Internationally, trade and investment agreements are giving media businesses the freedom to move money around without restrictions and to operate without government oversight. The World Intellectual Property Organization (WIPO), for example, seems interested only in protecting the interests of a handful of global media giants; individual creators get lost in the bargain.

So what are the rules? They are fairly simple. If you're a journalist, the picture is clear: the rule makers want all your rights—*forever*—and don't want to pay you more for taking them. When the *New York Times* issued its reprehensible all-rights contract in 1995, I called it an act of war against writers. If you're a writer of books, the rule makers want more rights up front, rather than allowing you to sell subsidiary rights down the road. And if you're a technical writer, the rule makers are demanding that you work for a temp agency that takes a big cut of your pay for very little in return.

So what do we do? The National Writers Union has laid out a three-pronged strategy for improving writers' working lives. The first prong is to arm writers with the information they need to negotiate better terms. This information is vital, since most of us have to deal as individuals with those who employ us. This *Guide* tells you what the lay of the land is, and what you can demand.

The second prong is to work together—as a union—to fight abuses like all-rights contracts and unfair terms for technical writers. The NWU does this on many fronts. For example, we backed a landmark lawsuit to fight the theft of our work in electronic media—and in September 1999 we won a historic victory.

The third element in this strategy is to create models and programs that enable us to shape and control our working conditions in the global digital environment. The NWU built the first-ever genuine licensing system for free-lance writers, the Publication Rights Clearinghouse, to make sure that you get paid every time your work is used. We countered the rip-off temp agencies with a union-friendly alternative so that technical writers can keep a larg-er share of their hard-earned money.

Beyond these tools and campaigns, though, we must work on our own perception of what it means to be an economically successful writer. We writ-ers are used to celebrating our individuality, our uniqueness, but we must also understand that individuals by themselves have very little power. We can gain power only by marshaling a collective voice. That's why we have a union.

Some of you may never have had the privilege of belonging to a union. In buying the *Guide,* you may be learning about the National Writers Union for the first time. So let me share with you what I think a union means.

The heart of a union is a common commitment to bring respect, dignity, and power to people at work. A union is a place to defend the weakest, not just the better-equipped or strongest, among us. It is a place to defend those who are different from us but who share a common bond. At its best, a union is a movement that sees ahead of the curve and that stands in the way of the few people of wealth who are bent on using their instruments of power to trample the many.

I'm glad you bought the *Guide.* But the best professional investment you will ever make is the check you write for your National Writers Union dues. Do it soon, and begin feeling a new sense of power.

About This Guide

The *National Writers Union Freelance Writers' Guide* is the second, revised and expanded, edition of a book initially published in 1995 as *The National Writers Union Guide to Freelance Rates & Standard Practice.* The NWU conceived the first edition in response to an almost complete lack of current, reliable information about freelance writing rates and publishing industry practices. Five years later, the *Guide,* representing the collective wisdom of writers like you, remains the only book of its kind. Unlike other writers' guides, it does not present what publishers say they do but rather what we know to be the real conditions of our daily worklives—and how the union believes those conditions should change.

The data in this second edition are largely based on three surveys of working writers conducted by the union. The first, taken in 1997, was a survey of business, instructional, technical, and electronic writers (whom the union refers to, collectively, as "BITE" writers). The second was a survey of writers participating in the NWU Job Hotline, conducted by the Hotline in the summer of 1999. The third, taken in the winter/spring of 2000, was a targeted survey of writers in various genres specifically intended to update and supplement the results of a large-scale survey of more than 1,200 writers performed for the *Guide's* first edition. The results of these surveys are augmented by other information collected by the NWU, by data gathered by other organizations, and by interviews with writers, editors, agents, and publishers. In a very few cases, this edition of the *Guide* reproduces statistical information from the first. We have done this only where we believe the information remains substantially accurate.

Part 1, "The Markets," begins with a chapter, "The Business of Writing," that includes information of general interest to all writers. It is followed by a series of chapters that address in greater detail the specific concerns of writers in particular genres. In addition to the areas covered in the first edition (books, journalism, technical writing, corporate/not-for-profit communications, literary magazines, and academic writing), this edition of the *Guide* includes new sections on instructional writing and on writing for performance. Recognizing the explosion in electronic media and the growing importance of the World Wide Web, this edition also includes a substantially expanded chapter on emerging issues in electronic publishing.

Part 2, "The Politics of Writing," offers a discussion of censorship issues and three perspectives on publishing-industry issues faced by writers who are members of underrepresented minorities—writers of color, writers with disability, and queer writers. Part 3, "About the Union," gives an overview of the National Writers' Union—its history and the services it provides to its members. Scattered throughout the book is a series of "Writing Life" essays in which writers working in the various genres offer first-person accounts of their careers and give experience-based advice to writers new to those fields.

The icons that appear in page margins throughout the *Guide* are meant to give instant visual cues to points of particular importance or interest. (A key to the icons appears in the sidebar.)

Written by working writers for working writers, the *Guide* is designed to be flexible and accessible. It is not meant to be a manual on how to become a professional writer but rather a convenient and useful reference tool for professional writers who want to improve their economic conditions.

Although this book is addressed primarily to writers, it is our hope that people who hire writers will also find it useful in negotiating fair contracts and compensation. Equitable, professional standards in all freelance markets will help writers and publishers work together more closely to bring forth better news stories, brochures, poems, manuals, features, books, scholarly articles—better *writing*—in a more just industry.

Icons: A Key

 NWU recommends. The thumbs-up icon emphasizes particularly important pieces of advice.

 Warning. The traffic-sign icon draws your attention to publishing-industry practices that you should be especially wary of.

 Website. The spider icon points out URLs of websites containing valuable information.

 Cross-references. Left- and right-pointing arrows tell you where in this *Guide* you can find additional information about a matter being discussed in the text.

PART 1

The Markets

The Business of Writing

Writing is a difficult business. As writers, we struggle with self-doubt, fear of exposure, rejection, isolation, writer's block, and a host of other psychological hobgoblins. But, as difficult as the emotions of writing are, most freelance writers will agree that the toughest thing about writing is making a living from their craft.

We are not talking about getting assignments and getting published. We are talking about pay rates and earning a fair share of the value we create.

The major reason for writers' economic plight remains our relationship with publishers

Even many full-time working freelance writers have a hard time paying their bills with what they earn from writing alone. In a survey of National Writers Union members conducted in 1995, we found that only slightly over 50 percent of responding writers had annual freelance incomes of more than $10,000. And these were not novice writers: close to 85 percent described their careers as "established" or "moderately established." By all indications, things haven't changed much in the intervening years.

Why are writers so poorly paid? The causes are complex and varied, but the major underlying reason for freelance writers' economic plight remains our relationship with the publishers and other businesses and organizations that hire us.

This relationship is defined by two interconnected factors: the absence of minimum standards for compensation and working conditions, and a profound power imbalance between writers and publishers. (Note: For the sake of convenience, *publisher* is used to mean "anyone who hires writers" and *freelancer* to mean "any independently employed writer.")

WRITERS AND PUBLISHERS

Samuel Johnson once said that "no man but a blockhead ever wrote except for money." His sentiment is in direct conflict with the widespread image of the writer as a gaunt artist pounding away at the keyboard in blind dedication to the craft, oblivious to cold, hunger, and all other adversity. This metaphor of writing as a self-sacrificing search for meaning and self-expression is deeply rooted in our culture and in the hearts of many writers.

The metaphor is certainly flattering, since it communicates the discipline and commitment required of a writer. But it is also deceptive and dangerous, because it perpetuates the view of writing as the fulfillment of one's creative urge, not a labor for which one gets paid.

It is incumbent on us to become our own business managers

This conception is, in part, responsible for the imbalance of power that exists between writers and publishers. Many writers consider themselves lucky to be published, regardless of how well they get paid, or in some cases whether they get paid at all. We fear and loathe rejection, and when someone likes our work well enough to pay us for it, we dare not risk alienating him or her by asking for a higher fee or a better contract.

Publishers, on the other hand, are not emotionally invested in the business. Their primary goal is to maximize profits, and the best way to do that is to minimize costs. The arithmetic is simple. It's in the publisher's best interest to pay the writer as little as possible.

This is not to say that publishers are mean, greedy people who live to cheat starving writers out of decent pay. They are, for the most part, honest people doing their jobs—acquiring the best possible writing at the lowest possible price.

The relationship between writer and publisher is thus inherently problematic, since it pits the interests of an individual against those of a corporate structure. Although these interests coincide to a certain degree, they are at odds in some crucial respects. And big corporations, especially, with their large financial and human resources, are invariably in a better position to protect their interests.

The problem is exacerbated by the fact that many writers feel uncomfortable with the *business* of writing—setting and negotiating fees, reviewing contracts, selling rights, and so on. By shying away from these issues, we often leave the decisions about how much we get paid, and on what conditions, to the publishers. Not surprisingly, the compensation and conditions we are given are frequently not in our favor.

To correct this imbalance of power, it is incumbent on us to become our own business managers. We need to learn to step out of the role of writer and into the role of entrepreneur. Until writers stand together and take an active, equal part in setting compensation rates and determining working conditions, we cannot hope to improve our economic and professional lives. We believe that, to do this successfully, writers need a union in which they can work collectively to make their individual lots better.

STANDARDS

"Fine," you say, "I am willing to roll up my sleeves and negotiate, but how do I know what value my work has in the marketplace?"

How does any of us know what our work is worth and what conditions are acceptable? We can all determine what we need to earn every month in order to live. We can say what we would like to get paid for a particular piece. Some of us can even tell which rights we want to sell and which we'd prefer to keep. But most of this is guesswork, and more often than not we end up accepting the publisher's "standard."

The fact of the matter, though, is that there are few real standards in the industry. Even individual publishers rarely have standards for rates paid to freelance writers. Rates are set more or less arbitrarily on a case-by-case basis. Many journalists, for example, have had the experience of doing a story very similar to one they had done for the same editor six months earlier, only to find that the fee is less than what they got the first time.

In a way, it's paradoxical even to speak of a freelance writing industry, much less of industry standards. We freelancers produce such diverse creations as romance novels, software manuals, political speeches, poems, newspaper and magazine articles, and textbooks. And the organizations that employ us to write range from the huge media conglomerates that own a great many consumer magazines and publishing houses to small electronics manufacturers, large foundations, government agencies, and literary magazines with shoestring budgets.

It is, of course, impossible to develop uniform standards for such a broad range of economic activity. It is, however, quite possible to look at the industry as a collection of individual genre markets and to begin to articulate standards for each.

This book does precisely that: it gives writers in the major freelance markets benchmarks by which to judge the value of their work in the marketplace and the working conditions afforded by their contracts.

RIGHTS

Legal rights in our work and the ability to sell and license these rights are at the foundation of writers' economic lives. To empower ourselves professionally and financially, we must understand the basic principles of the laws that grant us these rights, as well as the mechanisms for capitalizing on them. Let's have a look, then, at the concept of copyright and at the rights derived from it, at the concept of work for hire, and at what you need to know, in basic terms, when you consider selling any of the rights to your work.

Copyright

U.S. copyright law is based on a constitutional clause (in Article I, section 7) that empowers Congress to foster creative labor "by securing for limited times to authors . . . the exclusive right to their respective writings." The law thus essentially defines a writer's work as property that the author owns. This definition casts the relationship between writers and their works as an economic one, and the law is designed to safeguard an author's ability to profit from creative work by giving the author a monopoly, in the form of certain exclusive rights, to exploit the work for financial gain.

Works Eligible for Copyright. The Copyright Act of 1976 grants legal protection to "original works of authorship." What is an original work of authorship? Anything you write—that is, create rather than find or copy. For example, if you discover documentary evidence that J.F.K.'s assassination was indeed a high-level government conspiracy and publish a book based on this evidence, you will own the copyright to the book you write (that is, how you express the story or present the information) but not to the facts you discover.

To qualify for copyright protection, the work must be "fixed in any tangible medium of expression, now known or later developed." In other words, a poem you write on a cocktail napkin is eligible for copyright; one you write in the snow outside your lover's window is not. The issue of medium becomes particularly important as we move farther into the Electronic Age.

The Exclusive Rights. The current Copyright Act grants the owner of a copyright the exclusive right

1. *To make copies of the copyrighted work.* This means that no one is allowed to reproduce your work, in any form, without your permission. (There are some exceptions under the "fair use" doctrine, discussed below.)

2. *To develop derivative works based on the copyrighted material.* To put this simply, no one can transform your original work into something else—for instance, a movie producer cannot make a film based on a novel you've written—without your written consent.

3. *To sell, rent, lease, or lend copies of the copyrighted work to the public.* In other words, you have complete control over the life of your work and its distribution to the public.

4. *To perform the copyrighted work publicly.* Without your permission, no one can read from your work to an audience.

5. *To display the copyrighted work publicly.* Unless you agree to it, your poems cannot be plastered on billboards or posted on a website.

The right to *perform one's work by means of a digital audio transmission* is the sixth exclusive right, but this is limited to sound recordings.

By virtue of these rights, you, the author, have a legal monopoly in your work. The law, however, also provides that the author has the right to dispose of each individual exclusive right as he or she wishes. You can sell, lease, rent, license, or give away any of the rights. This makes it possible to sell various rights in the same copyrighted work to different buyers, possibly greatly increasing your income from the work. For example, you can sell the right to publish your book to hardcover, paperback, or electronic publishers; the right to print excerpts from the book to a magazine; and the right to make a movie based on the book to a film studio. The only condition governing the transfer of exclusive rights is that it be done in writing.

Infringement. Any violation of the six exclusive rights, except those specifically exempted in the Copyright Act and those designated "fair use," is an infringement of the copyright. For instance, if someone were to print and sell copies of your book without your permission, that would be an infringement. On the other hand, the copyright would not be infringed if someone bought a copy of the same book from a bookstore and then resold it.

Copyright infringement is punished in a variety of ways. A court may issue an injunction against the infringer, thus putting an end to the offending activity. It may order the publication or use to cease. All profits from the infringement may be awarded to the owner of the copyright. The copyright holder may also be awarded monetary damages and lawyers' fees. Even criminal charges may be filed against the infringer in some instances.

Despite the law's dim view of copyright violation, however, infringement is not always easy to prove and is usually debated in each individual case. Particularly murky and difficult are issues of "fair use."

Fair Use. The best-known exception to the six exclusive rights is that for "fair use," which is a very complicated concept.[1] The basic idea is that the use of copyrighted material without the consent of the copyright holder should be permitted for certain purposes that educate or inform the public.

This principle was codified into a statute for the first time in the Copyright Act of 1976. The Act states that "the fair use of a copyrighted work . . . for purposes such as criticism, comment, news reporting, teaching (including multiple copies for classroom use), scholarship, or research, is not an infringement of copyright."

The Act also provides four factors to be used in determining fair use:

- *The purpose and character of the use.* This consideration is designed to determine whether the user is likely to make money from the unauthorized use of the copyrighted material without paying its owner. For example, if a teacher makes copies of an essay of yours and distributes them to her students, this will likely be considered fair use. On the other hand, if she charges the students for the essay, she is unfairly infringing on your copyright.

- *The nature of the copyrighted work.* A scholarly article, for instance, lends itself to commentary and study by others and is therefore more likely to be used "fairly" than an erotic short story. Out-of-print works are more likely to be the objects of "fair" unauthorized use, while unpublished works can almost never be used in this way.

- *The amount and substantiality of the portion used.* (In other words, how much and what is taken.) Several paragraphs from an essay may be considered fair use, while a couple of lines from a poem may be seen as an infringement. There are no definitive guidelines for this. Of course, the more that is taken, the less "fair" the use.

- *The effect of the use on the potential market for or value of the copyrighted work.* This means that if, by scanning your pamphlet *Twenty-*

---

1. The other 13 exceptions to the six exclusive rights are, in general, industry-specific uses that have been approved by Congress.

five Survival Tips for College Freshmen into his college's computer network, a dean undermined your ability to sell the pamphlet on campus, the use would be considered an infringement of your copyright. The economic impact is the most important consideration in determining fair use.

Questions of fair use are important to writers not only in protecting our own work but also in using the work of others. As fellow authors, we should be particularly careful to make fair use of each other's writing. The easiest test for a fair use is this: if the use cheats the original author out of a sale, it is *not* a fair use.

Registration and Duration of Copyright. Your work is protected by copyright law regardless of whether or not it is registered with the Copyright Office. A work, however, must be registered before an infringement suit can be brought to court. (The work can be registered after an infringement has been discovered, but post-infringement registrations will not allow you to recover certain kinds of damages and attorneys' fees. So register! For information on registering your work with the U.S. Copyright Office, visit the Library of Congress's website, at www.loc.gov/copyright/.)

Copyright protection extends for the life of the owner plus 70 years. In cases of joint ownership, the term of copyright is the life of the last surviving owner plus 70 years.

Copyright Notice. Although notice of copyright (© [year][author]) is no longer required by law, it is advisable to make sure it appears on any piece of writing to which you hold copyright. If nothing else, notice tells anyone reading your work that you are claiming copyright in it.

Copyright Ownership. The law is very clear on this point: copyright belongs to the author or joint authors of the work. **Be careful about collaborations, because each author of a collaborative work automatically gets all the exclusive rights and can do whatever he or she wants with the work without ever informing the coauthor.**

There is an important exception to this rule about copyright ownership. The copyright of "works made for hire" belongs to the writer's employer or the commissioning party (under circumstances outlined under "Work for Hire," below). Also, keep in mind—and advise your heirs—that the Copyright Act permits you under certain circumstances to recapture rights you have sold.

There are materials that cannot be copyrighted at all—notably, most titles and short phrases and any U.S. government documents.

The Oregon Local of the National Writers Union has prepared an excellent website giving answers to frequently asked questions about copyright and providing links to many other sites containing information about copyright law. Visit it at www.oregonwriters.org/copyright.html.

Selling Rights

Copyright is one of the most precious possessions a writer has. From it derive the rights to our work that we sell, lease, and license to earn a living. Clearly, copyright is not a possession to be given away lightly. Many writers, unfortunately, let themselves be intimidated into relinquishing the copyright to their work.

Of course, holding on to the copyright of some types of work makes no sense since the subrights are virtually impossible to exploit. For instance, it is highly improbable that you could sell movie rights to an instructional manual for a forklift. On the other hand, signing over the copyright to a magazine article about propane poisoning among forklift operators might deprive you of the income from a potential television deal.

In general, unless you are fairly certain that you cannot derive any additional benefits from the copyright, do not sign over the copyright to your work.

What about the rights derived from the copyright? How do you know which to sell and which to keep? As a rule, the more single-purpose rights you can sell, the more money you can make from your work. For example, if in the agreement with the publisher of your most recent book, *Stories on Tap: A Winter in the Bars of Alaska,* you grant the publisher the merchandising rights (along with hardcover and paperback rights), you'll have to share the profits from the hot-selling caps, t-shirts, and jackets with the publisher. If you sell the merchandising rights directly to the company producing all the stuff, however, you get to keep all the money.

In general, when negotiating the grant of rights, consider what you might want to do with the work, what is possible, and who is best equipped to handle particular rights. The bottom line should always be how you can profit most from your work.

Work for Hire

It is crucial that writers understand the concept of "work made for hire"—or, as it is more frequently called, "work for hire"—because it completely

---

"Work for Hire" was prepared by Mike Bradley. © 2000 by Mike Bradley.

changes the rules of the game. In a generic sense, *work for hire* means work that you are hired to do as opposed to work that you do on your own. Sometimes it's explained as work that is done at another person's instigation or work that is not self-initiated. If you're hired as an employee, the work that you do for your employer is work for hire. For example, stories written for a newspaper by reporters on that newspaper's staff are work for hire. In contrast, if you're a freelance journalist and you pitch a story to a magazine, the story is self-initiated and it's not work for hire.

In copyright terms, "work for hire" has a set of much more specific meanings. Unless you're an employee, only certain types of works may be written as work for hire. Even with these works, strict conditions control whether the work-for-hire contract is valid. For example, an oral work-for-hire contract is invalid even though in all other respects it may be O.K.; so is a retroactive work-for-hire contract.

An oral work-for-hire contract is always invalid

In doing work for hire, a writer loses all rights immediately, so it's vital to determine whether a contract is using the work-for-hire designation legitimately. Nearly all technical writing and much business, education, and Web content writing are legitimate work for hire. On the other hand, few work-for-hire book contracts are legitimate because books seldom belong to one of the categories of work for hire as legally defined.

U.S. copyright law (Section 101, Copyright Act of 1976 [USC 17 §101]) requires that the following conditions be met in order for a work-for-hire contract to be valid.

- The work must be commissioned by the client, as opposed to the writer conceiving the work and selling it to the client. This makes it a work for hire in the general sense, that is, a work conceived by another party who hires the writer to create it.

- The work must be one of the types specified in the law.

- The contract must state that the work is a work made for hire. That is, it must use the words "work for hire" or "work made for hire"; if these words don't appear, it's not a valid work-for-hire contract.

- The contract must be a written contract signed by both parties.

Further, the law allows only these nine types of works to be written as work for hire:

- A contribution to a collective work—that is, a work in which a number of separate, independently copyrightable works are assembled into a collective whole, as in magazines or encyclopedias

- A part of a motion picture or other audiovisual work

- A translation

- A supplementary work (a "secondary adjunct to a work by another author," such as a product manual)

- A compilation (of non-copyrightable facts, such as TV or movie listings)

- An instructional text (a work "with the purpose of use in systematic instructional activities")

- A test

- Answer material for a test

- An atlas

Notice some of the types of written work that are generally not legitimate work for hire: books in a series and ghostwritten books (unless they're one of the valid types, such as translations), children's books, press releases, advertising copy, many analytical and marketing reports. Note, also, that if you write one of these kinds of works under an invalid work-for-hire contract, the work-for-hire aspects of that contract are unenforceable. Courts used to take a fairly loose view of mistaken work-for-hire contracts, but recent Supreme Court decisions have stopped that. A court will not enforce the copyright provisions of an invalid work-for-hire contract. You will own the rights even if you didn't intend to keep them.

There is a silver lining to work-for-hire contracts

After the legitimacy issue, the most telling difference between a work-for-hire contract and other kinds of writing contracts is that the former is a *service* contract in which the writer sells her labor rather than, as in traditional publishing, a *sales* contract in which she sells rights. In work for hire, the writer has no rights to sell—she loses all rights, and in a unique way. Through a legal fiction, the writer's employer or client is the author in the eyes of the law. As the writer writes each word, the rights to that word belong to the legal author (i.e., the client), not to her. This immediate loss of rights contrasts sharply with the practice in standard publishing contracts, where the rights belong to the writer until she transfers them, even if she is transferring all rights.

The immediate loss of rights is a serious matter—thus the importance of determining whether a work is legitimately a work made for hire. There is, however, a silver lining to work-for-hire contracts. Because the writer is performing a service, her work doesn't have to satisfy subjective standards of acceptability. Provided she hasn't breached the contract, the writer must be paid for every hour worked. If the client balks, the writer can sue in relatively inexpensive local courts instead of having to sue for infringement in prohibitively expensive federal court. This makes resolving disputes easier, because being sued is a heavy club to hold over a balking client's head.

CONTRACTS

When people think of contracts, they generally imagine devilish documents—pages and pages of ponderous legalese in triplicate—that make them sign away their first-born children and that are as likely as not to land them in court. Writers, in particular, seem to have an aversion to contracts. Maybe this is because the existence of a contract underlines the economic aspects of our profession, or maybe we are reluctant to ask for the conditions we want. Whatever the case, a great many writers work without contracts or do not pay attention to the contracts they sign.

This, to put it mildly, is imprudent. Contracts can and must be tools that help secure the compensation and working conditions we need and that protect our rights.

The Theory

Strictly speaking, any deal—or even any understanding—between two people is a contract, so long as it can be enforced by law. It does not matter whether the agreement is written or verbal. To be considered a binding legal contract, though, an agreement must represent a promise by each person entering the agreement to do something and an acceptance of each promise by the other.

An example will help. Let's say you want to write an article called "Teaching an Old Dog to Swim." You send a query to an editor you know at *Dog Fancy.* You and the editor talk things over and agree that you and she want to do business together. This, in itself, is not yet a contract. Then she offers to pay you $1,200 for a 1,000-word piece; you accept and promise to deliver the story in three months. You now have a contract, at least in theory.

The Reality

Now, let's look at real life. For writers, anything but a written contract is next to worthless. Verbal contracts are extremely difficult to enforce and therefore provide little legal protection.

In fact, the law requires written contracts in many instances. For example, throughout the United States, any agreement involving a task that will take longer than a year to complete—the writing of a book, for instance—must be made in writing to be binding. In many states, written contracts are required if any money is at stake.

Most important for writers, the U.S. Copyright Act demands a written agreement in instances where the owner of a copyrighted work grants exclusive rights in that work or transfers the copyright itself to another person (or organization).

Content

A contract should describe as explicitly and fully as possible all aspects of the agreement. The rights and obligations of each party are particularly important.

The contracts freelance writers deal with vary tremendously, as you might expect. At one extreme are the complex documents prevalent among book publishers; at the other are the assignment-confirmation letters used by many freelance journalists. (In such a letter, the journalist, after reaching a verbal agreement with the editor, spells out the terms of the agreement as she understands them and specifies that she must be informed in writing of any changes to the agreement.) There are some basic elements, however, that all writing contracts should contain, at minimum:

- *Scope of work.* A contract should always contain a detailed description of the work to be created, including content, editorial direction, and estimated length.

- *Rights.* The copyright of a work is by definition the property of the work's creator. It allows the author to sell individual publishing rights in the work. A contract should make it clear which publishing rights you are granting to the publisher, in what geographical area, and for how long. Beware contracts that seek to strip you of your copyright.

- *Fees.* The financial arrangement should be spelled out as fully as possible. This might include fees, advances, royalties, payment schedules, expense reimbursements, fees for additional work (such as rewrites beyond a certain agreed-upon number), and so on.

- *Time frame.* All deadlines have to be spelled out, along with procedures for extending deadlines.

- *Legal responsibility.* The contract should make clear the role and responsibility of each party in the event a claim or suit arises as a result of the work. The NWU strongly urges writers to try not to accept without amendment contracts that contain blanket indemnification clauses—provisions that place complete financial responsibility on the writer in case of a suit.

- *Termination.* The contract must clearly state the conditions under which the parties can break the agreement.

- *Disputes.* A procedure for settling disputes between the author and the publisher should be delineated by the contract. It is a good idea to specify arbitration as the primary method for resolving problems.

Negotiating

In some cultures, it is considered rude not to bargain at the marketplace. In others, it is looked on as simply foolish. In the United States, of course, we are not used to haggling; it is generally hard to get the manager of your local supermarket to come down on the price of frozen peas. But, even in this culture, no self-respecting businessperson accepts the first bid offered.

The moment a publisher offers you a contract, you are at the pinnacle of your power

Writers, unfortunately, tend to feel uncomfortable with the idea of negotiating. Many of us approach our business with the fear that if we ask for a higher fee, better terms, or even more reasonable conditions, we will simply be passed up for the next writer in line. As a negotiating posture, this attitude leaves a lot to be desired.

The crucial thing to remember is that, at the moment when a publisher (or any other client) offers you a contract, you are at the pinnacle of your power in the relationship. The publisher is saying, in effect, that you have something he or she wants.

If you view the situation this way, you begin to realize that you are in a position to discuss, and to a certain degree dictate, the conditions under which you would be willing to satisfy the publisher's wish. At this point, a dialogue can begin.

Ideally, you would open the discussion by presenting the publisher with your conditions in the form of a written contract. It is fairly rare in most freelance markets, however, for the writer to furnish the contract. Usually, the publisher provides the contract.

Most such contracts are written to serve as starting points for negotiations. They are, to one degree or another, "boilerplate"—language that generalizes terms common in the marketplace. There are, of course, certain points that are nonnegotiable, but you can at least talk about making changes to most clauses. Negotiating does not have to be bellicose. A lot can be accomplished through a calm exchange of positions, wishes, and needs.

The real trick to negotiating is having a carefully thought-out strategy. Consider what you want out of the deal. Then divide your wishes into categories based on desirability. For instance, you could look at the various provisions of a contract as (1) the things you would like but can give up without much pain, (2) the things you would give up only in exchange for something else, and (3) the things you absolutely cannot live without. You can then approach the negotiations with a series of demands and fallback positions. The goal is to get as much of what you want as possible, but not to back the other party into a corner where the only way out is to break off negotiations.

Finally, it is important to be realistic. Do not make wild demands, but be firm about asking for the things you want. By approaching negotiations in a professional, thoughtful way, you will make better deals.

In Case of Trouble

It is a fact of life that relationships between writers and publishers sometimes sour. It is essential that your contracts make provisions for such contingencies.

The situation you want to avoid is one where a dispute has arisen and you are forced to give in because you do not have the resources to fight a legal battle. Independently employed writers, even successful ones, are generally unable to take on the organizations with which they have contracts. **Therefore, negotiate hard to include an arbitration clause in your contract.**

Arbitration is a binding means of settling disagreements that arise between parties to a contract. It is less expensive and quicker than litigation. The particular advantage of arbitration is that it counters some of the power imbalance between writers and publishers.

There are several respected arbitration services throughout the country. The best known of these is the American Arbitration Association.

Negotiating over the Telephone

The most important part of negotiating a book or journalism contract is convincing yourself that you have a right to negotiate in the first place. Publishers count on the longtime practice of most writers to sign away all rights, no questions asked, in exchange for a correctly spelled byline. Your approach should be just the opposite: **Don't ever sign a boilerplate contract.** Publishers' contracts are written by publishers' attorneys for the sole benefit of publishers.

In addition, more than once I've heard a publisher tell me, "No one has ever asked for that before." **Don't be intimidated by this response.** Take it as a compliment. You have broken new ground for writers. (We thank you.) With a few exceptions, every publisher is willing to make concessions. Those that aren't—don't write for them. Dignity before byline—not to mention the additional income and the control over your work that come with negotiating.

In negotiating a book or journalism contract over the phone, follow these eight steps:

Step 1: "Self-hypnotize." Convince yourself that you're worth more than the boilerplate contract or you'll never convince the publisher. Two lines to say with conviction (practice speaking into a mirror before calling the publisher):

- "I am a professional writer."

- "That seems a little low to me." (I have to credit journalist Brett Harvey with this line. I can't emphasize enough how much this attitude has earned me. Say it slowly, then pause. Wait for the publisher to respond.)

Step 2: Know your contract. Book authors should refer to the book contract advice offered in this *Guide* (see pages 37–52) and, if they are NWU members, the *National Writers Union Guide to Book Contracts,* our Bible. Journalists should study the NWU's Standard Journalism Contract (see pages 97–101).

Step 3: Contact an NWU book or journalism contract adviser. If you're an NWU member, call your local or the National Office and request that you be assigned a contract adviser. Being able to tap into the NWU's contract advising network is one of the most valuable benefits of National Writers Union membership—for some members, this alone is worth the dues.

Step 4: Know your bottom line. In negotiating, you seldom get *everything* you want. The idea is to improve your contract as much as possible through compromise but not to be so rigid that you lose a potentially workable contract. On the other hand, not every contract is workable. What are your line-in-the-sand issues, the ones for which you would rather walk than compromise? Two rights to fight for in this so-called Information Age are copyright and electronic rights. As a book author, you want the right to profitably resell your books without penalty. What else matters to you? Only you know.

Step 5: Prepare an opening script and good notes. If you're comfortable on the phone and totally primed for negotiations, maybe an exact script isn't necessary. But remember the value of a good first impression in setting the tone of your conversation. A script is most important in helping you overcome your fear of negotiating. Write it down beforehand and practice repeating it until it sounds natural. Only then is it time to make your call or to accept a call from the publisher. Also, don't wing it or rely on memory during the negotiations. We're writers, not rememberers. Write down the points you want to make about every clause, including the first bids, the fallback bids, and the line-in-the-sand positions.

Step 6: Take notes during the negotiations. The act of note-taking empowers you and prepares you for the inevitable followup communications. Record dates of all phone correspondence, keep photocopies of all letters you send, print out all email correspondence, and record names of everyone you talk to, including secretaries.

Step 7: Take a day to think about your conversation before making any commitments. Don't feel compelled or pressured to make a snap decision over the phone. When you demand time to think, you are taking control. And, of course, the extra time allows you to psych yourself up and prepare a script if you need it.

Step 8: Be prepared to walk. Those writers who have no human dignity and are comfortable being stepped on can ignore this step. But, because you've read this far, you demand respect. You've already determined your line-in-the-sand issues in Step 4. If the publisher can't respect those terms, go elsewhere.

—Ken Wachsberger

Contract Help

The National Writers Union offers members help in contractual matters through its Standard Journalism Contract, the *NWU Guide to Book Contracts,* the "NWU Preferred Literary Agent Agreement," and other publications. The union also provides expert advice through its Grievance and Contract Division.

For more on the Grievance and Contract Division, see Chapter 14, "The Grievance Process," page 241.

Other writer's organizations, including the American Society of Journalists and Authors, the Authors Guild, PEN American Center, the Dramatists Guild, Science Fiction Writers of America, and Poets & Writers, also offer publications and advice about contracts.

Volunteer Lawyers for the Arts, with branches throughout the country, provides free or affordable legal services to artists, depending on income. For contact information, consult your local telephone directory or type "volunteer lawyers for the arts" into a Web search engine to find the website of your state's branch of the organization.

INDEPENDENT CONTRACTORS, AGENCIES, AND THIRD-PARTY EMPLOYERS

Many business, instructional, technical, and electronic writers—whom the NWU refers to as "BITE" writers—work for clients other than publishers, and many work under work-for-hire agreements in which the copyrights belong to the clients.

Traditionally, freelance BITE writers worked as independent contractors who set their own hours, controlled their own labor process, and were responsible for handling their own taxes. In other words, they ran writing businesses and were eligible for standard business tax deductions. Because clients report freelancer payments to the Internal Revenue Service on an annual 1099 form, the term "1099 contractor" is often used to denote this way of working.

By contrast, an "employee" is on the staff of a company, which directs and controls the employee's hours and labor process. Employees are paid an hourly wage or an annual salary. Income taxes are withheld from the employee's paycheck and reported to the IRS on an annual W-2 form, hence the label "W-2 employee." While employees can deduct some kinds of business expenses, they are not allowed to deduct the full range of expenses that independent contractors can deduct.

"Independent Contractors, Agencies, and Third-Party Employers" was prepared by Bruce Hartford. © 2000 by Bruce Hartford.

Some writers who wish to work as freelancers use agencies to help them find work. In such cases it is common for the writer to be "employed" (as either a 1099 contractor or a W-2 employee) by the agency rather than by the client. When a writer works through an agency, the writer is paid at a certain rate, and the agency bills the client for the writer's labor at a higher rate. In other words, the agency charges a markup on the writer's services. The NWU believes that a reasonable markup to compensate the agency for its job-finding and money-handling services falls within the range of 15 to 25 percent for a 1099 contractor and 22 to 30 percent for a W-2 employee, depending on the services the agency offers the writer.

Unfortunately, many agencies today are charging markups of 35 to 50 percent—markups that in our opinion are unreasonable and exploitative. These excessive markups harm freelancers in two ways. First, if the client is willing to pay that much for the writer's services, the writer could—and should—be getting a higher rate. Second, extreme markups may make the freelancer's services so expensive that the client will be less likely to extend the term of the contract or to provide additional work at that rate. Moreover, when freelance writers are paid as W-2 employees by an agency, they lose some of the business tax deductions they would enjoy as 1099 contractors.[2]

Agency markups of 35 to 50 percent harm freelancers

In recent years many clients have begun to insist that freelancers become W-2 employees of agencies (also called "third-party employers") even though the freelancers have found their jobs on their own without any agency involvement. Clients commonly claim that they are adopting this practice out of fear that the IRS will unilaterally reclassify independent contractors as "common law" or "de facto" employees and will impose large fines and penalties on the firm contracting the work.

The National Writers Union believes that freelance writers should be allowed to continue working in the traditional way as independent contractors. We also believe that forcing freelancers to work through third parties does not actually avoid IRS risks. In fact, this practice is actually detrimental to the client as well as writer. When an agency takes an excessive markup—one-third to one-half of what the client pays for the writer's labor and talent—the client's money is wasted.

---

2. In another exploitative practice, some corporations are now unilaterally converting their employees into pseudo-contractors as a way of stripping them of benefits and union protection. These employees are being told that in order to keep their jobs they must become "employees" of a temporary agency. This process, known as "permatemping," is strongly opposed by the NWU.

Agencies argue that their markups are paid by the client and not the writer and that, so long as the writer receives a "fair" rate, what the agency gets is none of the writer's business. This argument is absurd. The writer is doing the work; the agency just shuffles paper. If the client is willing to pay $60 an hour for the writer's labor and talent, the writer should be getting as much of that as possible. The agency's decision that, say, $35 an hour is a "fair" rate to pay the writer is capricious and exploitative.

Some corporate clients mandate that writers use a single favored temp agency

Some corporate clients are not only insisting that freelancers work through agencies, but they are also mandating that the writers must use a single favored agency. This creates a monopoly in which one agency has a lock on a client's business and therefore has no reason to compete for writers by offering better terms and services. The NWU's position is that writers should have free choice of agency. When we freelancers find jobs on our own but the client insists that we work through an agency, we should at least have the right to chose the third-party employer that offers us the best terms.

Some of the worst agencies, knowing full well that their markups are outrageous, now insist that writers sign contracts that prevent them from disclosing to the client (or anyone else) how little of the client's money is actually going to the writer. And they also try to get clients to agree not to divulge to the writer what they are actually paying for the writer's work. We strongly oppose such clauses. When deeds are done in darkness it is because the doer knows they cannot stand the light of scrutiny.

Most agencies offer no health, pension, vacation, or other benefits *or* they offer phony benefit plans that few can qualify for or actually use. To ensure that writers have some decent agencies to choose among, the NWU is now negotiating union contracts with some agencies that limit their markup and mandate real benefits.

For more information on these issues, visit the BITE Division section of the NWU website, at <u>www.nwu.org/bite/bitehome.htm</u>.

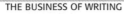

SELF-INCORPORATION

Some writers, particularly technical, business, electronic, and other writers who work under contract for non-publisher clients, are finding it advantageous to self-incorporate. More and more writers are turning to self-incorporation primarily because an increasing number of clients now hesitate to

---

"Self-Incorporation" was prepared by Bruce Hartford. © 2000 by Bruce Hartford.

hire and pay individuals on a direct 1099-contractor basis, as had been common practice for many decades. Clients who are afraid of contracting with individual freelancers are often willing to contract with a writer's corporation, particularly if the writer operates the business on a "vendor" basis.

Incorporation isn't for everyone, but for those with gross writing incomes over $50,000 per year, the business and tax advantages of incorporating may significantly exceed the additional costs.

More and more writers are turning to self-incorporation

To increase your chances of obtaining work from clients who hesitate to sign 1099 contracts, you should consider setting yourself up as a *vendor.* When you work as a vendor, your client pays your corporation and your corporation pays you. The client treats your business as it does other firms that provide goods and services. The client does not file a W-2 or a 1099 for you with the IRS, and you may work from a purchase order rather than a contract.

To be a vendor you must be incorporated *and* meet additional requirements mandated by your client. Besides incorporation, most clients require the following of their vendors:

- That you pay yourself a W-2-type salary equal to at least half of what your corporation is being paid for your services. You must also pay all federal, state, and local payroll taxes and other legally mandated withholding such as Social Security, Medicare, unemployment insurance, and so on.

- That you carry workers' compensation insurance ($500,000 minimum) and general commercial liability insurance ($1 million minimum).

Additionally, some clients may require that you have a business license. A few are beginning to require that you carry errors and omissions insurance. The Media Perils insurance that you can obtain through the NWU usually suffices for this. (For more information on the NWU's Media Perils policy, visit the NWU's website, at www.nwu.org.)

When you're a vendor, everybody's happy. The federal government is happy because you're paying yourself a salary from which the IRS can grab withholding taxes. The state is pleased because you are paying into its unemployment and other insurance programs. The client's glad not to have to worry about regulations regarding who is and who is not an employee. And you're content because, when the contract ends and you're out of work, your corporation can lay you off and you can collect unemployment benefits until your company finds another client and rehires you.

Regardless of whether they intend to become vendors or not, most writers who choose to incorporate do so as an "S"-type corporation. S corporations are designed for single individuals or a few partners. S corporations do not have to pay any federal income taxes. (Though, of course, profit and loss flow through to the corporation's shareholders, whose incomes *are* taxed.) State laws vary, but as a general rule state taxes are lower for S corporations than for other kinds of corporations.

Self-incorporation is not difficult. You can pay a lawyer several hundreds (or thousands!) of dollars to do it for you. Or you can get a book, forms, and software from Nolo Press (www.nolopress.com) and do it yourself for very little money.

The biggest headache of being a vendor is paying yourself your W-2 salary. The procedure is absurdly complex and time-consuming. The best way to handle this is to use a commercial payroll service to perform all the necessary transactions, reports, and deposits. If you pay yourself only once a month, a reliable service should cost no more than $30 a month.

Of course, if you're incorporated, you do have to submit two sets of tax returns, one for you as an individual and one for your corporation. The tax implications of being incorporated and operating as a vendor will vary according to your individual circumstances. Meeting with an accountant to discuss how to set up and run your business can be a very wise investment. And in the long run you'll save money by having your taxes done by a professional.

ERGONOMICS

Till now we've talked mostly about the financial aspects of a writing career. The effects of writing—day in, day out—on your physical health are just as important.

Computers can cause painful and debilitating repetitive strain injuries

While computers have been a boon to writers in many ways, they can also cause painful and debilitating repetitive strain injuries (RSIs). Repetitive strain injuries, also known as repetitive motion disorders or cumulative trauma disorders, are injuries to the musculoskeletal system of the upper body.

Many people equate RSI with carpal tunnel syndrome, a swelling of the tendons inside a passage in the wrist that puts pressure on the median nerve (which travels through this passage). Carpal tunnel syndrome, however, is only one of the many injuries to the soft tissue, muscles, ligaments, tendons, and nerves that can develop from using the computer. Bursitis, ten-

"Ergonomics" was prepared by Betsy Feist. © 2000 by Betsy Feist.

dinitis, trigger finger, and ganglion cysts are among the many other common RSIs. More obscure conditions include DeQuervain's disease, epicondytitis, and thoracic outlet syndrome. Symptoms include aching, tenderness, swelling, pain, tingling, numbness, weakness, decreased coordination, and decreased range of motion.

The most ergonomic work environment is the one that best fits you as an individual

RSI symptoms do not necessarily occur while or even immediately after working at the computer. You might, for example, be awakened during the night with pain, numbness, or a tingling sensation in your hands. It may therefore be easy to miss the connection between the symptoms and the work you do every day. **It is unwise to wait for the symptoms to become intolerable before seeking medical help; early treatment can make the difference between a few sessions with a physical therapist and a lifetime of pain.** Of course, it's an even better idea to avoid developing RSI altogether.

Among the factors that can contribute to RSI are these:

- *Repetition*—the cumulative number of times you strike keys or click the mouse

- *Speed*—the pace at which you work

- *Force*—how hard you hit the keys

- *Awkward or fixed posture*—sitting in positions that put stress on your body and remaining immobile for long periods

- *Lack of rest*—too many uninterrupted hours at the computer

- *Job stress*—including deadline pressure

Many of these risk factors can be controlled by changing your work habits. You can, for example, take frequent short breaks, vary your routine, and learn to strike keys more gently. Others can be addressed by modifying your furniture and tools.

People come in a wide range of shapes and sizes, so the most important point to keep in mind is that the most ergonomic work environment is the one that best fits you as an individual. Adjustability is key. You need a chair that can be adjusted to the right height for you and that gives your back good support. The keyboard, mouse, and monitor all need to be in the correct position for you, as do any papers you are working from. You also need good, glare-free lighting. Many people also need special eyeglasses for working at the computer.[3]

If you work from a home office, you are in control of your environment. An ergonomic upgrade can be expensive, however. The single most important purchase you can make is a good chair, one that is completely (and easily) adjustable for height, back support, seat angle, and so on. Other improvements—such as buying a keyboard tray or using a phone book to raise the height of your monitor—can be made inexpensively or for free. (There are lots of alternatives to the standard keyboard and mouse; different writers prefer different solutions.)

If you work at a client's office, it may be much more difficult to make sure that your workstation is ergonomically sound. Many workplaces are ergonomic nightmares, and, to make matters worse, independent contractors are often given the furniture and equipment no one else wants. You can make some small improvements on your own, such as bringing in an inexpensive copy stand or a firm pillow to use for back support.

At the time of this writing, The federal Occupational Safety and Health Administration was in the process of introducing ergonomics standards for workers who use computers. Once these are in place, employees will have legal recourse to ensure a healthful work environment. Current labor law, however, is at the very least ambiguous about how such standards apply to independent contractors.

---

3. There are many books that provide detailed information on RSI. One highly regarded source is Emil Pascareli and Deborah Quilter's *Repetitive Strain Injury: A Computer User's Guide* (New York: Wiley, 1994).

It's *Your* Business: Take Charge of Your Financial Life Now

Susan Lee, EA, CFP

It's all too common for freelance writers to get themselves into trouble over taxes. People often take up freelancing without spending a lot of time thinking about how this new way of earning a living will impact their economic life.

For more than 20 years, I've worked as a tax consultant, specializing in helping writers and other freelancers to get and keep their financial house in order. Over my career I've seen many too many cases in which people have needlessly ended up owing money to the Internal Revenue Service. It's sad. You take up freelancing because of the joy of being able to do what you love to do. If you're a freelance writer, you want your writing to be at the top of your agenda. But if you let yourself fall into "Tax Hell"—which I define as continually owing money and always having to worry about it—that joy is lost. You'll spend too much of your time worrying about how you're going to meet your obligations to the IRS and survive at the same time.

You don't have to end up in Tax Hell. But to make sure you don't, you must take command of your own financial life. We tax consultants provide some very useful services, but a consultant is not a nursemaid. Nor is a consultant a priest who can give you "absolution" at tax time. And—unless you're comfortable financially—you may not find it worth your while to hire a bookkeeper to do your basic record-keeping. In fact, if you're running a very small business, you *should* do your own bookkeeping, so that you'll have the greatest control over your own cash flow. In other words, freelancing isn't only what you do, it's also your business.

© 2000 by Susan Lee

The first thing you must do is look the realities of freelance existence square in the face. In some ways, it's not an easy life. Most freelancers periodically have to endure significant cash-flow problems. A typical story goes like this. Say you're a business writer. You book a job, and you feel rather secure. The job is scheduled to last a certain number of weeks, and you expect to have a check for, say, $5,000 waiting for you at the end of it. Well, the hard truth is that there's many a spill 'twixt the cup and the lip: the job may take longer than you'd anticipated, or it may fall through, or your client may not pay you for three months, or six months, or . . . .

In the meantime, you're desperate. Rent or mortgage payments, credit card bills, insurance premiums—none of your bills can wait till your check arrives. As you should know, the government requires that you pay estimated taxes on a quarterly basis (you may be penalized if you wait until Tax Day to pay all the taxes you owe for the previous year). If you're regularly setting aside money to pay those estimated taxes, you may succumb to the temptation of dipping into that fund to cover your immediate expenses. If you don't replace that money—or if you continue to delay paying the government—you'll begin to dread doing your taxes for that year: you may have left yourself without the money to pay what you owe. Make sure, then, that you plan for slow payers and no-payers. Using money allocated for taxes for other purposes, no matter how pressing those needs may be, is a short-term fix that often creates greater long-term pain.

If you're venturing into the freelance life after working a full-time staff job, take a close look at your spending patterns and financial records for the last several years to see just how much money you've needed to meet your basic expenses. But don't make the mistake of thinking that that's *all* you're going to need to survive as a freelancer. You'll need more—perhaps thousands of dollars more. You'll be responsible for many of the things that your employer formerly took care of. Maybe you're used to your employer contributing to a pension plan; now the responsibility of socking something away for your retirement is entirely yours. Health care? You'll be paying for your own insurance from now on. Vacation? From here on out, you won't be getting paid for time not spent working, so you'll have to figure your income flow into any holiday plans.

And then there's the bane of the freelance worker: Social Security tax. When you were a W-2 employee, your employer paid half. You paid the other half, but—since it was automatically deducted from your paycheck—you may have been only dimly aware of what a sizable chunk of your pay was being subtracted for that purpose. As a freelancer, you'll be footing the whole bill. Many beginning freelancers, all too aware of how little money they're making, think that they can't possibly have to pay taxes on their measly income. They're very, *very* wrong. In fact, as of this writing, you must pay Social Security tax on any earnings above

$400. For most freelancers in the lower tax brackets—and, unfortunately, that includes too many freelance writers—Social Security tax represents by far the greater share of the federal tax they pay.

There's more than one road to Tax Hell. Some freelance writers—those who get their work through agencies, for example—aren't technically "independent contractors." Instead, they stitch together a living by doing a series of W-2 jobs. The agencies, which are their "employers," give them paychecks from which federal, state, and Social Security taxes have been deducted. If this is how you are paid—especially if over the course of a year you work multiple, relatively brief jobs through many different agencies—you can all too easily be lulled into believing that your tax obligations are being met. Taxes *are* being withheld, so there's nothing to worry about, right?

Wrong. The problem is, because each of these jobs is so small, it may be that taxes are being withheld at a much lower rate than would be the case if withholding were based on your overall yearly income. I've known freelancers who made matters even worse for themselves by claiming multiple exemptions, further lowering the amount being withheld. In fact, if this is the way your income is structured, you might be wise to claim *fewer* exemptions than you're eligible for—to make sure that you're not faced with an unpayably huge tax bill come April 15.

A good tax preparer/consultant will be able to help you plan wisely. The trouble is, good tax consultants are expensive. If you're a beginner, you may feel that you can't afford a consultant's services. But think about it. Developing an ongoing relationship with a consultant who really knows what he or she is doing can be extremely beneficial over time.

Even if you use a tax preparer, however, it's more than likely that you won't be spending more than an hour or two with that person each year. Whether you work with a consultant or not, it's therefore incumbent on you to learn as much as you can about your tax situation, to make sure that every decision you make really works to your advantage. If you're an independent contractor who receives 1099s from your clients, that means familiarizing yourself with all the deductions that you can take—and keeping full, accurate, and well-organized records of your business-related expenditures. (The sidebar gives the major categories of expenses that you may be able to deduct legitimately.) It means being persistent in finding answers to any questions that occur to you.

If your ability to pay for a consultant's advice is limited, find other ways of obtaining help. For instance, many professional groups—including some locals of the National Writers Union—sponsor annual tax forums. A tax consultant comes in, runs through the basics, and takes questions from the audience. You may want to join a group that offers such a service, or, if you're already a member of a professional organization, you may want to take the lead in organizing such an event.

Tax-Deductible Expenses

Many freelance writers can claim the following expenses on their Schedule C. This list is not necessarily complete. Cases vary, and some freelancers may have legitimate deductible expenses beyond those listed here.

- Studio/office rent
- Office supplies
- Telephone
- Gas and electric
- Cabs, subways, buses
- Books, magazines, reference materials
- Secretarial services
- Promotion
- Film and processing
- Memberships in professional organizations
- Postage, messengers, private mail carriers
- Business insurance
- Tax preparation
- Travel
- Business meals and entertainment
- Business gifts
- Mortgage interest/taxes
- Equipment
- Agents' commissions (if included in income)
- Cultural events

Chances are, if your freelance worklife is at all complicated, you may still want to hire a professional to prepare your returns. If you don't have a tax preparer, finding a good one can be as difficult—or, if you're lucky, as easy—as finding a good doctor or lawyer. There are few hard and fast rules to guide your search. Relying on friends' recommendations can be a blessing—or it can be a disaster. There is, however, one guideline that may help: trust your own feelings, *go with your gut.* If you're an ethically fastidious person concerned about doing things properly, you may well want to walk out on a consultant who introduces himself by saying, "Don't worry about it, honey." (If you're a woman who doesn't appreciate being condescended to, that "honey" can be particularly aggravating.)

Try to gain as clear a sense as you can—and as quickly as you can—of the tax consultant's ethics. Do they match your own? Be clear about your own expectations and desires, as well. Do you want a god, or do you want a coach? Personally, I don't want to play God in my clients' financial lives; the coach role suits me much better—and I think it helps my clients more in the long run.

Finally, remember that, no matter how much power you entrust to your tax consultant, the responsibility for decisions made is ultimately yours. I cringe whenever I hear someone say, "Oh, I don't bother with taxes and stuff—I let my accountant handle all that." To me, that's about as naïve—and almost as risky—as saying, "Oh, I don't bother with my health—I let my doctor take care of all that."

The Books Market

The Industry—An Overview
by Denell Downum

Freelance writing can sometimes be as confusing as it is exhilarating, and this is never more true than when trying to navigate the byzantine world of book publishing. Publishing companies come in a wide variety of shapes and sizes and can be bewildering to a new author with a book or book idea to sell.

The most visible and best-known publishers are the large commercial houses like Random House, Viking, and Doubleday. They are known as general trade publishers, meaning that they publish across a wide range of genres for the consumer market. These publishers have the deepest pockets in the industry, so they can pay the highest advances and have the greatest capacity for distribution and promotion. On the other hand, their large scale means that many of their authors end up feeling ignored by overworked editors and indifferent publicists.

With the exception of employee-owned Norton, the major American trade presses are all owned by even larger parent companies, and the trend in recent years has been toward increasing consolidation. This threatens to have several unfortunate consequences—most notably, reduced competition among the major publishers, which could lead to lower advances and less desirable contract terms. Mass market rivals Bantam and Ballantine, for example, have both been acquired by Random House (which is in turn owned by the German media conglomerate Bertelsmann) and thus seem unlikely to bid against one another for manuscripts as vigorously as they once did.

One consequence of consolidation is already evident: the powers that be who control large media conglomerates expect their companies' book-publishing divisions to achieve high profit margins akin to those of other

© 2000 by Denell Downum. Amy K. Hughes contributed to the research for this section. Additional material was provided by Charlotte Dennett.

media (cable TV, films). These expectations are putting the squeeze on so-called midlist authors—writers of non-bestsellers, who were traditionally the backbone of the book-publishing industry, which was traditionally a business of low profit margins. Large commercial houses are less and less interested in taking on "small" books—even books that seem guaranteed to turn a moderate profit—and more and more eager to wager huge amounts of money on astronomical advances for celebrity books that promise huge returns.

For writers, industry consolidation means that we need to fight even more vigorously for fair advances and equitable contract terms.

Consolidation among major publishers has encouraged many writers to consider other options, including mid-sized independents like Grove/Atlantic and the vast array of small presses, specialized genre publishers, university presses, and book packagers. Writers often speak highly of small literary presses such as Milkweed Editions, Seven Stories Press, and Graywolf. Imprints like these are run by people who care deeply about publishing good books. Unfortunately, small presses are seldom able to pay more than a token advance (a few thousand dollars is the

Consolidation has encouraged many writers to consider other options

norm), and their limited distribution and promotion capabilities may mean that your book will not receive the attention it deserves.

Specialized genre publishers are a diverse bunch with little in common except a tendency to focus their efforts much more narrowly than the general trade houses. Thus the category includes John Wiley, a large corporate publisher of business, science, and technology books; mystery novel specialist The Mysterious Press; illustrated art book publisher Harry N. Abrams; and organizations like the Sierra Club, which publish a small list in a specific area of interest (in this case, nature and conservation) although their primary business is not publishing. Although many are fairly modest operations, specialty presses can be good options because they have a great deal of experience pitching their titles to particular markets.

In recent years, many university presses have broadened their lists, publishing more fiction and popular nonfiction in addition to scholarly monographs. Being published by a university press carries a certain intellectual cachet but not, generally, a sizable advance, although some of the better-heeled (such as Oxford and MIT) will splurge occasionally.

Book packagers provide yet another option for writers. These companies contract with publishers to do the editorial and design work for a specific book. The publisher then handles manufacturing (although some packagers oversee this, as well), distribution, publicity, and marketing. Packagers generally undertake complicated, design-heavy projects that publishers prefer not to produce in-house, such as illustrated coffee table books, multi-author projects, and series books that must be updated periodically. It is important to note that when a publisher hires a packager, the publishing contract usually names the packager, not the writer, as the author. The packager then hires writers and illustrators for the project, either on a royalty basis or as work for hire. Advances aren't huge and royalties are sometimes nonexistent, but packagers are often more open than publishers to hiring first-time writers, so they can be a good place for a fledgling writer to get a published book or two under her belt.

When a publisher hires a packager, the contract usually names the packager as the author

 A word of caution: Never become involved with a vanity press that will charge you to publish your book. Such presses (also called subsidy presses) almost never sell enough copies to allow you to recoup your initial investment, nor are they taken seriously by bookstores or other publishers.

Finally, electronic books ("e-books") and print-on-demand technology are growing forces in the book-publishing industry. Both of these technologies are covered in detail in Chapter 4 (see pages 114–120), but a few cautionary remarks about print-on-demand are germane here.

There are some advantages to print-on-demand services: for example, they give authors the ability to circumvent the gatekeepers (agents, editors) and to get published immediately for little or no cost and without having to fear that their books will go out of print. Too, the fact that such services operate via the Web gives authors access to a worldwide market. But there are important negatives, as well. For example, print-on-demand services generally offer no advances; authors get even less in the way of promotional help than they do from traditional publishers; and print-on-demand authors, unless they are already very well known, get minimal (if any) attention from reviewers. Some print-on-demand services differ little from vanity presses, and the same caveat applies.

Some observers are claiming that print-on-demand and e-books will ultimately eradicate traditional publishing altogether. That remains to be seen. In the meantime, the National Writers Union is watching these developments closely.

FINDING THE RIGHT PUBLISHER

When you are ready to sell your book, or book idea, the first major decision you will need to make is whether or not you want to use a literary agent. If your goal is to sell your book to a major trade publisher, you will almost certainly need an agent. Publishing lore is replete with tales of unagented books being rescued from the "slush pile" and going on to become bestsellers, but such instances are legendary precisely because they are so rare. Smaller publishers tend to be more open to unagented authors, as do university presses and packagers.

If you decide not to seek an agent, there are a number of things you can do to improve your chances of selling your book on your own. First, if you have any personal connections in the publishing industry, use them shamelessly. An editor may pay more attention to a manuscript if he knows the author is his uncle's college buddy's daughter. Second, investigate your options carefully before submitting your project.

If you have personal connections, use them shamelessly

Go to the local library and use a reference book such as the *Literary Market Place* (commonly referred to as *LMP*) or *Writer's Market* to come up with a list of houses that publish books like yours. Then go to a bookstore to make sure that the publishers you have selected are well represented and that the nature and quality of their books are comparable to yours. Third, always address a submission to a specific, carefully chosen editor. Industry reference books list the names of editors and sometimes indicate their areas of particular interest. It can also be useful to check the acknowledgments sections of recently published books, where many authors will thank their editors by name. Editors do move around frequently, though, so it's a good idea to call the publisher and make sure that the editor you are interested in is still there.

QUERIES

Once you have compiled a list of editors you are ready to put your submission together. Your cover letter should be concise (no more than one page), compelling, and carefully proofread—there is no quicker way to doom a book than to send a cover letter containing typos, misspellings, or grammatical errors. It can help to personalize the letter by mentioning a book you admire that was published by the same company or, better yet, that was worked on by the specific editor you are targeting. If you include a separate synopsis, it too should be brief. With your query, always send at least one sample chapter (several, if the chapters are very short), as a cover letter and synopsis cannot fully convey the flavor of your prose. Manuscript pages should be single-sided and double-spaced, and you should always include a self-addressed, stamped envelope for the return of your materials. Finally, don't hesitate to make multiple submissions. Publishers take far too long to evaluate submissions for you to approach them one at a time.

Patience and resilience are the two qualities you will need most as you begin your search for a publisher. Editors are generally slow to respond, and most writers receive many rejections before they sell their first book. But the wide variety of publishing companies increases the odds that your book is right for one of them. A thorough, persistent search may well be rewarded by a phone call from an editor eager to buy your book. Good luck!

Agents

Agents do much more than just get more money for the authors they represent. At best, agents nurture writers, advocate for them, and act as buffers in the potentially hostile business environment of publishing.

It has become close to impossible to get a trade book published by a large commercial house without an agent

Agents are critical elements of the publishing process, especially (though not only) for authors who hope to publish with large commercial presses. We asked participants in a targeted survey of NWU book authors conducted for this edition of the *Guide* whether they had used an agent to sell their latest book. Table 2.1 shows how they responded.

Word on the street has it that it has become close to impossible to get a trade book published by a large commercial house without an agent. The figures from a survey of book authors conducted for this edition of the *Guide* tend to bear this out. Of those who had published a book with a large commercial house during the past five years, 77 percent had used an agent.

The power that agents wield is both a blessing and a danger for writers. We have stronger allies in negotiating book deals, but it is also more difficult

TABLE 2.1. **REPRESENTED BY AN AGENT?**

Response	Percentage
Yes	49%
No	51%

to approach publishers directly. And, of course, having an agent means giving up as much as 15 percent of your writing income. (That an agent's fee of 15 percent is now much more common than the traditional 10 percent is borne out by responses to the *Guide*'s targeted survey of book authors. Of those using agents, only 24 percent pay at the lower, 10-percent rate.)

It also bears noting that agents, like all other players in the publishing industry, are not immune to changes in the industry. Like the large commercial houses that increasingly insist on high profit margins, some agents have developed their own "bottom line" mentality. It's not unusual for an agent, when approached by a new author, to think, "How big is this writer's market, and how much money does she stand to make for a publisher—and for me?" It's never been easy for an unknown writer to find an agent, and agents' selectivity is, if anything, on the increase. Nor are agents as likely to spend as much time as they once did on any individual author's work. Traditionally, agents would work with authors to improve manuscripts before submission. These days, they're more likely to farm out a manuscript to a "book doctor" (for a fee, of course).

Some agents have developed their own "bottom line" mentality

Having an agent to deal with the business side of writing also creates the temptation to wash one's hands of such matters. Agents—especially ones who return your phone calls—can be great, but it is essential that writers inform themselves about such critical issues as contracts, rights, advances, and royalties. Needless to say, if you do not take an active interest in your own business, you open yourself up to disappointment and potential problems.

AGENT CONTRACTS

Traditionally, the relationship between authors and agents was only formalized in writing as a clause in a publishing contract. It is becoming much more common, however, for writers and agents to enter into separate written agreements. The points below summarize the key issues in such contracts. (They are based on the "Preferred Literary Agent Agreement," published by the NWU and available to members.)

Key Issues in Writer-Agent Contracts

- *Scope.* The contract should spell out precisely what you are hiring the agent to do.

- *Authority.* The contract has to give the agent the right to negotiate on your behalf but protect your ultimate decision-making power.

- *Compensation.* The financial arrangement should be detailed as clearly as possible.

- *Termination.* A procedure for ending the relationship must be established.

Questions to Ask When Selecting an Agent

How much does she charge?
Most agents now charge a commission of 15 percent, rather than the traditional 10 percent. (Of book authors surveyed for this edition of the *Guide,* only 24 percent of those using agents paid the lower rate of 10 percent.) The commission usually does not cover mailing, copying, and telephone costs.

Does he require a written contract?
More and more agents do. Just make sure the contract is simple and that you are not under an obligation to keep the agent for more than one book.

Who are some of her clients?
Have you heard of them, and do these authors share your sensibilities? If the agent is reluctant to name clients, ask what well-known books she has sold.

How much does he like and understand your book?
You'll glean this not only from the agent's enthusiasm, but by where he sees it being published, his ability to discuss the book intelligently, and how much he thinks it is worth.

Will your book be auctioned or offered in multiple submission?
Multiple submission may get you a bigger advance, but may not be right for your book.

Does the agent have Hollywood connections?
You never know what kind of project has film or TV potential.

- *Assignability.* Make sure that the agent cannot just pass you off to someone else without your permission.

- *Modification.* The contract should only be subject to modification in writing.

- *Arbitration.* Should a dispute arise, arbitration is the best alternative to litigation.

Building a Better Book Contract

by Philip Mattera

Each book contract is a milestone in the life of a writer. Yet the excitement of having a publisher express interest in your work is usually followed by feelings of confusion and disappointment. You are dismayed to find that the contract sent to you for signing contains provisions that are either indecipherable or totally one-sided in favor of the publisher.

You should never simply sign on the dotted line

The National Writers Union believes that authors need not be powerless or uninformed when it comes to book contracts—whether or not you are represented by an agent. Book contracts are complicated documents that often reflect entrenched industry practices favoring publishers, but they are not beyond comprehension. This chapter is meant to give authors a basic orientation to contract issues, which are analyzed in much greater depth in the *NWU Guide to Book Contracts,* available to members only (in hard copy from the NWU national office or electronically in the members-only section of the union's website, www.nwu.org.

When considering an offer from a publisher, keep in mind that the contract sent to you is not a take-it-or-leave-it proposition; you should never simply sign on the dotted line. Certain provisions may have been agreed on orally by you or your agent and have to be regarded as given, but everything else in the contract should be considered up for grabs—though to varying degrees. Some provisions in the publisher's standard contract (known as boilerplate) are easy to change, some can be changed with difficulty, and some can only be changed if you are a "big name" or someone with a hot project. (The commercial book business is not egalitarian.) Still other provisions cannot be changed at all in individual contracts; dealing with these will require industrywide reforms of the kind advocated by the NWU.

RIGHTS

In evaluating a book contract, there are three basic types of rights to consider:

- *Copyright* relates to the question of who is the author (and thus owner) of the work for legal purposes.

- *Publishing rights* are the terms under which the copyright holder authorizes the publisher to print and sell the work.

- *Subsidiary rights* are the terms under which the copyright holder authorizes the publisher or others to produce (or adapt) the work in forms other than the primary edition.

Copyright

Copyright and work for hire are discussed at length in Chapter 1, pages 5 and 9.

Copyright consists of those rights and privileges guaranteed to the legal author of a work under federal law. These include, above all, the right to reproduce the work and the right to prepare derivative works. Under U.S. copyright law, the copyright in a literary work belongs to the person who writes the work from the moment the words are expressed in some fixed form. (The exceptions to this are situations in which the writer is creating the work as a work made for hire or in which the writer agrees to sign over all rights to the work to the publisher.)

Publishing Rights

Unless you are planning to self-publish, you as the copyright holder will need to find someone else to publish your book. In signing a book contract, what you are essentially doing is granting various rights to a publisher. These publishing rights (which derive from your copyright) are the terms under which that publisher can print and distribute your book.

There are three aspects of publishing rights to consider:

- *Format.* In most book contracts, the basic publishing right being granted by the author is the right to publish the work in an original hardcover edition. In some cases, the primary publisher will also want the right to issue the work in paperback and other formats. When a publisher intends to publish both the hardcover and paperback versions of a work, it will propose what is known as a "hard-soft" deal. Agreeing to a hard-soft deal can be advantageous, as long as the size of the advance on royalties reflects the broader grant of rights and the royalty rate for paperback copies is adequate.

- *Duration.* The customary practice in the United States is to allow the primary publisher to retain exclusive publishing rights for the duration of the work's copyright term (which is currently 70 years from the author's death), as long as the work is kept in print.

- *Geographical Scope.* The final publishing-rights issue concerns the extent of the geographical area in which the primary publisher is authorized to exercise those rights. Traditionally, the primary publisher would ask for the exclusive right to issue the work in the English language in the United States, its possessions, Canada, and the Philippines. Often the primary publisher would be granted the nonexclusive right to sell the English-language edition elsewhere in the world. In recent years, however, publishers have sought to gain increasingly broader geographical rights, and in many cases they demand exclusive world rights in English—sometimes in all languages. As with the granting of hardcover and softcover rights, it may make sense for an author who is less experienced or working without an agent to give the publisher world rights, as long as the size of the advance and other money provisions reflect the greater profit potential the publisher thus achieves. This tradeoff between the extent of the rights you grant to the publisher and the size of the advance applies to all aspects of the contract.

Subsidiary Rights

For discussion of subsidiary rights, see the subsection on subsidiary rights under "Royalties," below (page 43).

MONEY

How much money will you receive from the publisher, when will you receive it, and how will it be calculated?

Advances

An advance (sometimes called an "advance against royalties") is a series of up-front payments that a publisher agrees to give the author in exchange for the right to publish the book. The author is entitled to keep the advance even if the publisher does not sell a single copy of the work. Assuming copies are sold, the publisher credits the author's royalty account for so much per copy, according to the agreed-on royalty terms. Once the total reaches the amount of the advance—at which time the book is said to have "earned out" the advance—the publisher begins to make additional payments to the author.

When negotiating an advance, remember that most books published do not earn out their advances, and so the advance is the only compensation that most authors will end up receiving for writing the book.

Schedule of Advance Payments. When you consider the minimum advance you can settle for, keep in mind that the amount is usually paid out in several installments. This is particularly relevant if you are negotiating a contract based on a proposal and sample chapters—that is, when you have not yet written the whole book. Unless you have other sources of income, the advance will have to take care of your living expenses (and research costs) for as long as it takes you to complete the manuscript.

The advance will have to take care of your living expenses for as long as it takes you to complete the manuscript

The most common arrangement is for half of the total advance to be paid on signing of the contract and the remainder to be paid on acceptance of the completed manuscript.

Royalties

"List" versus "Net." Royalty payments are usually calculated in one of two ways. Either they are a percentage of the cover price of the book (the "list" or "gross" basis), or they are a percentage of the money received by the publisher after discounts are given to the bookselling retailer or wholesaler. The latter are known as royalties based on net. ("Net" may also be referred to as "the publisher's dollar receipts" or "net proceeds.")

Royalties were traditionally paid on the cover price. Occasionally, a publisher would complain that this arrangement was too onerous for books whose production costs were high (e.g., heavily illustrated works or reference volumes) and insisted on paying net royalties. What started out as a rare situation has become common practice among smaller publishing houses, university presses, and even for some types of works put out by trade publishers. When you accept net royalties, you are effectively cutting your income by at least 40 percent (i.e., the amount of the discount given to booksellers) for copies sold through retail channels.

Royalty Rates. Generally, royalty rates increase as more copies of a book are sold. These increases, known as step-ups or elevations, occur as certain sales milestones, or "breakpoints," are reached. (Note: Book contracts typically specify lower royalty rates for special categories of sales, including mail order, copies sold at a "deep discount," copies of the original edition sold abroad, and copies sold to book clubs.)

The most common rates for hardcover trade books are as follows:

- 10 percent of the list price on the first 5,000 copies sold

- 12.5 percent on the next 5,000 copies

- 15 percent on all copies beyond that

Paperback rights are of two types: "trade paperback" and "mass market." Trade paperbacks are the upscale softcovers, usually carrying a cover price of $15 or more, that are sold primarily in bookstores. For some mysterious reason, trade paperback royalties are almost always lower than those for hardcover editions. Moreover, the breakpoints are steeper (i.e., you have to sell a lot more copies to get to a higher rate), and sometimes rate elevations are not offered at all. The most common royalty rates for trade paperbacks are these:

- 7.5 percent of the list price for the first 10,000 to 25,000 copies

- 10 percent thereafter

Starting rates, however, can often be as low as 5 percent.

Mass-market editions are the less expensive paperbacks (usually with a smaller trim size) that are commonly sold in drugstores, newsstands, supermarkets, airports, and other outlets, as well as in bookstores. There is much greater variation in royalty rates for mass-market paperbacks—they can start as low as 4 percent and go as high as 15 percent or more—and the breakpoint is usually much higher, often 150,000 copies.

Royalty Statements. Publishers are supposed to make regular reports to the author on the sales of the book and the receipt of subsidiary-rights income. These royalty statements are supposed to be accompanied by a check for money due the author. Trade book publishers usually issue statements semiannually, while small houses and university presses usually do so annually. There is a lag of 60 to 120 days from the end of the royalty period to the date when the publisher is obliged to deliver the statement and make any payments.

The NWU believes that, in this day of computerized accounting, writers should not have to wait more than 30 to 60 days after an accounting period —which could be as much as 14 months after sale—to receive their royalty payments. The union's Book Division is working to improve this situation, as are agents' professional groups.

One royalty-related issue to which you should pay careful attention is the "reserve against returns." This is a longstanding publishing industry practice of holding back a certain portion of the royalties due an author.

Book publishing is an unusual industry in that its products are sold to retailers on what amounts to a consignment basis. If a bookstore does not sell all the copies of a book that it has ordered, it can return the unsold copies to the publisher, which must reimburse the store. Publishers' rationale for the reserve against returns policy is to avoid a situation in which the author ends up owing money to the publisher, which occurs if the number of returns exceeds the number of copies sold during a given reporting period.

Royalty statements often conceal more than they reveal

Although this situation is rare—since a number of circumstances must coincide to produce it—publishers insist on withholding reserves for every author. Usually, the best you can do is to try to limit the size of the reserve and/or the number of royalty periods during which it can be applied. (The *NWU Guide to Book Contracts* contains more detailed information on reserves against returns.)

Traditionally, royalty statements have concealed more than they have revealed. They are often cryptic documents that are not understood by most authors—or even by some agents.

In recent years, in part under pressure from writers' groups such as the NWU, some publishers have been revising their standard royalty forms and providing more of the relevant data. Some of these new forms are quite complicated, though they still usually leave out important information, including the size of the print run. In addition, publishers continue to insist on lag times of up to four months before royalty checks are sent out. Such delays are unjustified in an era of computerized accounting, but the industry has grown used to a practice that in effect gives publishers interest-free loans of authors' money.

It is usually not possible for an individual author to negotiate changes to a publisher's standard royalty form or the payment schedule; these kinds of changes will require industrywide reform.

Subsidiary Rights. Your book's money-making potential doesn't end with the North American hard- and softcover print editions. Foreign publishers may be interested in translating it and selling it abroad. If the print edition generates interest, the publisher or a third party may want to bring out an audio edition. A filmmaker or producer may want to option the work or buy the dramatization rights and adapt it for television or a theatrical film.

Close attention should be paid to the subsidiary rights provisions of your contract

How will you and the publisher divide the money that comes from licenses granted to others to make use of the work in forms other than the original edition? Since subsidiary uses of the work often account for the lion's share of the potential income, close attention should be paid to these provisions of your contract.

Deciding whether it is better to reserve—keep—various rights or to grant them to the publisher is a complicated matter. Traditionally, it was standard practice to allow authors to reserve certain types of subsidiary rights. These rights, sometimes called "secondary subsidiary rights," included British Commonwealth rights, foreign rights, movie/TV rights, and first serialization—that is, the right to publish an excerpt from the work before the book comes out. Increasingly, however, publishers want exclusive control over as many subsidiary rights as possible.

If you are an experienced author with a good agent, you should reserve as many subsidiary rights as possible. On the other hand, if you are working without an agent, your chances of selling these rights independently are not good. Thus it may make sense for you to give control over their disposition to the publisher.

If you somehow manage to reserve all subsidiary rights, then there is no need for the contract to contain a subsidiary rights clause. In most cases, though, your contract will list the various subsidiary rights that the primary publisher has the exclusive right to exploit. For each there will be an indication of how the proceeds from that right are going to be divided between you and the publisher. For most rights, publishers will ask that the income be split 50–50; when dealing with inexperienced authors, they often want this arrangement to apply to all rights.

Keep in mind that when the publisher sells subsidiary rights, it is essentially acting as your agent and ideally should only be entitled to the percentage taken by an agent, namely 15 percent. This argument, unfortunately, is not taken seriously by publishers. **It is not difficult, however, for the average author to get a greater than 50-percent share for the secondary subsidiary rights listed above. For translation rights, foreign English-language rights, and film/TV rights, most authors can, if they try, get anywhere from 60 to 80 percent. And the author's share of first serial rights is typically 90 percent.**

Electronic publishing issues are discussed in detail in Chapter 4, page 110.

Special attention should be paid to electronic rights, which once were considered throwaways, lumped together with trivial items such as microfilming. But with the explosion of new technologies, these rights are now coveted by publishers seeking to find new ways to sell the same material.

THE MANUSCRIPT AND THE BOOK

Many of a book contract's provisions pertain to the manuscript you are promising to produce. For instance, the contract should give some indication of the nature of the work, or at least a working title. (You may also wish to make your proposal a part of the contract.)

While the agreement should always specify the length of the manuscript to be delivered, as previously agreed on by the author and publisher, the contract should state that the word count is approximate, so that you are protected if the manuscript turns out to be somewhat longer or shorter. Also, be sure the deadline you agree to is realistic. If the publisher insists on a clause providing for cancellation of the contract in the event you don't deliver the manuscript, make sure the contract doesn't allow that step to be taken as soon as the deadline has passed; there should be a provision for a reasonable grace period.

Supplementary Materials and Permissions

Most contracts make it the responsibility of the author to supply supplementary materials such as photographs, artwork, charts, and graphs. If your book involves a substantial amount of such materials, try to get the publisher to share in the cost of their preparation.

When you plan to make use in your book of material that is covered by someone else's copyright (apart from short quotations), you will usually need to get written permission to do so. Often the publisher of that material will charge you a fee.

Most publishers make it the responsibility of the author to secure permissions, and most also require the author to pay all related fees. If you expect to use little or no copyrighted material in your book, this is not an issue to be very concerned about. **If, however, you are producing an anthology of numerous previously published pieces or, say, a work heavily illustrated with reproductions of artwork owned by someone else (galleries, museums), the time and money involved in getting permissions can be quite substantial.** In such cases it is not reasonable for you to absorb all the permission costs *unless* you are getting a large advance that was determined with permission costs in mind.

"Unacceptable" Manuscripts

Manuscript acceptance is one of the most contentious issues in book publishing. Numerous authors who sell books on the basis of a proposal find that, when they later deliver the full manuscript, the publisher claims the work is unsatisfactory and demands repayment of the advance.

All too often, rejections have nothing to do with the quality of the manuscript

Although publishers sometimes take this position based on an honest opinion that the work is substandard, rejections all too often have nothing to do with the quality of the manuscript. Among the real reasons may be that the house has been acquired by another publisher and ordered to pare its list, that the acquiring editor has left the company and no one else is excited enough about the book to take primary responsibility for it, or that the subject of the work is not deemed as "hot" as it was when the contract was signed.

Ultimately, it is not possible to compel a publishing house to put out a work it does not wish to publish. Good contract language can, however, make it more difficult for a house to reject a manuscript frivolously.

In addition, the right contract language can make it more difficult for a publishing house to demand repayment of the advance if it does end up rejecting the manuscript. The NWU has long held that, if an author writes the book, the advance should be nonrefundable. To allow the house to recoup the advance is to take all the publisher's risk out of the contract. If the publisher genuinely does not like what the author has produced, then it should simply cancel the contract and write off the advance as a business loss. The industry, however, has strongly resisted this principle, so until industrywide reforms can be enacted, authors will have to focus on the following contract fixes.

The contract should require that, when the manuscript is deemed unsatisfactory, the publisher must provide a detailed written statement listing the manuscript's deficiencies and must give the author an opportunity to revise the manuscript in a way that addresses the stated objections.

If the revised manuscript is also rejected, and the publisher insists on rejecting the work, then the author has to be concerned with getting back the publishing rights (reversion) and with the question of what happens to the advance.

Publishers have come up with a mechanism to make repayment of advances less burdensome: the "first-proceeds" clause. This is not as desirable as language making advances nonrefundable, but it is often the best an author can do.

A first-proceeds clause allows the author to avoid having to refund the advance directly

A first-proceeds clause allows the author to avoid having to refund the advance directly. Instead, the publisher frees the author to shop around the rejected manuscript to other houses. When the work is resold, then the first publisher is repaid out of the money received from the new publisher. A less desirable form of the first-proceeds clause states that if the work is not sold within a certain period (usually 12 months), then the author is obliged to repay the advance directly.

Editing and Production

The contract should state clearly that the publisher is responsible for the costs of production. The publisher should arrange for the manuscript to be professionally copyedited, and the edited manuscript should be sent to you for review. Although the publisher will insist on language saying that the manuscript must conform to standards of spelling, grammar, and so on, the contract should also state that no substantial changes in the content of the work may be made without the consent of the author.

Reviewing Proofs. Once the work has been set in type, you will be sent proofs for review. Traditionally, the author would first receive galley sheets to review and, after those had been corrected, page proofs. Today most publishers skip the galley-sheet stage and go directly from edited manuscript to page proofs.

Publisher contracts will typically require you to review proofs promptly. It is also common for contracts to state that the author is responsible for the cost of making author's alterations to the proofs when such costs exceed 10 or 15 percent of the original cost of composition.

Indexing. Authors should also be aware that most book contracts make indexing the author's responsibility. Composing the index is usually the final (pre-printing) step in a book's production, since indexing cannot be done accurately until pages have been finalized. You are often given a very brief amount of time in which to do the index. If you can't or don't want to do the index yourself, you will have to hire a professional indexer and, in many cases, pay for that person's services out of your own pocket. (Your editor may be able to recommend a good indexer to you.)

Production Decisions. Publishers typically insist on controlling the details of production, distribution, pricing, and promotion. On some of these issues—the cover price of the book, for example—it will be next to impossible for you to have any control. You should, however, try to negotiate at least a consultative role with respect to creative decisions, especially regarding cover design and dust jacket copy.

> *Try to negotiate at least a consultative role with respect to creative decisions*

Promotion
It is very difficult to get a publisher to make specific commitments about any aspect of promotion—such as advertising budgets or publicity tours—in the contract. Sometimes you can get a publisher to promise to promote the work "diligently, professionally, and to the best of its ability." Once the book is in production, you should communicate regularly (but not excessively) with the editor and publicity department to urge them to give as much promotional attention to your work as is reasonable, given the amount of "buzz" the project is generating. Editors and publicists generally encourage an author to prepare a list of magazines and journals to which review copies should be sent as well as a list well-known people of his or her acquaintance who might be persuaded to contribute complimentary blurbs for the book's back cover.

Failure to Publish
Be sure that your contract includes a clause that requires the publisher to publish the book within a specified amount of time. A deadline of 12 months is best, though many publishers insist on 18 or 24 months. Should a publisher fail to publish by the end of that period, the author must have the right

to terminate the contract unilaterally and recover all rights granted to the publisher. In such cases the author should retain any advances received.

Indemnification

One of the scariest possibilities facing writers today—especially authors of works of investigative journalism and nonfiction works on controversial subjects—is that they might be sued for what they have written. What sort of indemnification language should your contract contain?

It is not unreasonable for the publisher to ask that you promise that the work you are submitting is original, that it has not been previously published, that it does not infringe on someone else's copyright, and that you are free to grant the specified publishing rights. Most standard contracts will also ask the author to promise that the work is not obscene or libelous and that it does not invade anyone's privacy.

All of this is known as the author's warranty, and it is usually presented together with what is known as an indemnification clause, which makes the author responsible for any legal expenses and damages resulting from lawsuits that involve violations of the above promises.

Standard contracts will typically require the author to cooperate with the publisher's lawyers in modifying passages that may be obscene or libelous. That is reasonable, as is the provision that allows the publisher to cancel the contract if it turns out that the manuscript is not original or is unpublishable for legal reasons.

Sweeping language requiring you to pay the publisher's legal expenses in the event of a lawsuit is not reasonable

What is not reasonable is sweeping language requiring you to pay the publisher's legal expenses in the event a lawsuit is brought. Ideally, the contract will say that if you cooperate with the publisher's lawyers and modify the manuscript so that the lawyers think it will pass legal scrutiny, you should be free of all responsibility for legal expenses.

Publishers, supposedly concerned about those rare cases in which an author submits a completely plagiarized manuscript, usually insist on the inclusion of an indemnification clause. You might try to negotiate language that says you are responsible for legal expenses only when the plaintiff is successful, which means that you are not responsible for expenses relating to frivolous or unsuccessful claims.

For any book that is investigative or controversial in nature, you should try to get coverage under the publisher's libel insurance policy. (This is possible with many larger publishers but few small ones.) Beware of the deductibles contained in these policies, which may require an author to pay the first $50,000 or more in damages. Try to get the publisher to pay the deductible, or at least put a reasonable cap on your liability.

Although the NWU remains opposed in principle to indemnification clauses, we recognize that they are not going to disappear anytime soon. To help our members deal with this problem, the union in 1999 established the first affordable group "media perils" insurance policy for authors. This policy, which is available only to NWU members, covers libel, invasion of privacy, and many other forms of liability. It also serves as supplementary coverage for those authors who are included in publisher policies but are responsible for large deductibles. For more information on the NWU policy, see the section on Media Perils Insurance on the union website, www.nwu.org.

Arbitration

In most cases, authors who believe their contract has been violated by the publisher have only one legal option: to embark on costly and time-consuming court action. Since writers usually cannot afford to take this step, publishers will prevail by default. (NWU members have recourse to the union's Grievance Division.)

Expensive, exhausting litigation isn't the only legal means of resolving disputes, however. There is a more practical way for authors to seek justice, and that is through the system of arbitration. This is a process in which the parties to a contract agree to have any disputes heard by an impartial third party in a non-courtroom setting. The arbitrator then issues a ruling that is binding on the parties.

Some publishers agree to arbitration clauses in their author contracts as a matter of course, some will consent to the clause if the author requests it, and still others will never consent to it.

THE FUTURE

Book contracts also typically contain clauses relating to your future relationship with the publisher and the future of your book.

Option Clauses

Option clauses (sometimes known as "right of first refusal" clauses) are provisions that give the publisher the right to consider your next book project before you show it to any other house. Ultimately, you cannot be compelled to sign a new contract with the same house, but the option provision can seriously encumber your ability to offer the new work to other publishers.

The most desirable alternative is to remove the option clause entirely—a step that many publishers will agree to without much resistance. Others will remain adamant about keeping the clause. In that case, you should try to modify the provision in various ways:

- Do not agree to an option clause that requires you to submit a complete manuscript to the publisher for consideration. Instead, agree only that you will submit a proposal for the new work.

- If you write in different genres, specify that the option clause will only apply to your next work in the same genre.

- Set a strict deadline (say, 30 days after submission) by which the publisher must make an offer on the new project or decline to do so.

- Do not agree to language that binds you to the same terms as the original contract, and do not consent to restrictions on your right to reject the publisher's offer in favor of another offer—even one that is less lucrative. There may be circumstances in which you decide it is best to go with a house that is offering less money but other terms that are more attractive.

"Competing Works" Clause

Most book contracts have something called a competing works clause. This provision, which comes in various guises, is meant to prevent you from unfairly reusing the material from your book in a deal with another publisher.

Competing works clauses can often limit your career

The problem is that competing works clauses are often written in a way that can limit your career. The best alternative is to remove this clause entirely. If this is not possible, try to put a time limit on the restriction and limit the restriction to competing works on the same (not simply a similar) subject.

Out-of-Print Clause

The out-of-print clause (sometimes referred to as the termination clause) deals with the circumstances surrounding the decision of the publisher to take your book out of distribution.

If framed correctly, it can allow you to recapture rights from a publisher that may have failed to execute its responsibility of properly editing, packaging, and promoting a book. As it is often written, however, this clause can keep your book in limbo and make you wait years for a reversion of rights.

A proper termination clause will, first of all, clearly define what it means for a work to be out of print. Preferably, this should refer to availability of the book in its primary market. What this means is that the original publisher cannot claim the work is still in print if the only forms in which it is available are translations, audio cassette, or some other subsidiary form.

Next, the clause should require the publisher to notify you when it has decided to take the work out of print. This commonsense requirement is, however, almost never found in publishers' boilerplate. Instead, the typical language requires *you* to inquire about the status of the work. At that point, if the work is not available for sale, the publisher is usually given six months to decide whether to reprint it. It is only after that period of time, if the publisher has still not taken steps to reprint the work, that you are entitled to reclaim the rights.

Good out-of-print clauses are especially important now that print-on-demand arrangements are becoming much more popular

Good out-of-print clauses are especially important now that print-on-demand arrangements are becoming much more popular and economical. A publisher should not be allowed to let a work go out of print and then hold onto its rights based solely on the fact that it is making the work available on demand. **Once a publisher ceases to keep the work in print in the conventional sense, rights to the book should revert to the author, who can then seek another traditional publisher to republish the book or, perhaps, sign a deal with an on-demand publishing service.**

Revised Editions

Ideally, the contract you sign for a book will apply only to the original edition of the work; a revised edition will require a new agreement. This gives you an opportunity to negotiate better royalty rates if the book is doing well. It could also allow you to get a new advance, which may be quite important if revising the work will take a lot of time.

If this is not possible, try to get a clause that requires a new contract if the amount of revision exceeds a certain portion (say, 25 percent) of the original text. Also, for works that could be revised regularly, try to prevent the publisher from having complete control over the frequency of the new editions. If the revisions are expected to be less extensive and less frequent, then it may be difficult to avoid language that states that revised editions will be subject to the same contract terms as the original edition.

If so, be sure that the contract states that the deadline for the submission of the revisions is to be determined by the mutual consent of you and the publisher, to avoid the imposition of unreasonable timetables.

Rates and Practices

In the unregulated, irregular world of freelance writing, no market is as capricious as that for books. Book publishing is largely a "subjective" industry. The decision to publish a book is based on an editor's or editorial board's taste and on the publisher's guess of the book's market potential. That same guess, along with the publisher's drive to make a profit, dictates the terms of the publishing contract. A book considered a potential hot-seller will command a six- or even seven-figure advance, a large print run, and a serious promotional budget, while a book deemed of limited interest is likely to bring its author an advance of a few thousand dollars, a small print run, and no money for promotion. (In fact, large mainstream publishers today often won't even bother considering books whose themes have limited market appeal.)

Look at the book industry closely and you'll see much that appears irrational

But statements like these are only accurate as far as they go. Look at the book industry closely and you'll see much that appears irrational. Despite the greater caution that's sometimes seemed to reign in the industry during the past couple of years, comparatively huge advances are still being handed to celebrity authors for books that stand little chance of making that money back; meanwhile, advances for midlist authors with solid track-records (of moderate sales) seem static or may actually be shrinking.

A couple of things are clear. The commercial book-publishing industry is increasingly profit-driven. Of course, commercial book-publishing has always been a money-making enterprise, but, in the past, independent commercial publishers were comfortable with relatively low margins (of a few percentage points). The bestseller was deemed a rarity—an occasional, fortunate happenstance that could carry a publishing house along, enabling it to do little better than break even on all the other books it published. Today, nearly all big American commercial houses are owned by large international media conglomerates. The "suits" who control these businesses are looking to realize the same levels of profit from book publishing as can be earned in other media sectors—anywhere from 15 to 20 percent or more.

Media-industry consolidations and the radically different business philosophy that now drives most commercial book-publishing are really putting the squeeze on midlist authors—those whose books are unlikely to become bestsellers. The financial people who exert greater and greater control over acquisition and marketing decisions are intolerant of the small profits that even successful midlist books make. And consolidations—in which several, formerly independent houses might now be owned by the same media giant—mean that there's less competition for any given title. As bidding wars become rarer, advances are driven down. And as commercial publishing houses retreat from publishing serious nonfiction and literary fiction, many authors are forced to bring their projects to university presses and small presses that simply cannot give the kinds of advances that big commercial houses are capable of offering.

Media-industry consolidations are putting the squeeze on midlist authors

The bookselling business has also changed dramatically over the five years since this *Guide* was first published, and these changes, too, are intensifying midlist authors' pain. The "superstore" chains and the large online booksellers have driven many, many independent booksellers out of existence. The big retailers' ability to stock untold thousands of titles might seem to be a good thing for midlist authors, guaranteeing that their books will continue to be readily available to book buyers. The actual picture, however, is much more mixed. Many of the midlist books that have gradually gone on to become bestsellers have done so because of the informal promotional efforts of independent booksellers—the word-of-mouth they generate among customers whose tastes they know. As the independents go under, the chance lessens that your little novel will be a "sleeper" that will eventually sell hundreds of thousands of copies.

Adding to the uncertainty is the advent of electronic publishing. Issues regarding e-books and print-on-demand technologies are dealt with in detail in Chapter 4 of this *Guide.* Suffice it to say here, however, that the long-term effects of e-publishing on authors' economic lives and on the financial health of the book-publishing industry in general are very, very unclear at this point.

This section presents information that will give you a general idea of current conditions in the book marketplace. Except where noted, the data that appear in the tables are drawn from a targeted survey, conducted in the winter and spring of 2000, of National Writers Union book authors who had published at least one book during the preceding two years. The NWU's recom-

mendations are meant to serve as general guides—not hard-and-fast rules—
to help you deal with some of the tangible and intangible issues that come up
in considering a contract.

ADVANCES

In the topsy-turvy book-publishing environment, it is very difficult to say
what a good publishing deal is. Is a $20,000 advance reasonable? It might be
for a mass-market paperback with an initial print run of 50,000, but it's a so-
so deal for a hardcover with an anticipated run of 20,000.

In thinking about book-publishing deals, it is important to keep in mind
that there are a great many differences among publishers. What might be a
good offer from a small press, for instance, is generally grossly inadequate if
offered by a large trade house. And since there are so many intangibles that
go into a publishing contract and the experience of authoring a book, you
have to be clear about your primary concerns and the trade-offs you are willing to make to satisfy these. A large publisher, for example, may offer a bigger advance but may not give you the kind of editorial attention you want. A
smaller press, on the other hand, might accord your work a great deal of editorial care but might not have the resources to promote your book aggres-
sively. (By the way, although it is not unusual for small presses and university presses to offer authors no advance, larger trade houses always pay
advances, and certainly should be expected to do so.)

Trade Books

Table 2.2 shows the amounts of advances received by midlist trade-book
authors responding to NWU surveys.

TABLE 2.2. **ADVANCES: TRADE BOOKS**

Category	Min/Max	Prevalent range
Nonfiction hardcover	$0/$150,000	$3,000–$50,000
Nonfiction paperback	$1,000/$25,000	$5,000–$13,000
Fiction hardcover	$1,500/$150,000	$5,000–$20,000
Fiction paperback[a]	$1,500/$56,000	$1,000–$10,000

[a] Data derived from survey of NWU authors conducted for *The National Writers Union Guide to Freelance Rates & Standard Practice* (1995).

Children's Books

Amounts of advances received by NWU children's book authors are given in table 2.3.

TABLE 2.3. **ADVANCES: CHILDREN'S BOOKS**

Min/Max	Average
$4,000/$14,000	$7,500

Mass Market Books

Table 2.4 gives amounts of advances reported by NWU mass-market authors who responded to the survey conducted in 1995 for the first edition of this *Guide.* By all indications, these figures remain more or less accurate.

TABLE 2.4. **ADVANCES: MASS MARKET BOOKS**

	Min/Max	Prevalent range
Mystery	$5,000/$50,000	$5,000–$35,000
Romance	$1,000/$40,000	$1,000–$10,000
Science fiction	$3,500/$40,000	$7,500–$40,000
Western	$1,500/$35,000	$1,500–$10,000
Young adult	$1,000/$14,000	$2,000–$7,500
Other original paperback	$1,000/$35,000	$1,500–$10,000

Schedule of Advance Payments

The schedule of advance payments is a serious consideration in contract negotiations. Advances are paid out in installments, and it is important to make sure that you get as much of the money up front as possible. In what has traditionally been the most common payment schedule, writers have received half of the advance on signing and half on acceptance of the manuscript. NWU book authors indicated that this remains a dominant method of scheduling advance payments (see Table 2.5). A disturbingly high number of book authors, however—29 percent—reported that some portion (or all) of their advance was not paid until publication. **Since most authors must use their advances in order to work on their books and since the time-lag between acceptance and publication is often long, the practice of withholding advance money until publication is unacceptable.**

TABLE 2.5. **ADVANCES: SCHEDULE OF PAYMENTS**

Schedule	Percentage
Full payment on signing	25%
Half on signing, half on acceptance	46%
Full payment on publication	4%
Other arrangements (including some portion paid on publication)[a]	25%

[a]In these other arrangements, half the advance was generally paid on signing, with further installments doled out when certain milestones were reached (outline completed; some text completed; acceptance; publication).

"Earning Out" the Advance

The advance you get for your book is just that: an advance against the royalties you are expected to make on sales of the book. As copies of your book are sold, royalties are credited toward the advance you received. You get no royalties until the advance is "earned out." Table 2.6 shows percentages of NWU book authors who had and had not "earned out" the advance on their most recent book.

As you can see, many books' chances of earning out their advances are fairly low. The reasons for not earning out are complex and numerous, from

TABLE 2.6. **ADVANCES: EARNED OUT?**

Response	Percentage
Yes	28%
No	24%
Respondent did not know[a]	48%

[a]Includes those whose books had been published too recently for authors to know whether they would earn out their advances or not.

intense competition for shelf space to inadequate promotion to premature remaindering. What is important to understand is that most of these reasons are outside your control and that a book's sales performance is generally not a very realistic gauge of its quality. **Whatever the reasons, it seems clear that it is in most writers' best interest to negotiate for as high an advance as possible.** You get to keep the advance no matter how poorly your book performs, but, if you don't earn out your advance, you'll never see another penny in royalties from that book.

ROYALTIES

Royalties are calculated as a percentage of sales, usually with the rate going up as more copies are sold. In negotiating contracts, it is important to consider both the royalty rate and the escalations (the breakpoints at which rates go up) as well as the method used to calculate royalties—list price or publisher's net. The rate and the method of calculation can be used as counterbalancing negotiation points: for example, if you are getting royalties based on publishers' net, hold out for higher rates.

List or Net?

We asked the book authors we surveyed whether royalties for their most recent book were based on list or net. Their responses are given in Table 2.7.

Alarmingly, all of those who said their royalties were based on net reported rates that were *the same as or lower than* the prevailing rates based on list price. Also worrisome was the fact that 29 percent of book-author respondents reported flat royalty rates (ranging from 7.5 to 10 percent), whether based on list or net. **If royalties are based on net, the rates should be higher than those based on list. Flat royalty rates are not usually acceptable: if your book sells lots of copies, you deserve to share proportionally in its success.**

TABLE 2.7. **ROYALTIES: LIST OR NET?**

Response	Percentage
List	69%
Net	28%
Respondent did not know[a]	3%

[a]Or did not respond.

Trade Books

For trade books, standard escalations are as follows:

- For hardcovers: first 5,000 copies, next 5,000 copies, all copies thereafter

- For paperbacks: first 10,000 copies, all copies thereafter

Table 2.8 shows the prevailing list-based rates for trade books as reported by respondents to the targeted survey performed for this *Guide,* as well as the

TABLE 2.8. **ROYALTY RATES: TRADE BOOKS**

Category	Prevalent rates	NWU recommends (at least)
NONFICTION		
Hardcover		
First 5,000 copies	10%	10–15%
Next 5,000 copies	12.5%	12.5–15%
Thereafter	15%	15–20%
Paperback[a]		
First 10,000 copies	7.5–12.5%	7.5–12.5%
Thereafter	10–15%	10–15%
FICTION		
Hardcover		
First 5,000 copies	10%	10–15%
Next 5,000 copies	12.5%	12.5–15%
Thereafter	15%	15–20%
Paperback		
First 10,000 copies	7.5–10%	7.5–12.5%
Thereafter	10%	10–15%

[a]Several authors of nonfiction trade paperbacks reported a third breakpoint (at 45,000–50,000 copies) at which rates went up to 15 percent.

NWU's recommendations for minimum royalty rates. The latter are suggestions for *the lowest rates you should consider.* If you can get more, do it.

Mass Market Books

For mass market books, escalations tend to be at very high breakpoints, with the first often set at 150,000 copies. No matter how astronomical the numbers may be, however, it is essential to make sure that your contract specifies some escalations. The NWU believes the rates in Table 2.9 are reasonable minimum royalties for mass market paperbacks of all types (including mysteries, romance novels, science fiction, westerns, young adult fiction, and other original paperbacks):

TABLE 2.9. **ROYALTY RATES: RECOMMENDED MASS-MARKET MINIMUMS**

Breakpoint	NWU recommends (at least)
First 150,000 copies	7–15%
Thereafter	10–15%

Children's Books

For children's books, the common breakpoints are at the first 5,000 copies, the next 5,000 copies, and all copies thereafter. The NWU believes that the rates in Table 2.10 are reasonable minimum royalties for children's books. (Children's book authors should note that, when a book is a collaboration between a writer and an illustrator, royalties are often split 50–50.)

TABLE 2.10. **ROYALTY RATES: RECOMMENDED CHILDREN'S BOOK MINIMUMS**

Breakpoint	NWU recommends (at least)
First 5,000 copies	7–10%
Next 5,000 copies	8–12.5%
Thereafter	12.5–15%

Professional Books

For professional books, breakpoints tend to be set at the first 5,000 copies, the next 5,000 copies, and all copies thereafter. The NWU believes that the rates given in Table 2.11 are reasonable minimum royalties for professional books. Because royalty rates for professional books are commonly based on publisher's net, we have set recommended royalty rates higher than for trade books.

TABLE 2.11. **ROYALTY RATES: RECOMMENDED PROFESSIONAL BOOK MINIMUMS**

Breakpoint	NWU recommends (at least)
First 5,000 copies	10–12.5%
Next 5,000 copies	12.5–15%
Thereafter	15–20%

RIGHTS

As we hammered home in the previous section, you should strive to maintain copyright in your work. Copyright is your assurance that you will be able to reproduce your work and to derive income from it. By signing over the copyright, you give up your rights as the owner of the work.

We were heartened by the fact that, of trade-book authors responding to the targeted survey conducted for this *Guide,* only 7 percent reported that they had given up copyright for their most recent book to the publisher. Indeed, copyright ownership is usually not an issue with trade publishers. **Academic and small-press publishers, however, often pressure authors to sign over the copyright. This is exploitative, and you should never agree to such terms.**

Subsidiary Rights

Subsidiary rights often account for most of the income derived from a book. Therefore, it is essential to pay careful attention to the grant of subsidiary rights in your contract.

We wanted to know how often book authors are granting various subsidiary rights to their publishers and—more important—how successful pub-

lishers are at selling them. Table 2.12 shows how respondents to the targeted survey conducted for this *Guide* responded.

The low rate of success that these figures seem to indicate should be
taken with a grain of salt, since it is often difficult to sell subsidiary rights.
Even so, these statistics are disappointing.

A full
discussion of
subsidiary
rights appears
on pages
43–44.

TABLE 2.12. **SUBSIDIARY RIGHTS**

Right	Publisher handled	Publisher sold
1st serial	46%	3%
Dramatization	11%	0%
British Commonwealth	49%	17%
Foreign translation	49%	9%
Merchandising	43%	3%
E-book, CD-ROM	43%	3%
Audio	31%	3%

PRINT RUNS

The number of copies initially printed—the book's first *print run*—is a function of that same guess as to the book's market potential that we talked about
in the beginning of this section. If the print run is large, the publisher expects
the book to do well and is more likely to support it with aggressive promo-
tions and sales efforts. In general, publishers tend to reserve large initial print
runs for blockbusters, preferring to reprint if a book proves to be a hot seller.

Publishers are often reluctant to tell authors how large their print runs will
be—and authors are, surprisingly, sometimes not very interested in this valuable information. (Of authors responding to the survey taken for this *Guide*,
13 percent did not know the initial print run for their most recent book.)

Table 2.13, taken from the first edition of the *Guide* and still accurate,
provides prevalent ranges of first print runs for various categories of books.

TABLE 2.13. **PRINT RUNS**

Category	Prevalent range
TRADE BOOKS	
Nonfiction hardcover	5,000–30,000
Nonfiction paperback	5,000–30,000
Fiction hardcover	5,000–30,000
Fiction paperback	5,000–30,000
MASS MARKET BOOKS	
Mystery	25,000–80,000
Romance	25,000–100,000
Science fiction	25,000–75,000
Western	10,000–50,000
Young adult	25,000–75,000
Other original paperback	25,000–75,000
CHILDREN'S BOOKS	5,000–10,000
PROFESSIONAL BOOKS	3,000–10,000

EDITING

Complaints that book-industry editorial standards have fallen are widespread among writers and readers alike. To find out how their books had been treated, editorially, we asked authors participating in the *Guide*'s survey whether they thought their books had been given adequate editorial attention, whether they'd had the chance to review the edited manuscript, and whether any changes had been made to their manuscript without their approval before publication. Results are summarized in Table 2.14.

Although the practice of making changes without the author's approval appears to be a minor problem, the number of authors who did not feel their manuscripts had been given enough editorial attention is dismaying.

To compensate for the lack of editorial attention they feel their books will receive from their publishers, some book authors are employing independent editorial services to polish their books before submission. The growth of this practice points to a decline in editorial attention that (especially) commercial houses are giving the books they publish. Although we bemoan the fact that publishers are falling down on their editorial responsibilities, it's hard to fault book authors, who want their published work to be as good as possible, for using third-party editors. Two caveats are in order, however. First, editorial services are expensive. Second, although there are a lot of good, honest independent editors and editorial services out there, there are also a few unscrupulous firms eager to take advantage of unsuspecting authors. Beware of pie-in-the-sky promises, made by some illegitimate firms, that they can also agent your work and find you a publisher. **If you do hire an independent editor, take the following precautions: agree on an hourly rate or flat fee that you feel you can live with, and make sure that your contract stipulates that you will have the chance to review the editor's work after one sample chapter has been completed—and that you can terminate the contract at that point if you are not pleased with the work.**

TABLE 2.14. **EDITORIAL PRACTICES**

	Yes	**No**	**Did not respond**
Adequate editorial attention?	66%	29%	5%
Shown edited manuscript?	97%	3%	0%
Changes made without approval?	3%	94%	3%

PROMOTION

Among the most common complaints authors have is that their books are not sufficiently promoted. The blockbuster mentality dominant in the commercial publishing industry encourages a highly uneven distribution of marketing and promotion budgets, with most of the money going to pitch the few books that publishers pay huge advances for and produce in large quantities, hoping to fulfill their expectations of bestsellerdom.

Realizing that publishers aren't doing very much to promote most books, authors are taking on more and more of the work of promoting their books themselves. We asked respondents to the *Guide's* survey whether they thought their most recent book had received adequate promotion from the publisher and whether they had done any promotional work themselves. The results, which appear in Table 2.15, are telling.

We also asked respondents about the kinds of promotional assistance their publishers gave their most recent book. Table 2.16 summarizes those results.

These figures are chastening. It's obvious that most authors can't count on a publisher's doing anything, promotion-wise, beyond sending out review copies. That warning turns out to be the perfect introduction to the next "Writing Life" essay, in which children's book author Marcia Savin outlines the vicissitudes—and the rewards—of self-promotion. (By the way, the NWU publishes a guide to self-promotion, called *On the Road,* available to members.)

TABLE 2.15. **PROMOTION**

	Yes	**No**
Adequate promotion from publisher?	35%	65%
Self-promotion?	89%	11%

TABLE 2.16. **PROMOTIONAL ASSISTANCE GIVEN BY PUBLISHER**

Type of promotion	**Percentage**[a]
Sent out review copies	91%
Placed paid advertisements	31%
Arranged national book tour	8%
Arranged radio/TV appearances	20%
Arranged readings/signings in bookstores	37%
Nominated book for prize(s)	29%

[a] Percentage of total number of authors responding.

Self-Promotion:
The Seven Cardinal Rules

Marcia Savin

Like most new writers, when I sold my first book to a publisher, I thought the hard part was over. I had sold my book! Little did I know that now I would have to *sell* my book. The ink was barely dry on that first contract when my agent said, "Better be prepared to promote it. Or it might disappear without a trace."

My baby? The book I'd spent years of my life working on? Promote it myself? Me—who was raised to believe that tooting your own horn was the Eighth Deadly Sin? But I promoted. I spent time and money doing so. And it paid off.

The Moon Bridge, my children's novel set in San Francisco during World War II, came out in hardcover in 1992 (Scholastic). It's been in paperback a long time, and it's still doing well. The story is about two fifth-grade girls, Ruthie Fox and Mitzi Fujimoto, who find their friendship challenged by the anti-Japanese hysteria that followed Pearl Harbor.

It's no news that publishers spend a lot less energy on promotion than authors would like. If your publisher is not promoting your book, you can sit back and watch, or you can take the bull by the horns and do it yourself. From months of self-promoting, I developed seven "cardinal rules."

RULE 1: LEAVE NOTHING TO CHANCE
Like many new authors, I assumed that my publisher kept an eye on the books it published. But I soon found otherwise. Most publishers have so many books out they can't watch each one as closely as it deserves. At large publishing houses, different people and different departments handle each aspect of a book's journey from inception to sale, and no one seems to oversee the big picture. That's where you come in.

Get to know everyone involved in promoting, marketing, and selling your book. I did, and by trial and error I learned a great deal about publishing, as well. I came to know my publisher's head of sales, the publicity person, the school sales rep, and the person who arranges authors' appearances. I learned to call the toll-free sales number to find out how many copies of *The Moon Bridge* were left. If the number was low, I'd alert publicity myself to see about getting more printed. "We're almost out," I'd say, "and I've got two school visits coming up!" (They didn't have to know that we'd be lucky to sell 30 books.)

RULE 2: REMEMBER THAT NO ONE CARES ABOUT THE BOOK AS MUCH AS YOU DO

I was willing to promote my book, but I had no idea how to start. I decided to throw myself a book party and invite everyone I knew. It turned out to be one of the smartest things I did. My guests were full of ideas and offers of help. They knew bookstore owners and teachers and librarians, and they were willing to contact them. I thanked everyone profusely.

After the party, I prepared a flier, so my friends would have something to hand out to their contacts. I photocopied it, sent it to my friends, and waited for them to make their calls. And then I waited some more.

Friends forget. People are busy. I learned to nudge gently. If my first nudge didn't work, I'd try a second. That usually worked. If not, I'd send the friend a blank, stamped envelope for mailing my flier to his or her contact. That always worked. People cannot ignore a stamped envelope.

RULE 3: KEEP A RECORD OF EVERYTHING

Once I started contacting people, it wasn't long before I found that I was forgetting whom I'd nudged and when I'd done it. So I developed a system. I started a file and called it "Action" (to make me take some). I recorded each lead on a separate sheet of paper, assigned it a number and a date, and left a space on each sheet marked "Result." (This was in the days before I had a computer—it would be easier now.) I made myself open the file very day. Each time I had a new lead, I put it on top, so the sheets were in reverse chronological order, with the newer leads up front. The Action file eventually had more than 400 entries. Some paid off, some didn't.

RULE 4: BE PREPARED TO SPEND TIME AND MONEY

I was willing to spend the time to promote my book because it seemed like a job. I would put in hours, the book would sell, and I would earn money. But I soon learned I had to *spend* money as well. I paid for the fliers I distributed to my friends and the postage for mailing them out. I sent copies of the book to people who could get me a review or other publicity. And like the hours spent, money spent meant sales.

Tip: If you ever send anyone a complimentary book and you don't hear back (which, I found is almost always the case—see Rule 2), follow up with a brief note: "I just wanted to be sure the book wasn't lost in the mail." And—this is the important part—enclose a postcard addressed to yourself. On the back, write, "Received _____" and "Date _____." Like stamped envelopes, stamped postcards are hard to ignore. Usually the recipient will not only reply but will apologize for taking so long. You might even be sent a glowing review, as well!

RULE 5: PLAN YOUR BOOK-SIGNINGS CAREFULLY

Setting up a bookstore reading and signing can be as simple as walking in and asking. But remember Rule 1, and don't assume the store will do any publicity. Give them a blowup of the cover that they can display in the window. Provide them with handouts and mailing lists. Find out if they have their own mailing list: While it's nice to have the seats filled when you do a reading, remember that if the audience is composed entirely of your friends you aren't selling books.

Anytime you're doing a signing, reading, or visit, make sure the books are ordered well in advance—three weeks, at least. A week before your appearance, call the place to make sure the books have arrived. If you're going to appear at a local store, library, or school, drop by a week before the reading to be sure the publicity material is displayed.

RULE 6: CREATE YOUR OWN PUBLICITY

I put my energy into creating a market for my book. I sent notices to newspapers and magazines. Because I'd worked on community newspapers, I knew they were always short of material and that they like free photographs because photos cost them money. I also knew that press releases come in by the pound, so I never wrote press releases. I wrote the actual stories.

My Brooklyn, New York, neighborhood—like many neighborhoods—has a giveaway paper, read in laundromats and Chinese takeouts. I wanted publicity, but the only "news" I could come up with was the less-than-earth-shaking revelation that I, a local resident, had written a book. Nevertheless, I interviewed myself and turned in the story with a black-and-white glossy head shot. The paper printed it, verbatim. After it came out, neighbors stopped me on the street to tell me about what a great story the paper did on me. (My lips were sealed.)

The article led to a call from a nearby school, asking if I would speak to a class of gifted fifth-graders. Later, other teachers at the school asked for me, too. The PTA had a book fair, and more copies were sold. No one there had heard of my book before I wrote the article.

RULE 7: LEAVE NO STONE UNTURNED

Think of any organization that might be interested in your book. Does the book focus on environmental issues? Religious? Political? Is it about art or architecture? There are all kinds of special interest groups and organizations that need speakers, or articles for newsletters, or guests for radio programs. There are also many non-bookstore venues for selling books: museum gift shops, gardening centers, visitors' centers, even hardware or home supply stores may take your book on commission if they think it will appeal to their clientele.

Are you—or your characters—members of an ethnic group? I looked into Japanese-American groups and learned that there were Japanese-American dailies on both the east and west coasts. I wrote an article that focused on the internment camp aspect. Both papers printed it verbatim. I discovered review journals I hadn't known existed. Several were for multicultural books, like mine. I'd check to see if the journal's editor knew the book. If not, I'd ask my publisher's publicity department to send a copy. If the publicist balked, I'd do it myself.

Was it all worth it? I think so, and I'd do it all again—better, now that I know a bit more about what I'm doing. Remember: These days publishers don't just look at a manuscript. If you've published a book before, they also look at that book's sales. When you promote your book, you're not just keeping your book alive. You're making sure you'll be given the chance to publish others.

The Better Half: Ghostwriting and Collaborating

Catherine Revland

For many years, I made my living ghostwriting trade books, primarily for celebrities, and nearly always without credit on the cover. "And these people take full credit?" other writers would say, their voices rising in indignation. "That's dishonest!" More sympathetic types wondered about my psychological state, suggesting that perhaps I should go into therapy to explore why I would choose such a self-effacing way to make a living.

Success erases those suspicions. One book I ghostwrote sold over 500,000 copies in paperback. Of course, it would be nice to get my name on the cover. But a steady stream of handsome royalty checks can go a long way toward assuaging the disappointment.

The business of selling books has become one of mass-marketable names—recognizable names, with no unfamiliar ones trailing behind attached by prepositions. What's in a celebrity name? Lots of advertising and promotion money. Quite frankly, as far as the publisher is concerned, the ghostwriter's name doesn't add anything to a book's sales potential. In fact, the promotion people don't want to know about the celebrity's need for a ghostwriter. It's like hearing of a star athlete's reliance on steroids: they hope it isn't so.

But do not get depressed. Although the phenomenon of the celebrity book elevates the status of writers no more than it does the status of literature, it means a lot of work for professional book writers and a good opportunity to make some real money. I hope that the following advice, drawn from my own experience, will help you strike better collaboration and ghostwriting deals.

THE LETTER OF AGREEMENT

Negotiations are best begun at the initial meeting, when you and the person you'll be writing for are brought together by an agent, editor, or referral. This is the time to make it clear to your prospective client what hiring a book writer means. If by the end of the meeting a collaboration seems possible, a letter of agreement can be drawn up. It should cover the following points:

Credit

Ask for credit on the cover and spine of the book. When negotiating, try to make the client understand that, if your name does not appear on the book, it will cost you in terms of professional status.

If the client does agree to give you credit, what you're doing is a *collaboration*. But no matter whether you're given credit or not, the letter of agreement should specify that both you and the client will be party to the contract with the book's publisher, where you will be designated as the "writer" and the client as the "author" and where your differing responsibilities will be clearly laid out. Unless the publishing contract is signed by both parties, your part in the project can easily slip into work for hire, and you will not receive royalties.

If you fail to get credit, insist on 50 percent of the royalties as a tradeoff for giving 100 percent of the credit to your client. If your client is adamant about not giving you cover or title-page credit, try to get him or her to acknowledge you as the writer in the acknowledgments section. Without the protection of such a clause, I have been credited in ways that made my contribution sound more like moral support or that of a humble drone who corrected the punctuation. Being named as writer in the acknowledgments is your best referral for future ghost-writing jobs—apart from cover credit, of course.

Division of Responsibilities

The letter of agreement should make clear how the responsibilities are to be divided between you and the author. Although you are probably going to do most of the writing, the agreement should specify what the author is required to provide you in terms of documents, access to human sources (letters of introduction, etc.), and, perhaps most important, adequate time for you to interview him or her. You should not be expected to have to exercise telepathy in order to gather the facts, ideas, and anecdotes that the author wants in the book.

The letter of agreement should also make clear who is responsible for the various expenses incurred while writing the book.

Resolution of Disputes

When you first make the deal with the author, relations between the two of you are bound to be quite amicable. While you hope things will remain congenial, all too many collaborations end in ugly disputes. Unless your letter of agreement is carefully worded, you could end up out of the picture, with little to show for your work.

It's a wise idea to include provisions in the letter of agreement that say, first, that you cannot be removed from the project without just cause. Most likely such a provision will not allow you to remain on the project with an author who has turned against you, but it will strengthen your hand with regard to a second essential provision, which should say that you cannot under any circumstances be removed from the project until you and the author have reached agreement on compensating you.

If the relationship ends while you are writing the proposal, or after the proposal is completed but before a book contract has been signed with a publisher, you should get paid the full amount agreed on for the proposal, plus, if possible, additional money to compensate you for your removal from the project.

If a publishing contract has been signed, and you are a party to it, you cannot be unilaterally removed from the project. The contract will have to be canceled and a settlement negotiated. Even if you are not a party to the publishing contract, however, your letter of agreement should guarantee you a substantial settlement, the size of which should reflect the amount of work you've done by the time of the "divorce."

The Advance

Experience has taught me to tell prospective clients that I cannot write a publishable, salable book in less than a year, from proposal writing to final copyedit, and that it normally takes six months to produce a first draft. During this time, I must work full time to meet the deadline and must be fully compensated. I make it clear that the deadline is *my* deadline—that the project ends when the money runs out and I have to take on another full-time project. By specifying a time frame in the initial letter of agreement, you'll save yourself the months of anguish, frustration, and financial struggle that come when you have to underwrite the book's completion with your own money. I got carpal tunnel syndrome because of all the extra writing I took on to support myself while I finished ghosting a book after the advance had run out.

Tell the author what you think a reasonable advance is. These days, unless you are dealing with a big celebrity, six-figure advances are rare indeed. Explain to your prospective collaborator how much money you will require for a year's work—say a modest $40,000—and make it clear that if your share of the first half of the advance is not sufficient to cover that amount, he or she must make up the difference. In addition, the author must pay for your travel and transcribing expenses, which can be considerable. Using our very modest figure of $40,000 for the year—and remembering that book advances are usually doled out in two installments, on signing and on acceptance of the completed manuscript—it becomes obvious that unless the advance is $80,000 or more, you will need the entire first installment of the advance in order to write the book. Your collaborator can then receive the second half of the advance.

Royalties

If your author is a celebrity, or has the potential of becoming one, you may be in the blessed position of having an annuity for years to come if the book is a success.

In general, however, a book has to sell in five figures before the advance is "earned out" and you begin receiving additional royalties. As you negotiate the letter of agreement, you should keep in mind that you're quite likely never to see a penny in royalties beyond the advance. Do not, however, agree to accept less than 50 percent of the royalties. If your client insists on a bigger share, point out how much work you will be putting into the book for modest compensation and suggest that the prospect of half the royalties is a great incentive for you to produce the best book possible.

The Proposal

Before you write the book, you and the author are going to have to find a publisher, which means you're going to have to do a proposal. I usually negotiate proposals as two-month projects for which I *must* be paid. The author may balk, but it is absurd for the writer to work on spec. If necessary, you might have to agree to reimburse the client for the proposal fee out of the first royalties—*not* out of your share of the advance, since you might need all of that to write the book.

AGENTS: ONE OR TWO?

I have had the best luck getting a fair deal when the collaboration came through my own agent or from a referral I brought to my agent. In such cases, one agent works well for both author and writer (plus you split the agent's commission). Publishers and editors also prefer dealing with one agent, as two can be cumbersome. If the client already has an agent, however, I strongly suggest that you bring your own agent in on the deal, so that you have someone to help you negotiate the agreement and look out for your interests.

YOUR RELATIONSHIP WITH YOUR EDITOR

Once you have a contract with a publisher, be sure to develop a direct working relationship with the editor assigned to the project. The senior editor may meet with the author alone at a swank French restaurant, but the hands-on editor needs to know the person who is cranking out the drafts.

There is a bittersweet aspect to the "as told to" craft: the better you are as a ghostwriter, the more the book sounds as if the author wrote it. "Does not bear the

Collaboration Agreements: What They Should Cover

- *Exclusivity.* The collaborators should agree to work with each other exclusively.

- *Proposal.* If you are doing all the writing, try to get paid for developing the proposal.

- *Responsibilities.* The agreement should make it clear who will do what.

- *Agents.* Whether you have one agent or two, the relationship should be spelled out.

- *Income.* The financial arrangements have to be made as explicit as possible.

- *Expenses.* Clarify who will pay for expenses, especially in works that require a lot of illustrations or permissions.

- *Copyright.* Make sure the copyright is registered in both your names.

- *Bylines.* If both names will appear on the book, whose will come first? And how will the relationship between author and writer be phrased: "and"? "with"? "as told to"?

- *Term.* It is common practice to make collaboration agreements coextensive with the copyright of the book.

- *Assignability.* The contract should ensure that each party has the right to carry on with the work should his or her collaborator become unable to continue.

- *Premature termination.* Terms for termination of the contract should be spelled out.

- *Arbitration.* Arbitration is a less expensive alternative to litigation. Make sure your letter of agreement specifies that the parties will submit to binding arbitration should a disagreement arise.

mark of a ghostwriter," read the *New York Times*'s review of my greatest celebrity triumph. But the editors knew, and that is how a ghosting reputation is built.

IN CASE OF SUCCESS

It is every writer's dream to hit it big. Images of fat royalty checks and carefree days spent writing the long-postponed novel fill our heads. But even success has its pitfalls. Here are a couple potential problems to watch out for.

Piggy-Backing

Should your book sell well enough for the publisher to offer you a contract on a second book, you could be tripped up by an insidious device called piggy-backing (or joint accounting). When book contracts are piggy-backed, the advance for the second book comes out of the royalties from the first, which means, in effect, that you're paying your own advance. Make sure your agent protects you against this. The publisher—not you—should pay the advance.

"Authoritis"

If the book's a hit, be prepared for a change in attitude on the part of your client, who suddenly and happily has a literary reputation. By the time negotiations begin for a second book, "authors" are usually convinced they did write the first book, which everyone says sounds so much like them.

Because they've seen earnings from the book go from a pie-in-the-sky possibility to those lovely checks that arrive from the publisher twice a year, their perception of the percentage of royalties due them may also undergo a radical change. They may no longer like the idea of giving up 50 percent. If you're negotiating a second book deal with the same author, don't back down on this. Insist on the same percentage you had for the first book. Convince the author that it would be foolish and time-consuming to end a successful relationship and go bargain-hunting for another writer.

PERKS

Every profession needs perquisites, and those of celebrity ghosting can be especially nice.

Travel to Exotic Places

I and my tape recorder have traveled to private tropical beaches, the better spas, and mountaintop resorts—all those hideaways celebrities go to in order to have a little peace and quiet to "write" their books. Of course, I do not presume to suggest that we go someplace luxurious. I describe the ideal book-collaborating conditions as monklike, isolated, phoneless, faxless, email-free, and devoid of all the distractions of career and family. To the client this can translate into something like La Costa. Fine with me.

Benefits to Fiction Writing

I live to write fiction, which may or may not be sold or even finished, although both are the goal and grand obsession. I find that ghostwriting is a valuable way to sensitize my ear to people's unique ways of speaking. After several weeks of listening to the taped voice of my client and reading transcriptions, I begin to make seemingly unconscious word and style choices that are authentically the author's own. It is a joy to break out of the tyranny of one's own voice. Ghosting makes a writer keen to the nuances of an individual's speech—the word choices and sentence construction, the quirks and repetitions—and that developed sensitivity becomes a very useful tool in writing fiction.

The "Author" Does the Promoting

While I mentally roam around in the 1870s, developing the middle section of a novel, the author of my mini-bestseller is out on the radio-television-bookstore circuit, rushing from airport to airport, drinking weak coffee, promoting the book three or four times a day. Me, I get to stay home—and that's the best part. Home is the book writer's natural habitat, and, if I've been fairly paid, I can look forward to a few months holed up with myself before I have to go scare up the next project.

If collaboration and ghostwriting relationships are like marriages, I'm convinced the ghostwriter gets the better half.

The Journalism Market

Freelance journalism is an exciting and rewarding professional pursuit. You can choose the subjects you want to write about, interview interesting people, travel, and see your work in print in a matter of weeks or months—sometimes even days.

Freelance journalism can also be a frustrating and defeating cycle of killed stories, late payments, squabbling over expenses, and fighting for the integrity of your stories.

It is a rough world out there, and no journalist alive, no matter how talented and lucky, can claim to have reaped the rewards of the trade without having had to grapple with some of the confusing, undisciplined, and at times outright exploitative practices of the business.

There is no foolproof way to practice journalism without occasionally getting burned, but there are things you can do to protect yourself. Learn where the pitfalls are: the more you know about how the business works, the better able you will be to look after your own interests. Sharpen your business skills by becoming savvy at interpreting contracts, by learning how to negotiate better fees and terms, and by anticipating problems and dealing with them quickly and professionally when they do arise.

The Periodicals Marketplace

The freelance journalism market is vast. There are thousands and thousands of publications that hire freelance writers, ranging from national general-interest glossies, to special-interest and regional magazines, to neighborhood newspapers, to online periodicals.

The sheer size of this seemingly ever-growing market is a boon for freelance journalists. But the flip side of the market's size is its increasing fragmentation *and* its increasing consolidation. On the one hand, publications tend to focus more and more narrowly on precisely defined groups of readers, with editorial content dictated by demographics and advertisers. As a result, freelancers have to deal with larger numbers of publications and need to develop more sophisticated marketing strategies for their story ideas. On the other hand, the consolidation of more and more magazines under fewer large media companies means that all the magazines owned by a vertically integrated company are likely to impose similar—and similarly onerous—contracts on freelancers.

QUERIES

In this complex and competitive environment, queries are the lifeblood of a journalist. To make a living from writing, you have to generate a constant stream of ideas and pitch them effectively to publications that are likely to buy them. Query development is a three-part task: you come up with a good concept for an article, identify publications whose audience and editorial focus would be appropriate for the story, and then approach the publications with specifically targeted proposals.

Queries are the lifeblood of a journalist

Say you want to do a story on the use of steroids in pigeon racing. You have found a source in the bird-racing community and feel that you can get a real scoop. Where do you take the idea?

You go to the library and look up "pigeon" in *The Standard Periodical Directory* (Oxbridge Communications Inc., New York, NY). You find that there are several publications dealing with pigeons, among them *American Racing Pigeon News.* Bingo! You have found a perfect market for your story. The story, you feel, might have a broader appeal, so you decide to pitch it to *Parade* and *Audubon,* as well.

Clearly, you need to customize your proposal for each publication. For *American Racing Pigeon News,* an in-depth look at the practice of drugging birds and its impact on the sport would be appropriate. For *Parade,* you may want to propose an exposé about celebrities involved in pigeon "pumping." *Audubon* might buy an article about the effects of steroids on the pigeons themselves.

You get the idea: to market your stories effectively, you have to be knowledgeable about the marketplace and adept at meeting the editorial needs of the publications for which you write.

ASSIGNMENTS

Imagine. It is early Monday morning. You have dragged yourself out of bed and are trying to focus on the day's headlines while waiting anxiously for the coffee machine to pour the first cup. The phone rings. You give a start and rush to the phone, convinced that the IRS is calling to announce an audit.

Entering a deal without a written contract is asking for trouble

To your surprise and jubilation, it is the editor from *Forbes* to whom you recently sent a proposal for a feature story on e-business in Russia. She wants the story. You discuss the fee, expenses, and deadline, and you "shake" on the deal. Ecstatic, you charge the ticket to Saint Petersburg and begin packing.

Here we interrupt the daydream.

An assignment is a business deal, and entering a deal without a written contract is asking for trouble. An assignment is not finalized until you and your editor have agreed to mutually acceptable terms and have signed a contract that clearly spells out those terms.

Although at one time verbal contracts were the norm in the business, most publications now have their own "standard" written contracts for freelance writers. If you get an assignment from a periodical that does not have a standard contract, you should send the editor a letter of agreement outlining all the agreed-upon terms.

It does not really matter where the contract originates—with you or with the publisher. **It is essential, however, that you do not invest significant amounts of time or incur expenses before the deal is finalized with a contract.**

Some will ask, "What if the deadline is really tight? How can I wait for a contract?" In fact, some underhanded editors have been known to use this logic to avoid giving writers contracts. The answer is simple: *fax.* Today, you can complete negotiations and exchange signed contracts in minutes—provided both parties are willing.

CONTRACTS

Getting an assignment is a thrill. You feel desired, accomplished, and not a little high. It is very important, though, not to let yourself get so lost in the euphoria of the moment that you neglect to negotiate a good deal. The time of assignment is when you have the most leverage. The editor is excited about the story and is likely to be willing to meet at least some of your conditions.

We will now take a look at what constitutes a good deal by examining the various elements that go into a written contract between a freelance journalist and a periodical.

Rights

Traditionally, periodicals bought first North American serial rights only. This allowed them to publish the article once in the United States and Canada. To resell or reprint the piece, they had to get the writer's permission and negotiate a separate fee.

In the 1990s it became common for periodicals to attempt to seize a variety of other rights—such as syndication, anthology, foreign reprint, and electronic publication rights—for no extra fee. Then, some periodicals began offering contracts that asked the writer to surrender *all* rights in one fell swoop—again, without the writer's receiving additional compensation.

An all-rights clause in a magazine contract often reads something like this (minus the legalese): "Author assigns to publisher the exclusive right to publish the work throughout the universe in all media that have been or ever will be invented." After your eyes unglaze, you will realize that, by signing a contract like this, you relinquish all future control over that piece of work and any possibility of making money off its republication.

Of late, a less draconian but still highly objectionable kind of contract has become common, one in which the magazine requests exclusive one-time publication rights and nonexclusive (and ongoing) secondary rights in other categories.

The NWU holds that it is fundamentally unfair for periodicals to demand anything other than one-time publication rights without the writer's receiving additional compensation for republication. It undermines writers' earning potential, and it is economically extremely lopsided. After all, when you buy a magazine, you do not purchase the right to sell photocopies of the issue. There is a simple principle at play here: one fee, one use.

For the basic fee, negotiate to sell one-time North American serial rights only. Append to your contract a phrase like, "All other rights to be negotiated separately."

Rates

There seems to be no logic to how periodicals pay. There are some small publications that pay as well as national glossies and some established magazines that pay as little as regional startups. How do you compare one magazine to another?

The National Union of Journalists in the U.K. uses per-page advertising rates to estimate what a periodical's rate structure should be. This is a logical and reliable method. We will be using it in the "Rates and Practices" section of this chapter, below, and we recommend it as the best way to evaluate magazine pay rates. The rate a page of advertising commands in a particular publication reflects the publication's success and therefore its ability to pay writers. For example, in early 2000 *National Geographic* charged a little over $167,000 for a four-color ad page, and *Woman's Day* charged approximately $165,000. Clearly, both publications are in the same high "success" bracket and should pay writers on the same high scale.

For more on periodicals' ad and pay rates, see pages 88–93.

At present, things seldom work this way. Even individual publications often do not pay fair, consistent rates to journalists. A lot of intangibles—such as your relationship with the editor, the size of the periodical's inventory, and maybe even the day of the week—go into the determination of the rate a publication offers you. But, as radical as this may sound, you have a say in how much you get paid.

Under no circumstances should you accept the editor's first offer without negotiating. Always ask for more money. You will be surprised how often you will succeed.

Kill Fees

There is only one legitimate reason for a publication not to pay a writer the full fee for an assigned article: the writer's failure to deliver on the terms of the agreement. Unfortunately, more often than not, the kill fee is used as a means to shift most of the financial risk involved in producing a story to the writer.

It is essential that contracts spell out as precisely as possible the conditions under which the story can be killed

Certainly, circumstances sometimes arise that make it necessary to kill articles. A news event might make the topic obsolete; a story on the same subject may appear in a rival publication; or the writer and the editor may simply not agree on the angle for the piece. But isn't it profoundly unfair that we, self-supporting writers, should bear the brunt of these uncertainties?

A typical "guarantee" clause in a magazine contract reads something like: "In the event the work is not acceptable and cannot be revised to the publication's satisfaction, the publication will pay the author 25 percent of the agreed-upon fee." Such broad language gives periodicals complete discretion to kill stories. An article can be labeled unacceptable for a great variety of reasons. In fact, some publications assign more articles than they can use, expecting to kill as many as two of every three.

Editors have to take more responsibility—and assume more of the risk—for selecting writers and assigning articles. The editor, after all, has a kind of final power: if a writer fails to deliver, the editor can choose not to work with that writer again. But if you have done the work, you should get paid. We can again reverse the situation to see how absurd it is. If you buy a magazine and think it is badly written and designed, can you get your money back?

It may take a while for kill fees to be abolished, of course. In the meantime, it is essential that contracts spell out as precisely as possible the conditions under which the story can be killed and the amount of the kill fee, which should never be less than one-fourth to one-half of the original fee.

Payment Schedule

As important as how much you get paid is *when* you get paid. Your contract may promise you $3,000 for a 1,500-word story, but that will not do you much good if it takes forever to collect. You know how insistent landlords are about getting their rent on time.

Most periodicals contract to pay either on acceptance or on publication. Neither of these choices is advantageous to writers. Many publications carry very large inventories and therefore take months and months to review and accept articles that are submitted on deadline. It takes even longer for stories to get printed. In fact, some articles that are accepted are never published.

To make matters worse, you might have to wait up to several months after the agreed-upon payment time to get

Be firm and businesslike about collecting payments

your check. In the survey of NWU-member journalists conducted for the first edition of this *Guide,* we found it common for periodicals to pay 60, 90, or even 120 days after acceptance or publication. The followup survey performed for the present edition indicated that publishers are still too often guilty of such inexcusable lateness.

The best deal is one that provides for payment in full within 30 days of submission. It is your right to be paid as soon as you have rendered your service and not after the publication makes use of the product you delivered. Either that, or we should be able to pay for magazines and newspapers only after we read them. Payment on acceptance is second best; payment on publication is unacceptable.

In addition to trying to negotiate better contract terms, you have to be firm and businesslike about collecting payments. Always enclose an invoice when you submit your article. And do not be ashamed of reminding your editor about pending payments. You are not begging, simply running your business.

Expenses

The fee a periodical pays you for an article is meant only to compensate you for your work in researching and writing the story. Since it is often necessary to travel, make long-distance phone calls, and incur other out-of-pocket expenses to get a story, it is a widely accepted practice for publications to reimburse writers for such expenses.

Your contracts with periodicals should always include an "expenses" clause. This clause should detail the types of expenses that will be reimbursed and set a schedule for reimbursement. You will obviously have to supply receipts for the expenses, so a reasonable reimbursement schedule is 15 days after submission of receipts.

Editorial Control

Few experiences are quite as deflating and infuriating as reading an article of yours that's just been published only to realize that a glaring factual error was introduced during editing—or that it contains copy that you did not write and did not approve (and with which you may even disagree!). Unfortunately, these kinds of things happen fairly frequently when writers are not given an opportunity to review the edited version of a story.

Since your reputation and credibility ride on every byline, insist on seeing proofs of all your stories. A clause in the contract to that effect is a good way to protect yourself.

It is a good idea to take the "editorial control" clause one step further by reserving the right to remove your byline from the article—without losing the fee—if a dispute about the final form of the article cannot be resolved. In the event that you and your editor simply do not agree on what the story should look like, you will have a legal way to disassociate yourself from the piece and still get paid.

Revisions

As much as we writers may hate the idea, it is reasonable to expect that just about all stories need some rewriting. It is far from reasonable, however, to expect a writer to continue working on the same piece for months—for the same fee.

A good deal will specify the number of revisions covered by the basic fee. The NWU's position is that writers should not be expected to perform more than one substantive revision for the agreed-upon fee. The contract should specify that fees for additional revisions will be negotiated based on their extent.

There is no way to avoid rewriting, but you can prevent major disasters by making sure that you and your editor are very clear about the assignment. A detailed description of the assignment should also be included in the contract.

Arbitration

Disputes can arise even if one does everything "right." In a fight with a publisher, the writer is at a distinct disadvantage. Periodicals tend to be owned by corporations that maintain large legal departments. Few writers, on the other hand, have the money needed for a legal battle.

Arbitration is an inexpensive way to settle disputes, one that is within writers' financial reach. Organizations such as the American Arbitration Association offer arbitration services, with objective hearings and binding decisions. An "arbitration" clause should specify that the arbiter's fee will be shared by the publication and the writer.

A Final Word about Contracts

Contracts between writers and publishers usually originate with the publisher. It is vital that you remember two things about magazine publishers' contracts: (1) they are written by the publication's lawyers, who have their client's—not your—interests in mind, and (2) you should view them as starting points for negotiations, not as tablets from the mountain.

No matter how much your editor tries to convince you that the contract you've been offered is the periodical's "standard" contract, there is always room for changes. Negotiate. Cross out offensive language. Write in your own conditions. Do whatever it takes to make the assignment a good deal for you.

PUBLICATION

All right. You struggled to get your foot in the door at the hot new pop-culture magazine, *Eighties Now*. Your proposal for "The Comeback of Conspicuous Consumption" got a lot of interest, and you got the assignment. You negotiated hard and got a good fee and a solid contract. The story turned out well. You got paid (on submission). And then you waited . . . and waited . . . and . . . .

Many periodicals maintain huge inventories; so articles sometimes do not appear until months after deadline. One NWU survey showed that a delay of

8 to 12 weeks between submission and publication is common. For a monthly, that is "timely." But far longer delays are by no means unusual.

Unfortunately, there is little that writers can do to protect their articles from getting lost in inventory. You cannot write a publication date into the contract. At most, you can choose not to work for publications where you have gotten burned. And, if enough of us do that, we might just create an industry standard for timely publication.

Rates and Practices

Freelance journalists write for thousands of different publications, from national glossies and regional magazines, to online periodicals, to trade and professional publications, to newspapers of all sizes and circulations. It is obviously impossible to generalize about such a broad range of markets. Therefore, to make our discussion of rates and practices in journalism sensible, we present information for four kinds of publications for which freelance journalists write: consumer magazines, trade magazines, professional magazines, and newspapers. The online market is still developing; perhaps by the next edition of this *Guide,* we will be able to provide solid, meaningful generalizations about Web publications' rates based on writers' real experience.

For more on journalism issues in electronic publishing, see pages 120–127.

RATES

How do you know what is a reasonable pay rate to expect from a magazine? Books such as *Writer's Market* (published annually by Writer's Digest Books) list pay rates based on surveys of editors. The National Writers Union has its own online resource, the MagazineRates Database, that shows how much actual writers have actually received at hundreds of periodicals. This resource is for members only. But if you are not a member, or the publication you are interested in is not listed in that database, there is another way to figure out how much you should charge. In fact, we believe the method outlined below is the best way for writers to determine how much they should be paid for their work.

What is a reasonable pay rate to expect from a magazine?

In this *Guide,* we use the system employed by the National Union of Journalists in the U.K., in which pay rates are established commensurate with publications' advertising rates. This is an equitable and logical system, since it links a magazine's financial relationship with freelance writers to its economic prosperity.

Since most of us are not used to thinking of the rates we get from magazines as a function of what they charge for advertising, figuring out an acceptable rate for a specific magazine might take a little getting used to. But the system is easy to use.

Step 1. Find out the publication's rate for a full-page ad.

In Tables 3.1, 3.2, and 3.3, we've divided print magazines into three categories—consumer magazines, trade publications, and professional publications—and then further subdivided each category into groups based on the cost of one full page of advertising. Newspaper ad-rate structures are more complex, and so in Table 3.4 we have divided them up according to geographic scope. If the periodical you're interested in writing for is not one of those listed in the tables, you can find out its ad rates from the *Standard Rate & Data Service* directories, which are available at many libraries, or from the magazine's media kit, which anyone can get by calling the publisher's advertising department.

Step 2. Compare the periodical to others in its ad-rate group to decide what kind of rate to negotiate for.

For each group, we provide a list of examples of publications that charge those rates. Then we give you a range of rates paid to freelance writers in that group, along with the NWU's recommended freelance rates for the group.

For instance, if you are interested in *Glamour*, which in early 2000 was charging $99,510 per page of advertising and therefore belongs in Group 4, you would likely try to get $1.50 to $2.00 a word.

Before talking about money, arm yourself with as much information as you can. Ask the editor what the periodical pays for stories that appear in various sections, and talk to other writers who have written for the publication. And, if you're an NWU member, check the MagazineRates database on the union's website, at www.nwu.org.

Step 3. Consider all your needs and options before negotiating.

There are always individual considerations in valuing one's work. You may really want the exposure of a national publication, for instance, and therefore you might accept a relatively low fee from an editor who won't budge. Or you may need to pay for next month's groceries, and so decide not to hold out for an extra 10 cents a word.

But always estimate carefully how long a piece will take to write, including editing and fact-checking time. **Figure out how much you need to make for that period, and if you cannot get paid a living wage, reconsider.** Remember that magazine publishing is a business. No commercial enterprise should expect you to subsidize it, and unless you have somebody subsidizing you, you can't afford to work for too little.

(Note that these recommendations are for magazines where you work to earn money. If you are writing for a publication that supports a particular cause that you want to contribute to, you may want to accept a reduced fee or do the work pro bono.)

You might think it is unrealistic and self-defeating to ask for $2 a word if you are used to getting half that or less. But the fact is that freelance journalists are grossly underpaid, and it is up to us to begin to change the situation.

The recommendations we make here are meant to start an incremental change in the industry. There is a wide gap between current economic conditions in the freelance journalism market and the equitable conditions that should exist. The minimum standards we propose here represent the first step in bridging this gap.

Consumer Magazines

We subdivided the consumer magazine market into seven ad-rate groups, based on the cost of a full-page, four-color ad. Table 3.1 (pages 88–89) lists these groups, along with examples of magazines that fell within them in early 2000. The pay ranges listed here are based on rates that NWU members reported to the MagazineRates Database as well as on information provided by freelance journalists responding to the targeted survey conducted for this edition of the *Guide.* They do not represent a comprehensive survey of industry standards, but rather the personal experiences of a number of working journalists. The NWU Recommendations are essentially a compromise between what journalists reported they actually were paid and what we believe magazines should pay, based on their ad-rate structure. Remember that, in each case, our recommendation is what we believe to be a fair rate for *first North American serial rights only.* If you grant the publisher additional rights, you should be paid an additional fee or a higher per-word rate.

Trade Publications

Pay rates for trade publications can also be linked to the magazines' economic performances as expressed by their advertising rates. Table 3.2 (pages 90–91) shows the four ad-rate groups into which trade publications are divided, and corresponding per-word pay rates.

Professional Publications

Pay rates in professional publications can be considered in light of the publications' advertising rates, too. Since many professional publications are printed in only two colors or even just black and white, we looked at their ad rates for full-page, black-and-white advertising. The groups are shown in Table 3.3 (pages 90–91).

Newspapers

Newspapers, especially those that publish several editions, tend to have more complex advertising-rate structures than magazines. It is, therefore, more difficult to compare newspapers based on this criterion. A more practical way is to group newspapers according to their geographic scope. We identified four groups, as shown in Table 3.4 (pages 92–93): national dailies, national weeklies, state/regional, and local.

PRACTICES

The treatment writers receive from the publications we work for is just as important as how much we get paid. Such issues as kill fees, rights, and contracts are of universal concern. In these matters, however, there is no need to differentiate among publications. A local newspaper should treat freelance journalists as well as a glossy national magazine. That is why the National Writers Union is calling for consistent minimum standards of industry practice.

Unless otherwise noted, all statistical information presented below is derived from a targeted survey of NWU-member freelance journalists conducted in the winter and spring of 2000.

Contracts

Freelance writing is a business, and every story assignment is a business deal that should be concluded with a written contract. Many writers, however, seem to discount the importance of contracts. In our research, we asked writers whether they had used contracts in their most recent assignments; Table 3.5 (page 92) gives the results

The responsibility for this situation lies equally with publishers, of course. Editors will often give the excuse that there is no time to deal with a contract, especially if the assignment involves a time-sensitive subject. A fax machine, of course, quickly takes care of this obstacle to signing a written agreement.

Ultimately, we writers are accountable for our own businesses. If you sell a story to a magazine that does not use contracts, outline the agreement in a letter, sign it, and send it to the editor. This is a common practice in cases where assignments are made verbally, and it is highly advisable.

Many writers do not even protect themselves in this simple way, however. "I've known my editor for years," many writers say. "I don't need written agreements or contracts." It is true that publishing traditionally operated on

TABLE 3.1. **CONSUMER MAGAZINE PAY RATES (IN $ PER WORD)**

Ad-rate group	Examples of magazines in this group
Group 1: $200,000 and over	*Modern Maturity, Parade*
Group 2: $150,000–$200,000	*Family Circle, National Geographic, Newsweek, Reader's Digest, Sports Illustrated, Time, Woman's Day*
Group 3: $100,000–$150,000	*Car & Driver, Cosmopolitan, McCall's, Men's Health, Money, Playboy, People, TV Guide, US News and World Report*
Group 4: $75,000–$100,000	*Business Week, Country Home, Entertainment Weekly, Field and Stream, Glamour, Life, Parenting, Poolife, Popular Mechanics, Prevention, Redbook, Seventeen, Vanity Fair*
Group 5: $50,000–$75,000	*Allure, American Baby, Automobile, Child, Condé Nast Traveler, Ebony, Elle, Esquire, Fitness, Forbes, Harper's Bazaar, New York Times Magazine, PC Magazine, The New Yorker, US, Victoria*
Group 6: $25,000–$50,000	*Atlantic Monthly, Black Enterprise, Boating, Chicago Tribune Magazine, Good Housekeeping, Mature Outlook, Modern Bride, Muscle and Fitness, New York Magazine, Penthouse, Premier, Town and Country*
Group 7: $25,000 and under	*The Advocate, American Way, Art & Antiques, Cat Fancy, Cigar Aficionado, Hispanic, Interview, Mother Jones, The New Republic, Palm Beach Illustrated, Playgirl, Pulse, Vermont Magazine, Wine Spectator*

Ad-rate data from Standard Rate & Data Service directories.

handshakes, secured by the personal relationships between writers and editors. But publishing is not what it used to be; the editor with whom you establish a relationship today is quite likely to be gone tomorrow. In any case, you are not entering an agreement with the editor but with the organization for which the editor works.

Always protect yourself with a written contract or confirmation letter.

Low	Prevalent range	High	NWU recommends (at least)
$1.00	$1.00–$3.00	$3.35	$3.00
$1.00	$1.00–$2.00	$3.40	$2.00–$2.50
$0.50	$1.00–$1.50	$2.15	$1.50–$2.00
$0.50	$1.00–$1.50	$2.50	$1.50–$2.00
$1.00	$1.00–$1.50	$2.00	$1.50
$0.50	$0.50–$1.50	$2.00	$1.00–$1.50
$0.10	$0.50–$1.00	$1.00	$1.00

TABLE 3.2. **TRADE MAGAZINE PAY RATES (IN $ PER WORD)**

Ad-rate group	Examples of magazines in this group
Group 1: $20,000 and over	*AV Video Multimedia Producer, Computer World, PC Week*
Group 2: $10,000–$20,000	*Architectural Record, Electronic Design, Food Service Director, Restaurant Business, Web Techniques*
Group 3: $5,000–$10,000	*Chemical Processing, Derivatives Strategy, E Business Advisor, Editor and Publisher, Electronic News, Sacramento Business Journal, Software Strategies*
Group 4: $5,000 and under	*American Cinematographer, Fabric Architecture, Pastry Art & Design, Real Estate Forum, Vermont Business*

Ad-rate data from Standard Rate & Data Service directories.

TABLE 3.3. **PROFESSIONAL MAGAZINE PAY RATES (IN $ PER WORD)**

Ad-rate group	Examples of magazines in this group
Group 1: $10,000 and over[a]	*ABA Journal, Electronic Engineering Times, Defense Electronics*
Group 2: $5,000–$10,000[b]	*American Educator, Columbia Journalism Review, Environmental Science and Technology, Oncology Times*
Group 3: $5,000 and under[b]	*Academe, Bench and Bar, Library Journal, NJ Medicine*

Ad-rate data from Standard Rate & Data Service directories.
[a]Pay-rate data in this row based on 1995 NWU survey results.
[b]Some pay-rate data in these rows based on 1995 NWU survey results.

Low	Prevalent range	High	NWU recommends (at least)
$0.75	$0.75–$1.40	$1.40	$1.00
$0.30	$0.35–$0.80	$1.00	$0.75
$0.18	$0.25–$0.75	$0.75	$0.60
$0.10	$0.25–$0.65	$0.75	$0.50

Low	Prevalent range	High	NWU recommends (at least)
$0.33	$0.75–$1.00	$1.25	$1.00
$0.25	$0.50–$1.00	$1.20	$0.80
$0.10	$0.25–$0.75	$1.00	$0.60

TABLE 3.4. **NEWSPAPER PAY RATES (IN $ PER WORD)**

Geographic group	Examples of newspapers in this group
Group 1: National dailies	*New York Times, Los Angeles Times, Wall Street Journal, Washington Post*
Group 2: National weeklies	*LA Weekly, Village Voice, National Employment Weekly, New York Observer*
Group 3: State/regional	*Boston Globe, Chicago Tribune, Dallas Morning News, Miami Herald, Newsday, Phoenix Republic Gazette, San Francisco Examiner, Philadelphia Inquirer*
Group 4: Local	*Boston Phoenix, Buffalo News, New York Daily News, Newark Star Ledger, San Jose Mercury News, Tallahassean*

TABLE 3.5. **CONTRACT USE**

Freelance journalists writing for:	Used contracts	Did not use contracts
Consumer magazines	58%[a]	42%
Trade publications	56%	44%
Professional publications	40%	60%
Newspapers	25%	75%

[a] All percentages are for total number of articles reported.

Prevalent range	NWU recommends (at least)
$0.30–$1.00	$1.00
$0.30–$0.50	$0.50
$0.15–$0.45	$0.40
$0.15–$0.35	$0.30

Rights

Until fairly recently, publishers of periodicals were content to buy first North American serial rights only—that is, the right to publish an article once in the United States and Canada. If they wanted to reprint or resell the story, they had to get the writer's permission and negotiate a separate fee.

Periodicals are now frequently attempting to seize many other rights for no extra fee. To find out the extent of the problem, we asked freelance journalists whether their most recent contracts included a grant of rights other than first North American publication rights. We found that roughly half of writers for consumer, trade, and professional magazines had signed over additional rights, as had two-thirds of online magazine writers and an extraordinarily high 85 percent of newspaper writers.

Publishers' demands for any rights other than one-time publication rights are fundamentally unfair and economically inequitable. The National Writers Union has long called for the principle of "one fee, one use" to be adopted as the industry standard. For the basic fee, negotiate to sell one-time North American print publication rights only. Other rights should be sold separately.

Payments

When you get paid is almost as important as how much you get paid. Many publications contract to pay either on acceptance or on publication. (Payment on submission is more desirable, in part because it precludes the use of kill

TABLE 3.6. **TIMING OF PAYMENTS**

Type of periodical	On submission	On acceptance	On publication
Print magazines	25%[a]	49%	26%
Newspapers	10%	35%	55%
Online publications	29%	37%	34%

[a]Percentages are for total number of articles reported.

fees.) We asked freelance journalists when they were paid for their work. Results are summarized in Table 3.6.

The NWU strongly recommends that writers be paid on submission.

Kill Fees

The kill fee is an insidious device. It allows publishers to decide at the last minute—and at their sole discretion—whether to use an assigned article or not. And the only penalty they pay is a small fraction of the contracted-for fee.

The National Writers Union holds that a writer who fulfills the terms of his or her contract should be paid in full, regardless of whether the publisher decides to print the article. It is going to be difficult to convince publishers to stop using kill fees all at once. **If you cannot get kill fees out of your contracts, we recommend that you negotiate them up as high as possible.**

Expenses

It is often necessary to spend money on travel, phone calls, research fees, and so on. If writers were to pay these expenses out of the fees paid by magazines, we would have little to show for our labor. Unfortunately, a great many freelance journalists do subsidize publishers by paying the expenses they incur in researching and writing stories.

All reasonable expenses should be reimbursed by the magazine within 15 days of submission of receipts. Make sure your contracts include a clause that specifies what will be considered reasonable expenses and the maximum amount the publication agrees to reimburse. If you are going to exceed the agreed-upon maximum, call the editor and follow up with a confirmation letter.

Revisions

Contracts should specify that one revision of the article will be provided by the writer and that a separate fee will be paid for additional rewrites. Currently, this is rarely the case. We asked writers how frequently the number of rewrites was specified in their contracts. Table 3.7 (next page) gives the disappointing results.

Editorial Control

Freelancers often complain that their stories are changed without permission. We wanted to find out how prevalent this practice is. Table 3.8 (next page) shows what freelance journalists told us in response to our asking whether the stories they had written in the previous 24 months had been altered without their approval.

Writers have every right to see the final, edited versions of their stories before publication. After all, our names and reputations, to say nothing of professional pride, ride on every article.

Journalism contracts should include an "editorial control" clause that ensures that the writer will have the opportunity to review and make changes to the final, edited version of the article.

Response to Queries

Another concern that freelance journalists raise is the amount of time it takes publications to respond to queries. Table 3.9 (next page) shows what we found when we asked freelance journalists how long, on average, it takes periodicals to respond their queries.

Writing on Spec

Writing on spec—that is, doing the research and writing on your own time and then trying to sell the finished story—is one of those issues about which people tend to have very strong feelings. Some swear by it; others think it is preposterous. Our research showed that 59 percent of respondents write on spec, although most of these do so only occasionally. Of articles written on spec, 51 percent were eventually sold to a publisher.

In general, the NWU believes that writers should not write on spec. Submit queries rather than completed articles. It is difficult enough to make a living as a freelance journalist without assuming the financial risk of working on spec.

Some people might respond to everything we have talked about in this chapter by saying that it is easy for the NWU to talk about setting standards, but

TABLE 3.7. **REWRITES SPECIFIED IN CONTRACT?**

Response	Percentage
Never	53%
Rarely	29%
Sometimes	18%

TABLE 3.8. **STORIES ALTERED WITHOUT WRITER'S APPROVAL?**

Type of periodical	Yes	No
Print magazines	15%[a]	85%
Newspapers	14%	86%
Online publications	37%	63%

[a]All percentages are for total number of articles reported.

TABLE 3.9. **QUERY RESPONSE TIME (PRINT AND ONLINE PUBLICATIONS)**

Response time	Percentage
1–3 weeks	68%
4–6 weeks	8%
6–8 weeks	8%
More than 8 weeks	16%

that it is the individual writer who has the tough job of negotiating fees and contracts. In one sense that is true: as freelancers we all have to take responsibility for our own businesses. But the NWU also provides information, education, support, and grievance assistance.

The NWU Standard Journalism Contract

by Judith Levine

Fifteen or twenty years ago, journalism appeared in one medium: print. Contracts reflected that: publishers typically bought "first North American print rights," the license to use an article once in one publication. As the need arose, they would buy subsidiary rights—for instance, to include a piece in an anthology. Then electronic publishing was invented. With the advent of CD-ROMs and the World Wide Web, publishers hit on the concept of "repurposing" content in many different media. In the early and mid-1990s, they started asking writers to sign what are known as *all-rights contracts.*

With the advent of the Web, publishers hit on the concept of "repurposing" content

FIGHTING ALL-RIGHTS CONTRACTS

All-rights contracts usually contained a clause to the effect that the writer granted the publisher the right to publish the work in any and all media that had ever been or would ever be invented throughout the universe. (Apparently, the publishers and corporate lawyers who drew up these contracts were big believers in extraterrestrial forms of life!) The contracts gave publishers the right to reuse a writer's work in any way they saw fit, all for the price of a single use.

At about the same time, the National Writers Union created its own model contract for journalists, the NWU Standard Journalism Contract (SJC). The idea was that individual writers would submit this standard contract in place of an oral agreement or a publisher's contract; little by little, objectionable practices such as all-rights licenses, payment on publication, and kill fees would diminish. Eventually, as more and more writers demanded better terms, these practices would cease.

But submitting our own contract in place of a publisher's proved to be difficult because, as individuals, we were confronting contracts written by whole legal departments, which directed editors to impose the language. Though writers could get some changes, too often the editors stood fast on the basic rights clauses.

The NWU continues to promote the Standard Journalism Contract, however, so that writers, editors, and publishers can see what a fair contract—fair and reasonable to both parties—looks like. We also use it in our contract classes for journalists, where we teach writers how to conduct themselves professionally and to negotiate with editors for better terms and pay. And the SJC's language can still be used as a model for rewriting clauses of a publisher's boilerplate contract.

Use the SJC's language as a model for rewriting boilerplate clauses

In the last few years, writers' battles against all-rights contracts have been fairly successful. Pure all-rights contracts—contracts that ask for exclusive rights in all media for a one-time fee—are becoming rarer.

Instead, most publishers now ask for a combination of exclusive rights to certain media for certain periods of time—some of them perpetual—and nonexclusive rights to others. Some want all these rights without additional compensation to the author; others pay percentages of the original fee for subsidiary rights and offer to share the proceeds of third-party licenses. While the nonexclusivity of these agreements allows the writer to resell his or her work, a publisher's grant of rights in another medium may make it more difficult for the author to resell the work. For example, if a print publisher puts an article in an online archive, the author may find it more difficult to resell the work to an online publication.

The National Writers Union recommends that writers be paid for any additional uses, including making the work available in Web archives. The NWU believes that the rate you request will vary depending on the publication, the article, and how the publisher wishes to reuse it. For example, the rights to post a story in a Web archive may be worth as much as the original print publication of the article, since the writer could conceivably resell the story to an online publication. If a publisher wishes to resell an article to a third party, then the author should receive 50 percent of whatever the publisher realizes from the sale. If the publisher objects that it cannot track subsequent reuse and sales, the author should ask for at least $2 to $3 a word to cover all nonexclusive secondary rights. Increasingly, the difficulty of policing secondary uses is convincing NWU contract advisers that the fairest, most efficient strategy may be simply to get more money up front.

OTHER CONTRACT ISSUES

Writers should also be alert to other contract issues. The NWU Standard Journalism Contract says that the writer will provide a coherent and original article that fulfills the assignment. Having a good description of the assignment in the contract is essential, as a large proportion of disputes stem from misunderstandings over the nature of the original assignment.

In return, under the SJC, the publisher pays on submission (not acceptance or publication). There is no kill fee, which means that, providing the author has fulfilled the terms of the assignment, the publisher must pay the writer in full even if the article is never published. This protects writers from editors who change their minds and from changes in the publication's needs that are beyond the writer's control. If an editor assigns an article and the author fulfills the assignment, then the writer should be paid, even if the story never runs—just as a contractor is paid for remodeling a kitchen even if the client later decides she didn't want that green tile after all. The NWU contract also specifies that the publisher will share the cost of arbitration with the writer should a dispute between them occur.

Watch out for a new trend in contracts, the indemnification clause

Writers should watch out for a new trend in contracts, the indemnification clause, which says the publisher is not legally responsible should a lawsuit arise from the article's publication. These clauses are particularly problematic when the contract also says that the publisher has the right to edit the work without the author's permission, since it's unreasonable to hold the author responsible for content over which he or she has no control. The Standard Journalism Contract states that the publisher will defend the writer in the event of a libel suit. (The National Writers Union also offers its members Media Perils libel insurance as additional protection.)

Authors should refuse to sign contracts that give publishers retroactive rights to publish work purchased in the past in media not formerly contracted for without additional compensation to the writer. Some publishers, such as the *Boston Globe,* have recently tried to introduce such clauses to protect themselves from infringements of past contracts, following the NWU's victo-

Standard Journalism Contract

Contract between(Writer)_____

and (Publisher) _____

1. The Writer agrees to prepare an Article of _____ words on the subject of:

_____

_____

for delivery on or before _____ (date). The Writer also agrees to provide one revision of the Article.

2. The Publisher agrees to pay the Writer a fee of $ _____ within thirty (30) days of initial receipt of the Article as assigned above. (In other words, an original and coherent manuscript of approximately the above word count on the subject assigned, and for which appropriate research was completed.)

3. The Publisher agrees that the above fee purchases one-time North American hard-copy print publication rights only. All other rights, including the electronic reproduction, transmission, display, performance, or distribution of the Article, are fully reserved by the Writer.

4. The Publisher agrees to reimburse the Writer for all previously agreed-upon and documented expenses within fifteen (15) days of submission of receipts.

5. The Publisher agrees to make every reasonable effort to make available to the Writer the final, edited version of the Article while there is still time to make changes. In the event of a disagreement over the final form of the Article, the Writer reserves the right to withdraw his/her name from the Article without prejudicing the agreed-upon fee.

6. The Writer guarantees that the Article will not contain material that is consciously libelous or defamatory. In return, the Publisher agrees to provide and pay for counsel to defend the Writer in any litigation arising as a result of the Article.

7. In the event of a dispute between the Writer and the Publisher that cannot be resolved through the National Writers Union (NWU) grievance process, the Writer will have the option of seeking to resolve the matter by arbitration or in court. If arbitration is chosen, the Writer may be represented by the NWU in any procedures before the arbitrator. The arbitrator's fees shall be shared fifty percent (50%) by the Publisher and fifty percent (50%) by the Writer. Any decision reached by the arbitrator may be appealed pursuant to applicable law.

_____   _____
Writer or Writer's Representative   Publisher's Representative

_____   _____
Date   Date

ry in the *Tasini v. New York Times* lawsuit. In that case, a federal appellate court found that publishers do not have the right to republish works in databases and CD-ROMs without the author's express permission.

GOOD FOR THE INDUSTRY

The Standard Journalism Contract is a model that is part of a wider NWU campaign to expand writers' rights in a marketplace that all too often refuses to consider them. At contract orientation sessions, writers share information about editors, fees, publishers' contracts, and developments in the industry. They practice negotiating skills that are tailored to the union's standard contract but flexible enough for any contract. The union's experienced Journalism Division leaders, contract advisers, and grievance officers are available to help members decipher, negotiate, and amend contracts and to resolve problems if they occur.

The points emphasized in the NWU contract are good not only for writers but also for periodical publishing as a whole. Contracts that starve writers of rights, legal protection, and decent fees are death certificates for the periodicals industry, for good writers will no longer be willing or able to write for magazines, newspapers, or online publications. The Standard Journalism Contract is an important step toward improving writers' declining economic lot and gaining them a measure of equality in dealing with publishers. By establishing rules and standards where none exist, it helps restore fairness, professionalism, and civility to the periodicals industry.

Freelancing from Afar

David Lida

As a youth, I had two compelling fantasies: making a living as a writer and living in a foreign country. I began to realize the first in 1983, when I got a job at *Women's Wear Daily*. Seven years later, the second fantasy crystallized. My goal was no longer "a foreign country," but Mexico City, a place that had enchanted me during numerous visits.

I was 30. I had freelanced full time for two and a half years (after five on staff at *WWD*), thus building enough contacts in the magazine world to give me the confidence to make the move.

Professionally, I was as methodical as possible before leaving. I spent days in the library, researching every story angle that might interest any imaginable publication. I met with editors I knew and contacted others I didn't. These efforts resulted in a few assignments and the promise of more later.

Nonetheless, not long after I arrived in Mexico, I experienced the freelancer's familiar panic attack. In one day, I was hit with a one-two punch. An editor at *Connoisseur,* who had given me an assignment before I left, called to say the magazine had been taken over by a new editorial team, which no longer wanted the story. Another magazine, *Diversion,* which had encouraged me on two ideas, decided they wanted only one and offered so little money that it wasn't worth the effort.

Before moving I had bought a fax machine and was optimistic about long-distance communication with editors via this (for me) new technology. However, I soon realized that it was just as easy for them to ignore faxes as it had been to disregard phone calls.

Although as a New York freelancer I had been no stranger to insecurity, my sense of doubt was intensified by the lack of proximity to my sources of work. Fresh worries appeared: What if I never get another assignment? What if all the editors forget I exist? Will I be able to work in a taco stand?

Soon after the one-two punch, however, I was rescued by calls from two different publications: *Bride's,* which assigned me a honeymoon travel piece about Pacific Coast beaches, and *The Advocate,* which wanted a cover story about AIDS activism in Mexico. These were publications I hadn't even thought of soliciting when I lived in New York.

Their calls inspired me to become more expansive in my search for work. I don't claim to have found a foolproof method of staying alive as a freelancer in a foreign country. In fact, survival might require a different strategy from one place to another. But a mixture of doggedness and imagination helped me to consistently gain assignments in Mexico.

I looked farther and wider—not only editorially but geographically. When Canada announced that it would join the North American Free Trade Agreement, I went to the Canadian embassy in Mexico City and did research on that country's publications. After considering the Mexican population in California, I did similar research about L.A.–based magazines. I made a dozen blind solicitations.

Although this was an imperfect, almost arbitrary, way to do business, it bore fruit. The Canadian research resulted in an assignment from a supplement to the *Toronto Globe & Mail* about drawn-out, drunken Mexican business lunches. While the Los Angeles investigation didn't conclude with any jobs, one L.A. editor recommended me for a lucrative story for a Hong Kong airline magazine (about the different ways Spanish is spoken throughout Latin America). Similarly, I sent many of my articles to *Vogue's* travel editor in New York, and although he never gave me work, he recommended me to two other magazines that did.

The need to make a living also propelled me to spread my wings journalistically. I wrote about nearly every conceivable topic: politics, business, arts and entertainment, science, architecture, food, bullfighting. The exigencies of the freelance life drove me to learn more about Mexico in two years than I would have if I'd had a regular job or, I suspect, a regular journalist's job at a bureau or wire service.

Survival through lean periods was easier because Mexico City's cost of living is roughly half that of New York's. Therefore, I could take on certain assignments whose fees would have been lamentable for a New Yorker, such as $700 for a long profile of a woman bullfighter for *The Village Voice,* or $600 (plus $200 expenses) for a *New York Times* travel-section feature on an archaeological site in Veracruz. These paychecks were by no means extravagant, but my monthly rent, to give you an idea, was $330; a taxi from my apartment to the airport cost $7; and dinner out in an elegant restaurant ran about $25 (more modest meals were as little as $2). I have often thought I'd have had a tougher time if, instead of Mexico City, I'd fallen in love with Paris or Tokyo.

The slower pace of life in Mexico, and the fact that accomplishing anything takes more time than Americans are accustomed to, was annoying—but in another sense beneficial.

Let me explain. Once or twice a week, I would walk to the post office—an errand that took 45 minutes round-trip—because leaving letters in a mailbox is too risky in a country whose postal system is unreliable. These errands—as well as getting around an impossibly large and confusing city on assignments—were not wasted time. They awakened the process of discovery in me. I got to know the look, texture, and subtleties of Mexico City street life, which made my writing about Mexico more vivid.

In the course of these missions, I had a lot of time to think—not only about the articles I was working on but about my experience in my adopted country. When I wasn't working on a story, soliciting new work, or writing dunning letters, I spent a lot of time in cafés and cantinas—sometimes with other writers, sometimes with people who had nothing to do with my profession, sometimes alone.

I can't overemphasize the importance of those hours of peaceful reflection. Living in Mexico, where most people work to live and not vice versa, helped me learn to live in the present. In contrast, in New York much of our life is spent planning the future, in fast-paced blips and sound bites, brief encounters and harried phone messages. The constant struggle to survive fosters an ethic wherein moments of meditation make one uneasy. When writers have a free moment in New York, we ask ourselves: Why have I nothing to do? What should I be doing? (Soliciting another editor? Polishing a rewrite?)

I think many writers consider it a dirty secret that we don't sit down and write for eight hours a day—that some of our best work is accomplished walking around thinking, reading, or sitting in a café having a conversation. In contrast to the self-important atmosphere, breathless pace, and brutal expense of New York, the relative tranquillity of my life in Mexico made me comfortable with that reality.

If the cantinas were cozy, there were also some difficult aspects to working in Mexico. For example, press officers of most government agencies perceive their jobs as a variation on the old post of town crier: through communiqués or press conferences, they disseminate officially sanctioned information. Trying to obtain any other data—even harmless statistics with no controversial significance—can be an ordeal. A story for *Longevity* about pollution in Mexico City—an assignment I thought would be easy, given how much had been written on the subject—turned out to be a bureaucratic nightmare, demanding months of research from primarily hostile sources.

For one line of the story I wrote for *The Advocate,* I needed to confirm an accusation that the state-owned oil company tested all prospective administrative employees for HIV as a condition of employment. The company spokeswoman was nonplussed by my query and managed to stall for several weeks, claiming that the only person in the entire company who could answer my question was unavailable (a frequent tactic of Mexican bureaucrats). Since I didn't have a pressing deadline, I finally obtained a juicy, damning quote from her. Had I been working for a daily, I would have had to use a variation of "officials were unavailable for comment."

Even from nonofficial sources, obtaining information could be a trial. For example, the *hemerotecas* (periodicals libraries) of Mexico City have no card catalogs, computers, or indexes. If you don't know which issue of a particular publication you're seeking, you're damned to having to look through periodicals day by day, month by month, hoping to unearth the desired information.

Also, the culture of what has been called *mañana-ismo* is still in place. Although the situation has improved somewhat in the past few years, many Mexicans, even gung-ho businessmen, arrive late for appointments and sometimes don't show up at all. This is by no means judged as harshly as it would be in the United States.

Nonetheless, living in Mexico was a wonderful experience for me, and my first few months back in New York were very difficult. Although the phones invariably function, the library is computerized, and one o'clock really means one o'clock, New York seemed sterile, cold, and devoid of spontaneity. I missed Mexico terribly.

Sportswriting: The Rules of the Game

Ray Tennenbaum

I admit I sometimes wonder why I still haven't made my first million as a freelance sportswriter. But then I remember a guy named Jerry I used to work with when I was starting out as a staff writer in the high-school sports department of a big suburban daily.

A shy ex-drinker in his 50s with distracting personal habits—a stammer and a tendency to hold forth at excruciating length—Jerry was tormented by the elderly alcoholic who edited our section, and by just about everyone else. But he remained devoted to his job as editorial coordinator—where, with his encyclopedic knowledge of regional scholastic sports going back 20 years, he was indispensable. Jerry had all the local high-school coaches' phone numbers in his head, plus things like the records set at every track and field meet on Long Island, to the hundredth of a second.

One night he approached my desk—I probably looked like I was having a bad night, as usual—and, staring at me earnestly, said, "R-Ray, there's one thing you've got to remember all your life: you've got to do something you enjoy doing." I was startled by his heartfelt sincerity and by the realization that despite all the hard work he did and the abuse he suffered, Jerry enjoyed nothing so much as the action and excitement of breaking news and being able to watch the emergence of remarkable young athletes.

Well, me too. Doing what I enjoy is my excuse for being a freelance sportswriter, which these days is a little like trying to be a professional athlete without a team, since the multibillion-dollar sports industry is covered so deeply by newspapers and magazines. The good news is that Americans are ever-thirsty for information about sports figures and coverage of events. There's something almost sacred about sport, which has become our society's single most important measure of achievement and success.

For a writer, this makes for a rich lode. The national obsession with sport has created a world where social issues are catalyzed on the field of play as never before. In the last hundred years, the lives of figures such as Babe Ruth, Jackie Robinson, Muhammad Ali, and Tiger Woods have signaled epochal transformations in American society. The daily and weekly ebb and flow of a team's or an athlete's performance provides a ready-made serial melodrama that's enlivened by the off-the-field stuff. And sportswriting undoubtedly reaches a broader swath of American readers than any other kind of writing.

All these things give the sportswriter an excuse to have fun. Writing well—even distinctively—is demanded of sportswriters, and other kinds of reporting can seem humdrum by comparison. But best of all, there's the free ticket. You get to go to the game and get your fan jollies—and *then* you get to talk with the players.

The game of making a living as a freelance sportswriter is challenging and laden with obstacles. For one thing, you're competing with an entrenched network of beat reporters and staff writers. The papers and magazines throw a lot of money at coverage. Are you trying to wrest an assignment from one of them? Odds are, that magazine's got a dozen writers who could write a similar story (not to mention the fact that the magazine won't have to pay extra for the piece if it's staff-written). If you haven't got a track record at a publication, even pitching your story can be hazardous; if the editor hadn't thought to assign the idea you've cooked up, you may indeed see "your" piece in print—written by somebody else. Want to corner a megabucks jock for a five-minute one-on-one interview? With many of these guys, if you're not working for *Sports Illustrated,* . . . well, good luck. The only kind of ink some of them care about is the kind that splashes everywhere.

But winning at this game can be very rewarding. If you're thinking of embarking on a sportswriting career—and you want to manage it successfully—here are some things to keep in mind.

These are days of specialization for sportswriters, and you may find it helpful to establish a reputation for taking a particular, identifiable angle. One colleague decided to be Bobby Knight's Boswell, and now he plays the rapt biographer for other jocks and coaches. Another guy I know specializes in nostalgic interviews with old athletes; yet another decided to be the Max Weber of sports columnists. To make a living at sportswriting, a freelancer needs to be able to offer something that's consistently new and different.

It may or may not help to have worked as a staff writer. It may seem that the rule is, the further you've made it on staff at a newspaper or magazine, the better you'll do as a freelancer. But that's not necessarily the case. Plenty of celebrated beat reporters have gone out on their own and struck out, while worthy freelancers have enjoyed the sort of massive success that's gotten them prestigious magazine staff positions.

Nevertheless, you've got to start someplace. As with virtually every other sort of journalism, nothing beats daily newspaper experience, which—however maddening, intense, pressure-filled, and exhausting—is still the best place for any fledgling sportswriter to start out. (And it's not a bad place to go back to, either.)

You've got to make friends. Though you've read this so many times it's become old hat, it still bears repeating: networking is critical. And not just with editors. Snub publicists at your peril—they are crucial bridges for getting to the athletes, managers, and owners you need to speak to, and they're also some of the most careful and diligent readers you'll find. There's no telling what kind of connection a publicist might be instrumental in making for you. (I hate to think of how many editors I never would have written a word for had I not first met them at press parties.) Writers' associations, press conferences, outings, book signings, press trips—each of these furnishes the enterprising freelancer with an opportunity to meet the right people, and maybe to snarf up a free cocktail or three.

Just as important, you'll have to make some enemies. Conflict is a part of life, and—for better or worse in this bruising business—it's part of a writing career, as well. Sports fans don't much care for indecisiveness or equivocation. So, when you're writing, don't worry so much about presenting "both sides" of the story. Plenty of other writers will gladly supply the points of view that you neglect.

While few of us intentionally seek out discord, sooner or later something's bound to happen: someone will take exception to something you wrote or try to point out the error of your ways—often less than politely. When that happens, a bit of relish for combat helps—as does a thick skin. I've been threatened with exclusion from professional organizations because of things I've said in print; one argument with another writer nearly got out of hand; and a caddie once threatened to sue me over something I'd written. (In such cases, it also helps to know your rights—and, of course, that what you've written is accurate and true.)

The same need to stand your ground applies to less-public sorts of conflict, as well. No one wants a reputation for being difficult, but every so often there comes a point when a relationship has been jeopardized by the other party's conduct and you've got to cut your losses. An editor at a well-known tennis monthly sat on a feature I'd written for more than two and a half years. Occasionally I'd send in a revision and ask, very politely, when he planned to run it—and I'd get a dismissive response. Then I happened to run into a key figure in the story, who gave me a few new sordid (and newsworthy) details. I reworked the piece and sent it to the editor. When he called back, bursting with enthusiasm, within a day of receiving it, I mentioned that I'd need more money if he wanted to publish the newly revised version, and I named a fairly steep figure. He was angry and "disappointed," but he coughed up, and, more important, he never shelved anything of mine again.

The market conditions for print journalists are a source of frustration for all of us, and it can easily happen that you get locked into doing the kinds of assignments that, while they may once have been enjoyable and are still profitable, are no longer getting you anywhere. If you find that happening, you might decide to go elsewhere—say to a startup magazine or website that may not pay as well but that will give you a shot at higher-profile or more interesting assignments.

Along the same lines, if assignments are becoming scarce and you're forced to undertake other kinds of work, choose creatively. A couple of years ago I was having a hard time getting sportswriting assignments, so I fell back on computer consulting work. The Internet was just then coming on strong, and because of my experience I was able to persuade *Golf* magazine to let me do a story about golfers and the World Wide Web—a piece that eventually led to all sorts of related work.

Finally, keep in mind that the best way to make your way in the freelance sportswriting world is by single-mindedness. If you're independent enough to be a freelancer, odds are you've got the advantage of a distinctive point of view. And if you work long and hard enough in the freelancing sportswriting game, you, too, can start to change the rules.

CHAPTER 4

Electronic Publishing: Issues for Book Authors and Journalists

There's a new game in town, and just about everybody wants to come out and play. Publishing companies, Web entrepreneurs, retailers such as Barnes & Noble, technology giants like Microsoft, and writers of every description are all vying to establish a foothold in the burgeoning new field of electronic publishing.

Alarmists forecast the complete demise of the paper-and-ink book within the next decade

The future of the field is far from clear, as new technologies are developed and fall by the wayside practically overnight, and in many cases it seems as though the players are making up the rules as they go along. Predictions by industry insiders vary wildly, ranging from those who are dismissive of the new technologies to alarmists who forecast the complete demise of the paper-and-ink book (and thus the traditional publishing industry) within the next decade. Even if the more radical projections fail to materialize, one thing seems clear: the electronic revolution is already changing the book publishing and journalism industries, and further changes are on the way.

Before we discuss the pros and cons of these changes, a brief overview of the new technologies is in order. For freelance writers, electronic publishing has come to mean the distribution of articles, books, and other kinds of writing via some form of electronic media. These electronic media come in a wide variety of forms, but the ones that most frequently use the work of journalists, book authors, and business, instructional, technical, and electronic (BITE) writers are these:

- *World Wide Web sites of traditional (i.e., print) magazines and newspapers and of TV stations and networks.* Many traditional publications now have their own websites or have teamed up with other media companies to create a presence on the Web. A number of television networks also have websites that feature content produced by freelance writers.

- *Magazines that are published exclusively on the Web.* (The best-known of these are probably Salon and Slate.) Unlike the sites described above, they do not have paper-and-ink counterparts. But, like traditional publications, they "come out" (or are updated with new stories) on a regular basis, and their articles are not usually very different in style from print articles, although sometimes they feature audio, video, and more photographs than could be included in a traditional magazine or newspaper spread.

- *Commercial/not-for-profit websites.* More and more freelancers are producing informational and promotional text to be used exclusively on business websites. Moreover, many technology-savvy writers with programming skills are creating and maintaining, as well as writing and editing, these websites.

- *Electronic databases.* Electronic databases such as Lexis-Nexis, which are distributed via CD-ROMs or (increasingly) on line, take the content of entire issues of newspapers and post them on a searchable database network. Traditional publishers sell the content of their publications to database companies, which in turn sell access to that content to consumers.

- *Reprint services ("fax-on-demand").* These services deliver reprints of published articles via fax. Computer users can search the services' archives on the Internet and then order any article online.

- *CD-ROMs.* Once thought to be a major threat to traditional publishing, books and anthologies on CD-ROMs are not turning out to be as effective, or as popular, as anticipated. The exceptions are encyclopedias and similar reference books. Because an entire series of reference volumes can fit on one or two compact discs, people who use such books are turning to the discs for convenience's sake (it's much easier to store two feather-light CDs than it is to store 25 heavy books).

- *Electronic books.* The newest kids on the electronic media block, e-books are just starting to hit the mainstream market. They are books in electronic format that can be purchased on the Internet and downloaded to computers or electronic reading devices such as Rocket eBooks® and Softbooks®. Most of the several thousand titles now available as e-books are well-known bestsellers or classics, but the number of offerings available in this format is increasing rapidly. Sales, however, have been limited thus far, largely because of the high cost of the electronic reading devices.

- *Print-on-demand books.* These products are "electronic" in the senses that (1) they are sold and ordered via the Web and (2) developments in printing technology have made print-on-demand possible and affordable. Otherwise, print-on-demand books—more fully explained in the sidebar on page 119—are, in physical terms, good old-fashioned paper-and-ink commodities.

Now that we have an idea of the types of electronic media out there, what opportunities and perils do they present to the freelance writer? On the

What opportunities and perils do electronic media present to the freelance writer?

positive side, electronic publishing clearly provides an increased number of venues for our work. Journalists and BITE writers can write original content for a dizzying array of websites catering to almost any imaginable interest. They can license electronic reprints of articles originally printed by traditional publishers, and they can sell the rights for the use of their work on an electronic database or CD-ROM.

Book authors, meanwhile, can circumvent traditional publishers entirely by publishing their books online, while those with a paper-and-ink publisher can license e-book or CD-ROM versions of their work. The existence of electronic versions of books, coupled with the new print-on-demand technology, also makes it much easier for authors to republish their out-of-print works.

But there are also serious perils for writers eager to get in on the electronic game. Traditional publishers realized several years ago that electronic publishing might become very lucrative, and many have changed their standard contracts in an attempt to grab electronic rights from authors, often for little

or no additional fee. **Beware of any attempt on the part of a publisher to seize your electronic rights without providing you with additional— and fair—compensation.** (The sections of this chapter that follow provide more detailed advice on e-contract issues to book authors and journalists.)

Even for writers who do manage to exploit some of the earnings potential of their electronic rights, the World Wide Web can be a dangerous place.

Internet users tend to pride themselves on the open and democratic nature of the Web, but unfortunately this very openness has led to a culture that often pays little heed to the rules of intellectual property. Written work is often copied and posted on websites and databases without compensation and sometimes without attribution. This clearly diminishes the value of the work. Why pay to reprint or read an article that is widely available for free? There's not a lot that individual writers can do about this situation (except to protest and, if you're up to it, to threaten litigation when you find your work being used inappropriately), but as a group we must stand together to demand the establishment of responsible standards for the use of intellectual property in electronic media.

The open and democratic nature of the Web has led to a culture that often pays little heed to the rules of intellectual property

Overall, the lack of standards in the rapidly evolving world of electronic publishing makes it essential for us as writers to make our voices heard *now.* Are writers going to be fairly compensated for each electronic use of their work or will publishers be able to use sweeping contract language to seize all electronic rights? Will book authors find their work held hostage by publishers who claim that the existence of a print-on-demand version allows them to consider a book "in print"? Will the online community respect authors' rights to their intellectual property?

Such critical issues are being decided right now, in the course of the chaotic rough-and-tumble that characterizes these early days of electronic publishing. That's why it's so important that we fight to make sure that electronic rights are handled fairly in all our contracts.

Because many forms of electronic publishing are so new, and because the industry is changing so quickly, we have not been able to provide the precise data about rates and practices that we have given for other markets. The National Writers Union is carefully reviewing conditions in electronic publishing, and by the time the next edition of this *Guide* is published we should be able to offer a great deal more in the way of specific information about the actual conditions faced by e-writers of all sorts. In the meantime, by adhering to general principles of fair and equitable treatment in all of our negotiations, we as writers can help to ensure that this new game will take place on a more level playing field.

Brave New Books

by JoAnn Kawell

If, like me, you think that reading is a sensual act that goes beyond scanning words on a page to include the physical experience of holding a book and caressing the paper and cloth it is made of, you may find the idea of electronic books about as appealing as cybersex. But whether or not any of us feels inclined to do our own reading on computer screens, as writers we need to recognize that the age of e-books has already dawned. The new era holds both new promise and new perils for authors. Here, I'd like to suggest how those of us who have so far remained on the margins of the impending e-book revolution can become more aware of both.

The age of e-books has already dawned

Books in all genres are now being published and sold in electronic form via websites, disks, CD-ROMs, and even email. These "e-books" can be downloaded and read on desktop computers, laptops, personal digital assistants (PDAs), or special, portable "reading devices" such as the Rocket eBook® Pro and the SoftBook® Reader—or, for those of us still wedded to ink-on-paper, printed out from the digital file.

No one can predict exactly how, or how fast, this trend will transform the book-publishing industry. Naysayers point to the failure of CD-ROM "books" to catch on as widely as predicted a few years back. But, as of mid-2000, giant online bookseller barnesandnoble.com had more than 2,000 e-books available for direct downloading from its website into Rocket eBook Readers, and Portland, Oregon–based independent powells.com carried more than 3,000 e-titles.

Thousands of other titles can be purchased, in various electronic forms, from e-publishers' own websites. E-book publishing was pioneered by these mostly small, Web-based firms, which issue only electronic editions, never producing a single paper print run of the works that make up their lists, though some now also provide print-on-demand copies of certain titles (see sidebar, page 119).

Initially, many of these online publishers specialized in science fiction, romance, and erotica. The avid readerships of these genres were willing to put up with scrolling plain ASCII text on their computer screens—previously the only form in which small e-publishers issued their works. More recently, however, Web-based e-publishers are issuing a full range of fiction and nonfiction books, and many of these publishers have begun to issue editions compatible with portable readers or with one of the new e-book software systems for desk, laptop, and handheld computers. Glassbook, Microsoft, and Night Kitchen are three current makers of such "reader" software. In general, these systems aim at making the experience of reading a book on a computer more like that of reading a paper book. The layout, typeface, and graphics of the e-book can be identical to the print version, and, instead of scrolling through the text, the reader can "turn pages" by clicking a mouse.

In 1999, industry observers predicted that the advent of these formats would greatly expand the market for e-books of every kind. In response, many traditional trade publishers started to issue at least some of the books on their lists, fiction and nonfiction, in electronic as well as good old-fashioned hard- and softcover print editions. Bestselling author Frank McCourt's 1999 memoir 'Tis, for instance, was available as a Rocket eBook title shortly before the hardcover release.

But it was the March 2000 release of Stephen King's *Riding the Bullet* that marked the industry's turning point. The wildly popular horror/suspense writer published his novella *only* as an e-book, available, in most cases for free, from various websites. Within days, hundreds of thousands of people had downloaded the book and the special software needed to read it. By midyear, even the most traditional of the big trade houses were looking into e-book editions. In July, Random House announced the creation of a new division dedicated to e-book production.

The release of Stephen King's Riding the Bullet *marked the industry's turning point*

It's easy to discern the biggest potential benefits, for writers, of the Brave New World of e-books. Because the expense of physically producing and distributing a book is minimized—there are no printing, shipping, or warehousing costs—electronic publication means, at least in theory, that many more works by many more authors can be published. There's no reason—again, at least in theory—for any publisher to concentrate only on potential blockbusters, and if the biggest presses insist on doing so, new independent publishers will (or perhaps already do) fill the gap. What's more, when a book can be downloaded directly from the World Wide Web, would-be readers everywhere have ready access to it, greatly increasing sales potential.

But in the new cyberworld as in the old regime of paper and ink, these two areas—rights and royalties—pose the greatest challenges to writers intent on protecting their interests. And electronic publishing makes the task more complicated, not less, since this is a world in constant flux, where both the players and their ways of doing business seem to change radically every six months or so. It seems safe to predict that the still somewhat separate realms of Web-based e-publishers and paper-based trade presses will eventually converge. Indeed, given current business trends, the two realms are likely to merge. The recent merger of online giant AOL with Time Warner, followed by the launch of Time Warner's Web-based publishing company, iPublish, is clear evidence of such a trend. For the time being, however, traditional trade publishers and specialized electronic publishers present somewhat different issues for writers trying to get the best possible e-contract terms. Here, based on the experience of some seasoned negotiators of such contracts, is a brief overview.

It seems safe to predict that the realms of Web-based e-publishers and paper-based trade presses will eventually converge

TRADITIONAL PAPER-BASED PUBLISHERS

In the very near future—probably within the year—it seems certain that the standard book contracts offered by nearly every publisher, from the largest multinational to the smallest independent, will include a clause that makes specific reference to e-book editions. Elaine English, a Washington, D.C., attorney whose firm specializes in media and publishing law and literary agentry, has already represented both publishers and writers in negotiating many such provisions. English believes that a writer should aim, above all, to "maximize the flexibility" of e-book clauses. Because this is such a rapidly changing area, she says, publishers that do not wish to publish or license e-editions immediately have been open to agreements that call for e-book clauses to be negotiated later, when the publisher decides to issue an e-book edition of the work. What publishers have not been open to, however, is allowing authors to retain e-book rights (perhaps to use them to negotiate their own e-book licensing deals) even when the print publisher has no intention of exercising e-rights in the foreseeable future.

Many book contracts signed in the last decade or so have made some reference to "electronic rights," and some publishers now claim that a general grant of electronic rights is enough to allow them to issue or license an e-book edition. English, however, argues that a grant of rights to publish or license an e-book should be very specific and should include three elements: (1) the right to distribute the work online, (2) the right to make the work part of an electronic database, and (3) the right to publish the work in a print-on-demand edition. Authors should also strive to retain the right to review e-book licensing deals made by their publishers. English says an author reviewing such deals should make sure that e-book licenses are *not* exclusive because some e-book systems are currently incompatible, and an exclusive license for, say, a Rocket eBook edition would seriously limit a book's market.

Currently, the most contentious e-book contract question is this: What's a fair royalty rate? Because e-books are so much cheaper to produce than traditional paper books, the Authors Guild argued in a 1998 public statement that "publishers should benefit from higher profit margins, and royalty rates for authors should soar." For the same reason, the NWU has generally taken the position that authors' e-book royalties should be higher than those that have become standard for hardcover or paperback editions. The Guild criticized the licensing deals NuvoMedia was making with publishers, in which the eBook Reader maker and e-book distributor barnesandnoble.com were together retaining 60 percent of e-book sales revenues, with the remaining 40 percent going to the publishers. According-ing to the Guild, "Some publishers are asking authors to take much less than the 50% share of electronic book licensing income," which the Guild said "has been the industry standard."

A grant of rights to publish or license an e-book should be very specific

A 50–50 split of 40 percent of sales revenues would give the author the equivalent of a 20-percent royalty, but Elaine English says the best e-book royalty provisions she has so far seen in trade house contracts have only been around 15 percent. And a more common current practice, which English says is becoming "a trend among trade publishers," is that of merely extending the hardback royalty provisions of their contracts to e-books, which in most cases results in a royalty rate of significantly less than 15 percent. English's firm has had some success in getting publishers to agree to provisions reopening the royalty clause if the standard industry payment moves upward from 15 percent. The problem with such clauses, English says, is that "there's no easy way to judge what the industry standard is."

NEW ELECTRONIC PUBLISHERS

By contrast, in the personal view of established e-author and NWU member Sharon Reddy, "Most professional electronic book publishing contracts are extremely fair." Describing the prevailing practice among firms that specialize in electronic publishing, Reddy wrote in mid-1999 that "the author royalty is 25–50% of the sale price per book sold, royalties are paid frequently, [and] the contract is for only electronic rights and for a specific term, usually a year and thereafter renewable."

It's worth noting, however, that while many electronic publishers do ask for more limited rights grants and do pay significantly higher royalties (or the equivalent), in percentage terms, than do the trade houses, most e-publishers sell their e-books at a low "cover" price, usually $2 to $6, while—at this writing—trade publishers are listing most e-editions at prices close to those of hardcover editions.

What's more, some observers believe that the adolescent e-publishing industry still has a few image problems to overcome. Many electronic book publishers, including a division of one of the best-known, 1stBooks Library, are "subsidy" publishers, little more than old-fashioned vanity presses updated to cyberspace. They publish almost any work submitted but charge authors hefty "set-up" or other fees. Reddy advised would-be e-authors to avoid these kinds of firms. According to Reddy, what defines a "professional" e-publisher is, "in one word, editing." That is, these publishers work with authors whose manuscripts they accept to improve the work for publication. She calculated that about a fifth of 300 or so electronic publishers were professional "royalty-paying publishers with 'traditional' book editing policies."

The adolescent e-publishing industry still has a few image problems to overcome

But others argue that, just as the MP3.com website, which allows any interested musician to sell inexpensive, downloadable recordings of their music, is said to be democratizing the popular music industry and making a wider range of music available to the public, online subsidy publishers can play a similar role for writers and their readers. A Science Fiction Writers of America guide says that "subsidy e-publishing can be a good solution" for writers "who don't want to go through the submission process" required by non-subsidy publishers. Certainly, while authors published by the old vanity presses were faced with the thorny problem of having to personally persuade bookstores to carry their books, Web-based publication handily solves that distribution problem.

Authors whose works are Web-published by any of the electronic firms also face the daunting task of making their work known in an increasingly frenetic cyberworld, where thousands of websites compete for visitors' attention. Some online subsidy publishers offer promotional services—for an extra fee—but many of these seem to be of dubious value. Many of the non-subsidy publishers take some steps to promote their authors' e-books, but most authors find it necessary to take a do-it-yourself approach to selling their work. One website for e-authors (www.geocities.com/SoHo/Suite/9474/pressrelease.html) includes a guide to putting together your own promo package—advice that's potentially helpful to authors of paper-and-ink books, as well.

Both the Science Fiction Writers of America and the writer's tipsheet Inkspot have compiled useful online guides (www.sfwa.org/Beware/epublishers.html and www.inkspot.com/epublish/articles/epublishfaq.html) to help authors evaluate both subsidy and non-subsidy e-publishers. "Writer beware" seems especially important advice in this particularly fast-changing sector of the pub-

What Is Print-on-Demand?

"Print-on-demand", or POD, means that each paper copy of a book is printed from a computer file and bound only after a customer "demands," or orders, it. POD books can be ordered from a growing number of sources, including publishers' websites, online bookstores, and kiosks in traditional bookstores. In 1999, a spokesman for a Bertelsmann subsidiary announced projections showing that POD may make up as much as 30 percent of all book production within three years.

Some companies now specialize in producing POD versions of works originally issued by traditional publishers but that have gone "out of print" in the old sense—that is, new paper copies are no longer available for sale from the original publisher. Other firms, like Xlibris, produce POD books that have never been published in a traditional sense. In 1999, the Authors Guild made an agreement with an e-publisher to issue POD editions of out-of-print works for which the rights have reverted to Guild authors. But NWU President Jonathan Tasini has cautioned that some traditional publishers might use POD availability to argue that an author's work is still "in print" even though there are no more copies in the warehouse. Under the provisions of some current book contracts, this would prevent rights to the work from reverting to the writer.

—JoAnn Kawell

For more on the Grievance and Contract Division, see Chapter 14, "The Grievance Process," page 241.

lishing industry. The NWU's Grievance and Contract Division monitors e-publishers, as it does other publishers, based on information received from members, and it is always a good idea to ask an NWU contract adviser to review an e-book contract before you sign it.

Right now, no one can be sure exactly what shape the e-book world will eventually take or precisely what kinds of e-contracts will be best for writers. Attorney English says that "the industry is evolving" and so it's best not to "take absolute positions" on royalty splits or other points. But she cautions writers not to passively await the results of this evolution because, she says, we "run the risk of settling into the ways things were done when there was no money" in e-publishing. Together, writers must press publishers to raise current e-book rates, which are rapidly becoming "industry standards." As Steven Zeitchik, writing about the future of e-books in the August 23, 1999, issue of *Publishers Weekly*, noted, "The music experience seems to indicate that [industry] standards are most favorable to content-providers"—that's us—"when the providers help to establish them." Zeitchik pointed out that in 1995 few in the music industry believed that digitally distributed recordings would be widely available, while only four years later 17 million people were downloading MP3 singles or even whole CDs from the Web every day.

Negotiating Web Rights

by Todd Pitock

On an online writers' forum, an editor made a curious remark: that, after doing extensive research, she'd concluded that there is "no such thing as electronic rights." A knee-jerk response would have been to scream, "What? Are you a fool?!" But, once she'd explained herself, it became clear what she meant, and her point was a valid one: "electronic rights" is too broad a term. Databases, CD-ROMs, and the Web are all separate "electronic" uses.

The remarks below address online, or Web, writing. This is the area of electronic publication that's expanding most rapidly, with online magazines, corporate sites, and a variety of publishing forms unique to the medium.

Notwithstanding the pain that many electronic-rights contracts have

---

inflicted, the Web has, on balance, been an incredible boon to savvy writers. Although Web-based publishers have not, as a rule, generated huge revenues, they're viable because they're free of two of the most burdensome costs of print media: production and distribution. This means that many are able to offer rates that are competitive with—and often much better than—those paid by print publishers.

Of course, print publishers have rushed to get online, too. Some careful writers have managed to get additional fees from those publishers for the republication of their stories on the Web or to retain rights in order to relicense online rights to other Web publishers.

The changes brought about by the World Wide Web are massive, and they can tilt the balance of power in favor of writers who familiarize themselves with the market and with certain key issues. Content, Net-nerds like to say, is king. We writers, then, are the kingmakers.

> *The Web has, on balance, been an incredible boon to savvy writers*

What follows is a brief survey of Web-rights licenses. Note: we say "license" for a reason. Writers need to stop talking about "selling" stories. The National Writers Union's position is that paying one fee should not give a publisher rights in perpetuity—unless that fee is substantial. Publishers have to re-up their licenses to use their URLs. There's no reason why, if a writer's work has value, a publisher should not pay an ongoing royalty to continue using it. This is standard practice where other forms of intellectual property are concerned, and writers ought not to be excluded from it.

There are, roughly speaking, three types of Web-related licenses:

- Licensing original content to an online publisher

- Licensing online rights to the original print publisher

- Licensing the right to reprint an article online to a separate online publisher

When it comes to licensing content that has not been previously published to an online publisher, the negotiation is similar to what would occur in the world of print. As with any market, writers need to become familiar with prevailing rates, and they should establish their own "floor" when it comes to the fee that they're willing to work for. That's a highly subjective matter, with some writers refusing to work for less than $1 per word, while others, who need to build a portfolio of clips, may be willing to settle for less.

To find out about prevailing rates, consult other writers. Find out what terms they have gotten. (You may, by the way, be surprised at how much things can vary at the same publication.) Both the NWU and the American Society of Journalists and Authors publish information on rates. The NWU's MagazineRates Database—available online to members only, at www.nwu.org—contains information on the rates paid to journalists writing for hundreds of print and online publications.

For tips on negotiating contracts, see pages 12–17.

Don't be afraid to ask up front what a publication pays, and don't be afraid to negotiate. Editors respect professionals, and they understand that professionals, by definition, write for money.

Online publishing does differ from print in a couple of ways. For one thing, Web wordcounts tend to be low, so even if the word-to-fee ratio is respectable, the overall fee may not be sufficient. Some writers argue, with justification, that wordcount-based fees are not a good way to measure value. Still, they remain the industry's main method for determining fees. In addition to setting a floor—the minimum per-word rate for which you'll take on an assignment—you should also estimate how much work a given project will involve before deciding how much you'll need to be paid. How many sources does an editor expect to see in your story? Will the editor provide you with sources? If not, and if the Web publication does not have a widely recognized name, how difficult will it be to reach those sources and convince them to talk to you?

Wordcounts remain the industry's main method for determining fees

Another difference between online and print publications has to do with the duration of the license. In the old days of print-only publication, periodicals were typically given one-time serial rights that lasted only as long as an issue was available for distribution or sale. Articles appearing online, however, can stay up on a website forever, and some Web publishers say their most valuable electronic asset is their easy-access index of previously published articles (what's commonly called an "archive"). Unfortunately, the value your article adds to a website reduces its potential long-term value for you, the writer.

If readers can already find your article online, why should another online publisher pay you to republish it? The solution to this quandary—one that's increasingly accepted by online publishers—is a *time-limited license.* At the expiration of the mutually agreed-on term (the minimum tends to be one week and the maximum one year), the publisher and writer can renegotiate an appropriate fee if both sides want the article to continue to appear. **The NWU's Standard Webzine Contract (available on the NWU's website) suggests that the initial license last for as long as it takes for the website to refresh its main page—one day, one week, one month, or whatever.**

Many print publishers want writers to grant them Web rights for no additional fee. There is, however, a principle to defend and a material reason not to give those rights away. The principle is that all of society understands that you pay as you go, and each use deserves a separate fee. The material reason is that there is a growing number of online publications that pay—and pay well—for online rights. If you give Web rights to a print magazine that also publishes a Web edition, you may not be able to license your story to another Web publication, and you, the writer, will take the loss.

Some writers will say, "Oh, well, I don't have an online market for my piece anyway." But keep in mind that the online world is burgeoning. What doesn't exist today may well exist tomorrow.

If, on the other hand, there already is an online market that's likely to be interested in a story of yours that's appearing in print, you should use that information when you negotiate. If you're writing a story for a print magazine for $1,000 and you know of an online magazine that, if it were to accept your piece, would pay $700 for the online rights, tell your editor. At the very least, the print magazine

The online world is burgeoning—what doesn't exist today may well exist tomorrow.

should cover your potential loss by paying you a substantially higher fee. And, remember, in many cases today, online markets are better financed and pay more than print publications, particularly newspapers.

Define your contract terms as narrowly as possible. If, say, TodaysAngler.com wants to buy online rights to your story on chasing the wild blue marlin, you should:

1. *Get as much money as you can.* If TodaysAngler.com's fee is not sufficient, see if DeepSeaTrawler.com pays more. There may be limits to how much you can cast about, but, at the very least, you should know what various publications in a given market pay.

2. *Put a time limit on the license.* No one should get rights in perpetuity—certainly not unless they pay commensurately for those rights.

3. *Make sure your contract defines the specific online market.* For instance, you might give TodaysAngler.com a three-month license that's exclusive to all *fishing-related* websites only.

You won't always get what you want, but you should at least be familiar with—and go for—terms that are most advantageous to you.

"Hyper" Text: If You're Writing for the Web, Keep It Snappy

Cate T. Corcoran

I'll never forget the editor at Cnet who told me I had to rigidly outline exactly what I would say in my forthcoming 4,200-word story about an obscure Internet standards-making body—*before* I had reported a word of it. Nor can I forget the editor at Ziff-Davis's now-defunct The Site who told me, "Don't bother doing any reporting" for a story I was writing about online diaries. But these experiences weren't typical, and, despite the scare stories you may have heard, standards for online journalism aren't necessarily looser or more exacting than those for print. Nonetheless, online writing has some unique characteristics.

The biggest difference between writing for online publications and writing for print periodicals is that, in general, Web publications pay worse. During the five years I have been freelancing full time, I have found that online publications typically pay about 50 cents a word, whereas all the print magazines and newspapers I deal with pay $1 a word or more.

The relatively poor pay for online work is offset, however, by the fact that Web magazines are relatively easy to break into. And I have also found that writing for online publications can help you take your writing career to the next level, whatever that might be.

Say you've never published anything in your life. The Web is definitely where you want to get your start. Or say you're a fairly experienced freelancer. Maybe you've been supporting yourself by writing for niche or regional publications and you want to break into the national press. There's nothing like having a story published in Salon, Slate, or the *New York Times* online edition to bridge the gap between where you are and where you want to go.

Web magazines gave me the opportunity to write more ambitious general-interest features than I would have had I just stuck to print. And writing for online publications helped me quickly move up the ladder from periodicals with less prestige to those with greater readership and influence.

There is, of course, a strict hierarchy of periodical publications, with national general-interest magazines at the top, national newspapers and big-city magazines in the middle, and pretty much everything else—whether print or online—at the bottom. Your best way of getting a foothold on this ladder is to begin by writing for smaller-circulation print newspapers and/or webzines, both of which are always in need a lot of material and are therefore relatively open to new writers. If you've already published a story in, say, the *San Francisco Chronicle* or Feed, you stand a better chance of getting a go-ahead from an editor at a national newspaper such as the *Los Angeles Times, Washington Post,* or *New York Times.* After that, you might write just a tiny squib for a magazine such as *Vanity Fair* or *Playboy*—but once you can stick one of those big names on your resume, you're definitely on your way to the top.

(By the way, the only exception I've found to this rule is at the glossy women's magazines, where having been the editor's college roommate is usually the best way to get in the door. Oops, you didn't go to Vassar or Brown? Sorry, you're out of luck.)

Really, there are only two basic things you need to know about writing for the Web:

- Online writing should be short and snappy

- Sex, technology, and controversial opinion sell

A lot has been written about how the Internet makes it easy to publish *New Yorker*–length works of journalism or in-depth investigative stories accompanied by full notes and supporting documents. The fact is, however, that most people don't really like to read online—or not for very long stretches of time. Maybe that's one reason so many Web-related terms begin with the prefix "hyper." Most Web-users have short attention spans. They like to click around, look at dirty pictures, and repeatedly ask each other, "Hey, how ya doin'?" in chat rooms. That's why brief (600- to 800-word) but sizzling opinion pieces on hot, controversial topics are such a popular format at so many online magazines. Make it personal, confessional, gossipy, funny, or outrageous—but, above all, make it snappy.

Online magazines want concise, straightforward prose. Even if you're writing a long-ish feature story—of, say, 1,200 words—it had better be more tightly organized and to-the-point than what you would ordinarily find in print.

Twelve hundred words is quite a long piece for the Web, but there are, of course, exceptions. Salon, for one, regularly publishes 3,000- or 4,000-word stories. But Salon and similar online magazines have come up with a number of innovations to keep readers clicking along. The type is large; stories are broken up into neatly digestible screenfuls of about 800 words each; and tantalizing subheads ("My Stint as a Porn Star") function like soap-opera cliffhangers to propel readers onward.

Naturally sex is a hot topic—who would've guessed?—as is technology (since, by definition, everyone on the Web uses a computer). Breaking news is also very popular, but as a freelancer you're unlikely to be in a position to supply much of that.

Writing for online publications generally doesn't require a great deal of technical knowledge. Some editors like it if you can insert a few HTML tags into your documents before submitting them, but most just want plain unformatted text, usually sent to them in the body of an email rather than as an attachment. (HTML tags are simple bits of code that instruct a Web browser to display a word in bold, italic, or whatever. For example, in this sentence, the word <B>animal<B> would appear in bold.)

Some publications may also require that you supply a list of relevant links or related websites, for use either in the story itself or in a sidebar. (These function much like footnotes or a "recommended reading" section in a book.) Say you're writing a story about visiting Paris in the springtime; your editor might want to include a sidebar of related websites, such as those for the Paris Chamber of Commerce and Industry, or Air France, or some general travel sites. When the story appears on screen, readers can immediately go to those sites simply by clicking on the links. The webzine Suck has made a high art out of this practice by embedding links whose only connection to the story is a sly pun or insider joke. There are various shortcuts to embedding links in a story, but basically all you have to do is to cut and paste a site's URL (Web address) into your text.

You don't have to be a tech-head to publish online. Many prestigious outlets—NYTimes.com, Playboy.com, Slate, Salon, Feed, Suck, Women.com, Discovery Channel Online, and Word—are general-interest sites. Rates at some of these publications match or come close to those paid by similar print publications.[1]

There are a few kinds of online formats that you won't encounter in print. Cnet, for example, had the unusual idea that magazine stories could be broken into stand-alone, interchangeable, reusable pieces of content that somehow when taken together would add up to a whole, coherent article. This is not the case. As I mentioned above, the editor asked me to plot out multiple pieces of

---

1. For a very thorough list of places to publish online—and for excellent advice on writing for the Web—I highly recommend Anthony and Paul Tedesco's *Online Markets for Writers* (New York: Henry Holt, 2000).

a huge article before I even knew what I was going to say so that the heads and subheads could be put into the database ahead of publication. As it turned out, what Cnet really wanted—and what it ended up with—was not a magazine story in the conventional sense but something more closely resembling a series of mini–encyclopedia entries on various subtopics ("How the Consortium Works," "What the Consortium Does," and "Who's in the Consortium") under a larger topic ("Who Rules the Net?").

You'll also run into informational websites that try to combine the usefulness of a database with an editorial point of view. Examples include Monster.com, About.com, and Snap.com. Writing for these ends up being not all that different from writing for print, though in some cases the bulk of your task will be to find the best other websites on the topic you're writing about so that you can include links to those sites in your piece.

Few and far between are the sites that will ask you to include video, sound, or music with a story. A notable example is Discovery Channel Online, where "articles" resemble multimedia presentations.

Virtually everything else you need to know to succeed as an online writer is the same stuff you've got to know to make a living writing for any medium. Running a successful freelance business is a little bit like being able to get dates. According to that infamous advice book *The Rules,* a popular woman is one who is fun and easy to be with but who doesn't put up with poor treatment from anyone. Likewise, in your writing business you should be professional, polite, and easy to work with.

But you should always ask for more than an editor offers, whether it's money or terms. Being too eager for work or agreeing too readily to whatever an editor lays on the table is the mark of an amateur. By no means should you put up with unreasonable demands—unfortunately, all too common in publishing—such as working on spec or giving up all rights for less than $2 to $3 a word. In several cases, editors—after a series of polite proddings—have raised their rates for me because they knew they couldn't get the kind of quality they were looking for at the prices and terms they originally offered. I know other journalists who've had the same experience.

Remember that good, reliable writers are hard to find. Strive to be one of them, and editors will always need you more than you need them.

The Technical Writing Market

Most people—or those who are aware that the profession exists—assume that technical writers work in the computer industry. Many, of course, do. Computer-industry technical writers plan and write documentation for computer hardware, software, and systems. They create user manuals, online help systems, and websites, usually working closely with engineers, programmers, testers, and information managers. Such writers don't only work for computer companies, however; some are employed by telecommunications companies and other firms that develop and customize hardware, software, and systems.

Not all tech writers do computer-related work

But not all tech writers do computer-related work. Some work for manufacturers, developing (for example) documentation and user manuals for various kinds of products. Others work for financial institutions. And yet others are employed in scientific and medical fields or for the pharmaceutical industry. Today, the largest technical writing markets are these:

- Computer hardware/software

- Financial and corporate

- Government and not-for-profit

- Telecommunications

- Defense/aerospace

- Biotech/medical/pharmaceutical

The boundaries separating technical writers from other kinds of business writers are, unsurprisingly, somewhat fuzzy. This *Guide,* however, distinguishes

Portions of this chapter are adapted from *Breaking into Technical Writing,* a seminar handbook developed by the NWU Technical Writers Trade Group, and *Launching a Career as a Technical Writer,* a handbook produced for a symposium of the same name held at Polytechnic University, Brooklyn, in October 1999 and cosponsored by the National Writers Union and Polytechnic University. Used by permission.

between technical writers per se—those writers engaged in writing documentation, manuals, and similar products for the computer and other industries—and other business writers, whose concerns are addressed in Chapter 6.

TYPES OF TECHNICAL WRITING

Technical writing positions are defined by the market or industry for which the writer works as well as by the *intended audience* for the work, the specific *kind of work* performed, the *platform* used, and the *employment mode* under which the writer works.

Intended Audience/Kinds of Work

The kind of work a technical writer does as well as the kind of background he or she needs are determined in large measure by the audience for the work. The most common audiences—and the kinds of materials produced for them—are as follows.

Traditional Technical. Traditional technical writing is aimed at a limited audience of professionals in the field. Among the kinds of work produced by writers in this sector are

- Programmers' manuals

- System administrator guides

- Repair and maintenance manuals

- Scientific papers and research reports

- Technical specifications

To succeed in this sector, you have to know what the specific audience needs and you must be familiar with its technical jargon. Usually, a technical background in the subject area—perhaps a college degree in the field—is required. Writers who write for professional audiences in commercial markets usually command high pay, but, in most cases, writing scientific papers and research reports doesn't pay as well.

Technology Education. Writers in this sector explain technology to general, nontechnical audiences. Among the kinds of documents they produce are

- Hardware and software user manuals for consumers

- Operating and procedure instructions

- Reports to lay (or semi-technical) readers

Essentially, these kinds of jobs require you to learn something and then teach it to others via a written or online document. To do this kind of technical writing you need have only as much technical background as a typical reader would possess (in other words, not much).

Training Materials. Writers in this sector—sometimes known as *instructional designers*—develop training courses and instructional materials used by those who teach technology topics in various markets. These materials can be in various formats and media, including written text, video, multimedia, and CBT (computer-based training). For this type of writing, you need only as much technical background as the audience for which the course material is intended. A background in teaching may also helpful for this kind of work.

Techno-Business. Writers in this sector produce grant requests, environmental impact statements, technical product documentation for industries (such as the pharmaceuticals industry), and so on. Requirements vary.

Websites. Writers in this sector work on corporate or government websites. As in other sectors, you need as much technical background as the audience you are writing for—which can range from a great deal for a highly technical internal website to very little for a site oriented toward the general public. You also need to know Web technology.

> **Web work is more stratified than other types of tech writing**

Web work is more stratified than other types of tech writing. The kinds of positions available include

* *Website design/architecture.* This is the highest and best-paid level and requires both design training and extensive knowledge of Web technology.

* *Website administration.* Also very well paid, website administration requires extensive knowledge of Web technology.

* *Website content provision.* This means writing material for websites administered by someone else. Pay for Web content varies widely. In most cases, the only Web technology you need for this is HTML coding, which is quite easy to learn.

Platforms

The different types of computer operating systems are called *platforms.* Different technical writing markets require knowledge of different platforms.

Windows. In case you hadn't noticed, let us point out that the Windows operating system created by Microsoft Corporation has, over the past decade, taken over the world. The Windows market is huge. About 95 percent of all computer users work on Windows, which runs on IBM PC–compatible computers (in other words, PCs). This means that there is lots of Windows-based tech writing work—and that there will continue to be lots of such work for some time to come.

While most writing work for companies producing products for the Windows platform is consumer-oriented, there is some highly technical work intended for Windows system administrators, engineers, and programmers. Windows-based technical writing covers numerous genres: you might write game manuals, for example, or educational materials, business software manuals, or any of a vast number of other kinds of documents.

Windows programs are easy to use. Most documentation mostly consists of guiding the user on how to get from here to there. (For example: "To print, pull down the File menu and select the Print option. Enter the number of copies you wish to print and press Return.") Since it's relatively easy to document Windows tools, there are lots of tech writers using this platform, and the pay rates are average.

Macintosh. Apple Corporation makes both the hardware (Macintosh computers) and the Mac operating system. The Macintosh market is relatively small. Apple's future, once in grave doubt, has improved over the past couple of years, but even so only about 5 percent of desktop computers are Macintoshes. This means that there are many fewer Mac-based jobs than Windows-based jobs.

Most writing work for companies producing products for the Mac also tends to be consumer-oriented, but here again there is some highly technical work for system administrators, engineers, and programmers. As with Windows-based tech writing, Mac-based tech writing covers many genres. Like Windows programs, Macintosh programs are easy to use, and most documentation involves instructing users on how to get from here to there. As with Windows-based tech writing, pay rates are average.

UNIX. The UNIX operating system runs on computers from Sun Microsystems, IBM, Silicon Graphics, Hewlett-Packard, and others. This powerful platform is favored by many large corporations, government agencies, educational and research institutions, and Internet/Web companies.

UNIX companies build a wide range of products, from those used by ordinary consumers to those that require advanced degrees simply to operate. Some UNIX manuals are similar to those written for Windows or Mac products and are read by customers who may not even know they are working on a UNIX machine. Other manuals are extremely dense and technical, while most are somewhere in the middle. Note, however, that even for the simplest, nontechnical manuals, most employers expect you to have at least minimal familiarity with the UNIX operating system because you will be working on their UNIX machines and they do not want to spend time training you in basic computer skills.

The UNIX market is very small (about 1 percent of the total), but it is growing fast and will grow faster as the Internet and Web continue to explode. Many of the corporations that use UNIX are in the San Francisco Bay Area (Silicon Valley), Greater Boston, and other high-tech centers, which means that it is a large market for tech writers in those areas. (As an aside, it's worth pointing out that tech writing markets differ greatly from region to region.)

It can be a real challenge to document a Web application

The complexity of the systems using UNIX means that there are relatively few tech writers capable of using UNIX, and UNIX documentation therefore tends to be better paid than writing for Windows or the Mac.

The Web. The Web is a *metaplatform*—that is, it runs on PCs, Macs, UNIX computers, mainframes, TVs, and other kinds of devices. It is also a meta-market in that Web writing comprises all kinds of writing. Articles, books, stories, poetry, drama, comics, corporate reports, product descriptions, marketing pitches, and so on are all now appearing on the Web, but these, of course, are not technical writing. Technical writing for the Web can be categorized into three basic kinds:

1. *Website technical writing* usually involves creating the connective material and links that form the site's structure. With a few exceptions, this kind of writing is usually not very technically demanding.

2. *Web software technical writing* involves documenting software products that website creators use to build and maintain sites. This kind of writing ranges from nontechnical to highly technical depending on the kind of customer that the product will be used by.

3. *Writing online manuals for online software applications* is a just-emerging kind of Web tech writing. The technical complexity varies according to the kind of application.

The Web continues to grow explosively, which means that tech writers employed in Web industries have plenty of work—now and for the foreseeable future. Because documenting Web products requires a wide collection of skills and a high degree of technical sophistication, pay rates can be very good. However, many Web companies are small startups on shaky financial foundations, and there are far more failures and bankruptcies than pots of gold at the end of IPO rainbows.

Employment Modes

Typically, technical writers work on staff for corporations, as employees of or contractors to agencies, or as independent contractors to corporations. The distinctions among these types of employment are significant: they affect the amount you are paid, your tax situation, and the way you work.

Working as a Staff Writer. Many corporations maintain separate writing departments, or assign staff writers to other departments. When you work as a staff writer, you receive company benefits (health insurance, vacation and sick time, employee savings plans) and have taxes withheld from your paycheck. While telecommuting is becoming more popular in some areas of the country, most staff writers work on site in the corporation's offices.

For beginning tech writers, it may be easier to find a staff job

For beginning tech writers, it may be easier to find a staff job than to land contract assignments. Because corporations often provide on-the-job training for their own products or services and for the tools needed to do the job, managers are often willing to hire someone who may not have extensive experience but who has good communication skills and who demonstrates the ability to learn quickly.

Unfortunately, staff jobs are not usually "lifetime" jobs (or even long-term jobs), as they once were. The volatility of financial markets and the regrettable popularity of downsizing have made employee status only slightly more stable than contractor status.

The good news, though, is that wages and benefits for staff tech-writing positions have risen steadily over the past decade. Salaries and benefits packages for staff technical writers are tracked on an annual basis by the Society for Technical Communication; the STC's salary surveys since 1997 are downloadable as PDF files from the STC's website, at www.stc-va.org/fjobstart.htm.

Working as a Contractor. Contract technical writers work on distinct projects. While corporations expect contractors to have the skills they require and are not often willing to provide extensive training, they generally pay more for a contractor's experience. Some contract jobs allow you to do a portion (or, more rarely, all) of your work from your home or your own office. Because tech writers must generally work very closely with other technical personnel, however, many contract jobs require the writer to be on site for the duration of the contract.

Of course, there are disadvantages to being a contract technical writer, as there are in any field of freelance writing. Contractors must provide their own insurance and are not entitled to standard benefits (e.g., paid holidays and vacations). They may face periods of unemployment, particularly in the last quarter of the year. Managers often expect contractors to have advanced technical expertise and sometimes set tighter deadlines than they would for staff writers. On the other hand, contractors have much wider control over their labor process and their hours of work and generally more freedom and independence in shaping the work itself.

There are several ways in which you can work as a contractor:

- *Agency Employee.* Agencies find jobs for technical writers, screen resumes, arrange for interviews, and handle payroll checks. When you work for an agency as its employee, you are considered a "W-2 employee" and the agency deducts taxes from your check. Some agencies offer vacation and some benefits for contractors. The level of benefits, however, usually does not match that offered by a corporation to its employees. These days, this is fast becoming the most common employment mode for technical writers. **That freelance technical writers nowadays are increasingly unable to find work except through agencies—or, alternately, are forced to join the employee rosters of agencies even when they have found their jobs themselves—is extremely problematic and in many ways unfair to writers.** For a full treatment of this critical issue (which affects writers in other fields, as well), see "Independent Contractors, Agencies, and Third-Party Employers," page 18.

- *Independent Contractor to an Agency.* Some agencies allow contractors to maintain independent (or "1099") status. In this case, the agency arranges for interviews and handles your paycheck but does not deduct taxes from your gross pay. At the end of the year you receive a 1099 form from the agency and are responsible for your own tax payments. Because of IRS regulations, it is becoming more difficult to work as an independent contractor through an agency without incorporating your business. In New York State, for example, most agencies will accept you on a 1099 basis *only* if you are incorporated. For more on self-incorporation, see Chapter 1, page 20.

- *Direct Contractor to Corporations.* This is probably the most desirable status, but it is also the most difficult to arrange. Here, you find jobs and negotiate contracts and rates directly with the employer. Since the employer is not paying a percentage of your rate to an agency, you are likely to earn more money. If you're seeking work as a direct contractor to corporations, it may be very helpful to incorporate your writing business, which may also, if you fulfill certain other requirements, give you the option of working as a "vendor" to corporations.

FINDING A TECH-WRITING JOB: THE BASIC STEPS

Finding a job is a journey with several steps. You must target your market; make sure you're prepared for the kinds of jobs you want to apply for; take the time to ensure that your resume, portfolio, and other written materials are in as good shape as possible; and then, of course, you must look for work. Let's look at each of these steps in greater detail:

Targeting Your Market

Choose the audience you want to write for, the kind of writing you want to do, and the industries and markets you want to work in and then shape your strategy to hit those targets.

- *Choose your audience.* Decide which audience you are best suited to write for: technical, nontechnical, training, marketing, business. Even if you feel you could write for any, focus on one or two.

- *Choose your industry.* Almost every area of the economy now uses technical writers of one sort or another. If you have any experience at all in a particular industry—even if that experience is not as a writer or not of an especially technical nature—that's an advantage you should use to leverage work. The more knowledgeable you are about an industry, the easier it is to find work in it.

Almost every area of the economy now uses technical writers

- *Choose the kind of work you want to do.* Is your goal to become a Web designer or administrator? A writer of user manuals? A technical editor? It's wise to keep that goal in mind—and to try to shape your career to achieve it.

- *Don't box yourself in.* On the other hand, it's also wise to be somewhat flexible. A single area of specialization is not enough, because there may not be any jobs open in that field when you need one. No one, however, can keep up to date in many different areas. Successful technical writers tend to have two to four areas of specialization.

Making Sure You're Prepared

Once you've chosen your audience, your industry, and the kind of work you want to do, prepare yourself to find work in that market. You might want to consider going back to school. These days, many colleges offer certificate or degree courses in technical communications. In some areas of the country, particularly on the east coast, it's getting more difficult to land yor first few tech writing jobs without a certificate or degree. In other areas, such as Silicon Valley, few working tech writers have degrees or certificates. Before investing in formal education, you may want to check the help-wanted ads in your area—or to talk with local tech writers—about the importance of a having degree or certificate in your market.

A course should help you produce portfolio pieces that you can show prospective employers

If you decide to go the degree/certificate route, keep two things in mind when choosing programs and courses. First, try to find out whatever you can about the recent industry experience of the program's teachers. The teacher's industry experience is far more important than what the course description says. If your aim is to work for the computer industry, a teacher whose main experience is in aerospace may not do you much good.

Second, the course should help you produce one or more portfolio pieces that you can show prospective employers. The *greatest value* of taking a course is to build your portfolio. Unless the course requires at least one major piece of work that you can show to a manager, it's not worth your time.

Getting Your Written Materials into Shape

To succeed as a contract technical writer, you need to create and constantly update and maintain several different kinds of material:

- *Materials about you.* These consist primarily of resumes, cover letters, and references. If you are intending to work as a contractor, you also need business cards and stationery, both of which should include your email address and the URL of your personal website, if you have one.

- *Database of leads and contacts.* Looking for work is itself a lot of work. Like any large project, it needs to be organized, and the better you track your data the more efficient you will be in finding work.

- *Portfolio of Samples.* Your portfolio—the collection of written samples that you've produced—is one of your most important job-finding tools. Make sure it's as good, comprehensive, and up to date as possible.

Your resume and portfolio are so important that they deserve a bit more discussion.

Creating and Using Your Resume. A poorly conceived, poorly written resume—one that's guaranteed to languish in cyberspace—does you no good whatsoever. To create a successful tech writing resume, you've got to understand what happens between the time it leaves your computer and the time it lands on a prospective employer's desk.

The crucial thing to realize is that, for most of its journey, your resume won't be read by human beings—it will be handled by computers. Computers will receive it and store it. (Faxed resumes will be scanned with OCR—optical character recognition—technology and stored as electronic files.) Computers, not human beings, will do most of the work of "interpreting" your resume and selecting it from among thousands of others.

> *For most of its journey, your resume won't be read by human beings*

Say a company decides that it needs a tech writer to document its widgets. The company uses Macintosh computers and Microsoft Word. The manager contacts a recruiter, asking the recruiter to send resumes of people who know widgets, know Word, and use a Mac. The manager doesn't want to see *anything* else.

The recruiter's database might contain thousands of resumes. (Recruiters collect resumes by placing ads in newspapers or on billboards, radio, TV, or the Internet. Often, the job descriptions in these ads are extremely general. The ads ask people to send in their resumes, and those resumes are scanned or placed directly in the resume database.)

The recruiter searches her resume database by using the keywords "widgets + word + macintosh." She is *not* searching for full phrases or sentences, but rather for keywords so that her computer can reduce those thousands of resumes down to the 20 or 30 that fit the bill. **Your resume should therefore be simply formatted with many keywords.** (Note: Check your resume carefully for misspellings. Many managers will immediately toss a document that contains even a single misspelling. Also, keyword searches don't compensate for misspellings. If you misspell a keyword, your resume will not be found.)

The recruiter's search brings up several dozen resumes that contain all three keywords. From that, she culls the best candidates. She hands the short list to a low-level employee who calls you to see if you are available.

Recruiters generally only read about the top third of the resume, so put your most important information at the top. In fact, you may find that the recruiter who calls you won't have read your resume at all. Your resume may explicitly state that you wrote *Widgets for Dummies* and that you host the popular TV show *Men Are from Mars and Widgets Are from Jupiter,* but the caller will still ask if you know anything about widgets.

Don't assume that the recruiter understands the job. The recruiter probably has a humanities degree and knows nothing about widgets. You should be ready to explain widgets to her. The better she understands widgets, the better she can present you to the manager.

Once she's talked to you and the other people whose resumes her computer search pulled up, the recruiter will present the best candidates to the manager. She'll set up your interview. Be flexible and available. Don't make conditions or talk about having to take your cat to the vet.

Always get the manager's name and telephone number "just in case something comes up." And then call the manager and discuss the job. Since the recruiter will rarely know what a widget is—and since the job description may not have been very clear—you want to make sure that you are not going to waste time by going to the interview. Discuss the skills, duties, and salary range with the manager. Managers appreciate these calls; they don't want to waste an hour on a pointless interview, either.

When you attend the interview, bring along *three* clean copies of your resume. It's not unusual for a recruiter to lose part of your resume; the copy she's faxed to the manager may look awful; or the manager may have misplaced it in the disorder of his desk.

Building Your Portfolio. The most important thing managers look for is completed work similar to what they need. A good, thorough, up-to-date portfolio is vital to your career.

Photographers, art directors, and fashion models have leather-bound portfolios that they lug around from interview to interview, but a tech writer's portfolio is really just a collection of everything (and anything) you might ever want to show a prospective employer. When you go to an interview, choose the one or two samples (three at the very most) that most closely resemble what the prospective employer is interested in. (This is another reason to find out as much as you can about the job before arriving at the interview.)

Without experience, obviously, it's not so easy to put samples together, but there are a number of ways you can build a portfolio before you find your first job:

- *Take classes or enroll in a degree or certificate program for technical communication.* As we said earlier, *make sure that the courses you select are designed to help you produce portfolio-quality work samples.*

- *Volunteer to write something for a not-for-profit organization.*

- *Build your own website.*

- *Help a working tech writer on a project.* Writers who have a lot of business often find that they must subcontract portions of some projects.

Looking for Work

The next step, after targeting your market and shaping your portfolio to hit that market, is to register with online job boards. Here are a few of the most important ones: www.dice.com, www.headhunter.net, www.brassring.com, www.monster.com, and www.careermosaic.com.

Most such sites allow you to post your resume and/or fill out a questionnaire about your skills. **Do not pay to be listed on an online job board.** Most sites are free, and it's the free sites that employers and recruiters search. Keep in mind that most of those who search such sites are recruiters and brokers—that is, temp agencies. If you're looking for staff work, that's fine, because the employer pays the recruiter. If you're looking for contract work, it's still a good way to find jobs, but the downside is that you'll end up getting less money because the agency that hires you as a temp will take a big cut of what the client pays for your work.

In addition to registering with an online job board, there are a lot of other things you can do to find work:

- *Register with the National Writers Union Job Hotline.* The NWU Job Hotline lists contract and staff jobs for NWU members. When you find a job through the Hotline, you pay the NWU a finder's fee of 10 percent of the first four months' income from that job—much less than the typical agency markup. For Hotline information, visit the NWU website, at www.nwu.org/hotline.

- *Search job banks.* The Society for Technical Communication (www.stc-va.org) and other trade associations run job banks, as do most universities that have technical communications programs.

- *Network.* Many of the best jobs are "invisible." News about these jobs is most often passed by word of mouth, and personal recommendations are the biggest single factor in who gets hired. *So network!* Attend NWU meetings.

Attend meetings of professional and trade associations like the Society for Technical Communication. Go to trade shows and schmooze, meet people, and collect their business cards for your contacts database. Call up people you know in the industry and ask them if they know anyone looking for writers.

- *Consult black marks on dead trees.* Check the Sunday edition of your local major daily for job leads. Look in classified ads under both "technical writer" and "writer." Check out the corporate display ads because they sometimes list technical writer openings. Look at employment-oriented publications such as *High Technology Careers.* (These are usually free on news-racks, or you can subscribe.)

- *Read the trade publications.* Articles about new technologies or corporate profiles can provide useful leads.

- *Advertise your services.* A few contract tech writers advertise themselves in Yellow Pages listings, newspaper classifieds, display ads in trade publications, and the like. Before you do this, be aware that it's expensive—and it's very unclear whether such ads actually produce results.

- *Get lucky.* Managers only want to hire experienced people, but sometimes their clocks are ticking a little too fast for them to find the writer of their dreams. They have deadlines to meet. If they can't find an experienced writer, they eventually have to hire whomever they can get. If you land on their doorstep at exactly the right moment, impress them with your enthusiasm, and convince them that you're a quick learner who's determined to succeed, they might just hire you.

CONTRACTS

Freelance journalists and other freelance writers often—and unwisely—work without a contract. It is much rarer for technical writers to work without a written contract (or the equivalent). This does not mean that tech writing contracts are unproblematic, however. Like all freelance writers, technical writers should commit themselves to becoming skilled negotiators.

For general information on contracts and negotiating techniques, see pages 12–17.

"Boilerplate" Contracts and Purchase Orders

Since technical writers tend to work for corporations, and quite often for huge corporations, most of their clients are likely to have a boilerplate contract. It is vital to remember two things about such contracts: (1) they are written with the client's, not the writer's, interests in mind, and (2) they should be seen as starting points for negotiations, not as immutable pronouncements.

By its nature, boilerplate is designed to be changed. Negotiate. Cross out unfavorable terms. Write in your own conditions. Do whatever it takes to make the contract a good deal for you.

The same goes for purchase orders, which are increasingly replacing contracts in tech writing. Purchase orders serve the same purpose as contracts, spelling out the terms of the agreement between writer and client. Purchase orders are particularly likely to have boilerplate language inappropriate for a freelance writing project—for example, specifying that payment is due 45 days after delivery of the product or service. **Watch out for such boilerplate and modify it, using a letter of exception signed by the manager who is hiring you.**

Negotiating with Agencies—Some Tips

As has already been noted, unless you develop a network of former employers and colleagues, you will probably find most of your work through agencies. In fact, in some markets today, it is all but impossible to find technical writing assignments *except* through agencies. Some tips on negotiating with agencies are therefore in order.

When a corporation requires contractors to work through an agency, the writer agrees on a rate with the agency, and the agency adds its markup to the writer's

Boilerplate contracts should be seen as starting points for negotiations

rate to form the billing rate it charges the corporation. The corporation pays the agency, and the agency pays the writer. The agency pockets the markup, which today commonly ranges from 33 to 50 percent percent of the total hourly fee.

Most contractors are paid by the hour or by the "professional day." An hourly rate is preferable, since the day rate usually stipulates that you receive a fixed sum for working for 8 to 10 hours and are paid for additional hours starting with the 11th hour.

When you negotiate a rate with an agency, there are several important points to remember:

- *Ask about details of the assignment.* Your recruiter may not have as much technical expertise as you do and may be able to ask for a higher rate from the corporation based on your knowledge.

- *Remember that the first offer is probably not the highest possible rate.* Asking for a higher fee—one that you would be more "comfortable" with—elicits a positive response surprisingly often.

- *Choose agencies carefully.* Some are quite reliable and will pay you whether or not the corporation has paid them. Some, unfortunately, wait to pay you until they've received payment—or they are simply unreliable.

RATES & PRACTICES

The statistical information given in this section represents the real experience of actual writers working in the field, and thus we believe the data present a reasonably accurate, if necessarily incomplete, picture of current conditions in the technical writing market. We also provide NWU recommendations for rates and acceptable practices to help you make better deals in the future.

Rates

It is difficult to settle on an "average" rate or salary for technical writers. Each industry in which technical writers work has its own prevailing rates. Even within a single market, rates may vary considerably based on the kind of product being written. Pay levels also vary from region to region, and, of course, more experienced technical writers generally command higher rates than those nearer the beginning of their careers. Beyond these factors, pay rates depend to some degree on the overall state of the economy, the current condition of the industry, and supply and demand.

Consulting the information on rates presented below is just a first step toward determining a fair rate for a given job. You should also note the rates offered in newspaper and website listings, and you should talk to other technical writers to determine the rate you can expect.

Table 5.1 gives the hourly rates for six major classes of *contract* technical writing reported by respondents to a nationwide survey of NWU-member business, instructional, technical, and electronic writers conducted in 1997. (Some data, as noted, are supplemented by information from two other, more recent surveys.) For each type of writing, three pieces of information about rates are provided: (1) the minimum and maximum reported hourly rates; (2) the prevalent range of rates in the market; and (3) the range of rates recommended by the NWU.

In interpreting Table 5.1, please note the following. The ranges of rates presented here represent hourly wages both for independent contractors and for tech writers who found their jobs through agencies. It's safe to assume that, in general, work found through agencies will pay less—sometimes significantly less—than work contracted directly with a client. This difference is borne out by a 1999 survey of independent-contractor and temp agency–employee technical writers conducted by the Society for Technical Communication. In that survey of 370 writers, published in the June 2000 issue of the STC's magazine *Intercom,* agency-employee respondents reported hourly rates ranging from $22 to $55; independent contractors reported rates ranging from $25 to $75 per hour. (Rates in the STC's survey were not broken down into specific markets or kinds of work done.)

TABLE 5.1. **TECHNICAL WRITING: HOURLY RATES**

Type	Min/Max	Prevalent range	NWU recommends (at least)
Software documentation[a,b]	$25/$140	$50–$75	$50–$80
Hardware documentation[b]	$15/$150	$50–$85	$60–$85
Engineering	$15/$70	$25–$60	$35–$60
Medical/ pharmaceutical[a,b]	$15/$150	$35–$100	$40–$100
Scientific (nonmedical)	$25/$114	$35–$75	$45–$75
Financial	$25/$187	$30–$60	$40–$60

[a] Data supplemented by *Freelance Writers' Guide* survey of technical writers conducted winter/spring 2000.
[b] Date supplemented by NWU Job Hotline survey conducted summer 1999.

Getting Work

In a targeted survey of technical writers conducted in the winter and spring of 2000, we asked respondents to estimate what percentage of their jobs they had lined up through a variety of sources. As Table 5.2 demonstrates, less than one-quarter of the total jobs reported were found through agencies. This relatively low figure may seem surprising given what we've said about the increasing dominance of agencies in today's tech writing market. The result, however, is undoubtedly skewed by the fact that respondents were, in general, established technical writers with pools of clients to draw on for repeat work.

TABLE 5.2. **SOURCES OF WORK**

Source	Percentage of jobs reported[a]
Repeat business from existing clients	39%
Agencies or job postings on the Web	26%
Personal networking	17%
Referrals from existing clients	8%
The NWU Job Hotline	7%
Job openings posted in newspapers	2%
Cold calls	less than 1%
Personal brochures and mailings	less than 1%
Job fairs or trade shows	less than 1%

[a]Jobs worked during the previous two years.

Incorporation

Some technical writers find that there are a variety of advantages to self-incorporation. We asked respondents to our 2000 survey whether they were incorporated, and, if so, whether they paid themselves a W-2–type salary. Table 5.3 combines the responses to these two questions.

TABLE 5.3. **INCORPORATED?**

Response	Percentage
No	64%
Yes, and pay themselves a W-2 salary	29%
Yes, but do not pay themselves a W-2 salary	7%

Employment Modes/Contract Types

We found that technical writers work under a variety of employment modes, ranging from independent 1099 contractors, to temporary W-2 employees of agencies, to corporation-to-corporation vendors. Table 5.4 summarizes the prevalence of various employment modes among writers responding to our

TABLE 5.4. **EMPLOYMENT MODES**

Response	Percentage
Respondents worked directly for clients on a 1099 basis/work-for-hire contracts[a]	53%
Respondents worked directly for clients on a 1099 basis/did not know or recall contract terms	less than 0.5%
Respondents worked as temporary W-2 employees of clients	less than 0.5%
Respondents found jobs themselves but were paid as 1099 contractors by an agency	27%
Respondents found jobs themselves but were paid as W-2 employees by an agency	less than 0.5%
Respondents found jobs through agencies and were paid as 1099 contractors by agency	1.5%
Respondents found jobs through agencies and were paid as W-2 employees by agency	2%
Respondents worked as vendors to clients ("corporation-to-corporation") and paid themselves W-2–type salaries	3%
Respondents worked as vendors to clients ("corporation-to-corporation") and did not pay themselves W-2–type salaries	less than 1%
Respondents worked as vendors to agencies ("corporation-to-corporation"), which billed the clients, and paid themselves W-2–type salaries	12%

[a]Or the functional equivalent—for example, "assign all rights" contracts.

2000 survey. (Percentages are for total number of jobs reported during the previous two years. That such a small number of respondents reported having found work through agencies is probably an artifact of our sample, which was mostly composed of long-established technical writers.)

Given the nature of technical writing, it's not surprising that work-for-hire and the functionally similar assign-all-rights arrangements prevail so universally among 1099 contractors. In the technical writing field, work-for-hire is acceptable.

 For detailed discussion of work-for-hire, see pages 9–12.

Fee Structure

In our 2000 survey, we asked technical writers how they structure their fees: whether on an hourly, per-project, per-page, or other basis. We were pleased to find that nearly 80 percent of technical writers generally charge an hourly rate.

Given the complexity of many technical writing projects, it is often very difficult to estimate how much time you will need to complete a project. Unfortunately, most writers tend to underestimate and—if they agree to a flat fee—end up working much more and earning much less than they expect. In an hourly fee contract, you avoid having to pay a penalty if the project goes awry. Your clients are also less likely to drag their feet during the project if they are paying you by the hour.

If you do charge on a per-project basis, try to build a maximum number of hours (a "ceiling" or "not-to-exceed" limit) into the contract and a provision for renegotiating the fee upward should the project go over that maximum.

Timeliness of Payment

We also asked freelance technical writers how many weeks after invoice they get paid. Table 5.5 summarizes their responses.

TABLE 5.5. **TIMING OF PAYMENT**

Range	Weeks after invoice
Soonest	1
Prevalent Range	2–4
Longest	16

There is nothing as infuriating as working long hours on a project for which you have negotiated a good contract and not having enough money to pay the rent because the client takes months to pay your invoices. One way to try to protect yourself against this is to specify the terms of payment in the contract. The ideal arrangement, obviously, is to be paid no later than ten working days, or two weeks, after invoice. If, after negotiation on your part, your client still insists on taking more than 30 days to pay your invoices, you might want to consider offering a 2-percent "prompt payment" discount of the invoice total if it is paid within 10 working days. You might also consider adding a late-payment penalty of 10 percent for invoices paid later than 30 days after the invoice date.

Expenses

We asked technical writers in our 2000 survey how often their expenses are reimbursed by the client. Table 5.6 indicates the results.

There is no reason that a writer should have to subsidize any part of a client's business. Make sure that your contracts stipulate that all reasonable expenses will be reimbursed. Specify the types of expenses considered reasonable and the maximum amount of reimbursement. It is also a good idea to have the client approve expenses before you lay out your own money. Remember to save all receipts to turn over to the client when billing for reimbursement.

TABLE 5.6. **EXPENSES REIMBURSED?**

Frequency	Percentage
Never	29%
Rarely	29%
Sometimes	14%
Frequently	14%
Always	14%

Bylines

We have all certainly written our share of pieces we would rather not put our names to. If you are particularly proud of the manual you just wrote for a new auto-assembly robot, however, you have every right to a byline. It's not just a matter of pride, though. A byline may be your only way of proving that a piece of writing is your own.

Unfortunately, as Table 5.7 indicates, there is a tendency for tech writers not to get credit for their work.

TABLE 5.7. **BYLINES RECEIVED?**

Frequency	Percentage
Never	29%
Rarely	14%
Sometimes	36%
Frequently	14%
Always	7%

Indemnification

A fairly high proportion of technical writers are asked at least some of the time to indemnify themselves against legal liability resulting from their work, as indicated by Table 5.8.

Indemnification clauses in contracts require you, the writer, to assume legal responsibility for "errors and omissions" in your work. This is vastly unfair, since the work you do for a corporation will in all likelihood be produced as "work for

TABLE 5.8. **REQUIRED TO PROVIDE INDEMNIFICATION?**

Frequency	Percentage
Never	43%
Rarely	15%
Sometimes	21%
Frequently	21%

hire" or the equivalent (and will not "belong" to you in any legal sense), because your work will be based on information given to you by employees of the corporation, and because what you write will undoubtedly be checked, rechecked, and re-rechecked for accuracy and completeness by your managers. The corporation, not you, should assume full legal liability for the work.

The Media Perils insurance available to NWU members provides protection against liability arising from errors and omissions–type claims. If you are sometimes required to sign contracts containing indemnification clauses, you should consider enrolling in this plan.

Non-Compete Clauses

Non-compete clauses restrict your ability to work for competitive firms within a given industry, generally for the period of the contract and for some specified time after the contract ends. There's a certain logic to the non-compete clause—no business wants you to be simultaneously lending assistance to a directly competitive firm and (perhaps) disclosing its plans and strategies to that other company—and some non-compete clauses are more or less acceptable. (In fact, you'll gain in professional stature if you're scrupulous about informing clients about any potential conflicts of interest.) The trouble is, some non-compete clauses are worded so comprehensively and/or extend the period during which you're prohibited from working for a competitor for such a long time that they would, if obeyed, unfairly restrain your ability to earn a living.

In our 2000 survey, we asked technical writers how frequently they were required to sign non-compete clauses. Table 5.9 summarizes their responses.

The NWU believes that non-compete clauses should be carefully worded so as not to interfere with a writer's ability to earn a living.

TABLE 5.9. **REQUIRED TO SIGN NON-COMPETE CLAUSES?**

Frequency	Percentage
Never	43%
Rarely	14%
Sometimes	29%
Frequently	7%
Always	7%

The Corporate/Not-for-Profit Market

We live in an increasingly "scribal" culture, one in which writing has become a specialized and highly valued skill. Businesses and not-for-profit organizations have, of course, always hired freelance writers, but today the market is bigger and more varied than ever. There's virtually no end to the different kinds of projects that freelance business/not-for-profit writers get involved in: speeches, advertising copy, press releases, brochures, employee manuals, annual reports, catalogs, newsletters, website text, grant proposals, project proposals, ghostwritten articles for trade publications, videoscripts, advertorials, white papers . . . . The list could go on and on.

This huge and diverse market is a boon to writers

This huge and diverse market is a boon to writers and would-be writers. As the rate information in this chapter indicates, freelance writers working for businesses and other organizations generally earn a much better wage than their journalist and book-author counterparts. (Of course, many freelance journalists and book authors augment their incomes by picking up temporary business-writing gigs.)

This is not to say that freelance writing for businesses and other organizations is problem-free. Freelancing is tough. It's hard to develop and maintain a list of steady clients. Periods of drought—when you just can't seem to scrabble together a living, no matter how hard you try—aren't unknown, even to the most experienced of freelancers. And there are businesspeople and not-for-profit agency officials who can be every bit as truculent, unfair, miserly, unclear about what they want, and just plain hard to work for as the worst publishing industry honcho. Problems with getting paid in a timely fashion—or getting paid at all—may be rarer for business writers than for, say, freelance journalists, but they certainly occur.

GETTING STARTED

Too, it can be difficult to break into freelance business writing. (For the sake of ease, we'll mostly talk about "business" writing from here on out, though what we say applies to writing for not-for-profits, as well.) As with every kind of writing, it's hard to land an assignment unless you've got samples to show—samples, moreover, that belong to the same general universe as the assignment you're pursuing. The decision-maker who's looking for someone to write website text for an international construction company won't necessarily be impressed by the well-turned phrases of your college paper on the *commedia dell'arte.*

> *If you're a beginning writer you may find it worthwhile to take a staff job*

Journalists—especially those who come to the table with a sheaf of clips on business-related topics—may have an easier time than other writers in breaking into the business-writing game. But if you're a beginning writer who has little work to show, you may find it worthwhile to take a staff job—as a proposal writer, say, or as the editor of an in-house newsletter (or in any of the vast number of writing-related staff positions that exist in the business world)—and to stay in that job for a couple of years before venturing into the freelance arena. Besides giving you credibility as a writer and a portfolio of produced work to wow prospective clients, working a staff job can begin to supply you with all-important contacts *and* with the body of knowledge you'll need to succeed as a freelance writer in a given field.

Like most writers, freelancers who work for corporations and not-for-profits tend to specialize in one, two, or a very few areas. Certain skills translate across boundaries (there's a knack to writing lively catalog copy, and it may not matter much whether the catalog is selling dresses, gourmet food items, or electronic gadgets), but, in general, business writers try to develop a certain level of expertise in specific industries, professions, or markets. It's hard to land an assignment writing for a bank if you know nothing about financial services or for a drug company if your pharmaceutical vocabulary doesn't extend beyond "penicillin" and "Prozac."

If you're considering taking a staff position, it makes sense to exercise some care in choosing the kind of company you'll work for. When you do go freelance, it's more than likely that you'll be pigeonholed according to the work you've already done. If, for example, it's your dream to become a freelance grant writer for private social-service agencies, it may not be wise to take a job in the communications department of an aircraft manufacturer.

In the Information Age, formerly well-defined boundaries between different kinds of jobs are tending to vanish

If you're just starting out—or even if you have a fair amount of experience under your belt—you may also want to think about augmenting your writing skills with some high-level computer skills. In the Information Age, formerly well-defined boundaries between different kinds of jobs—like the traditional division between the writer and the designer—are tending to vanish, and it's very likely that you'll increase your employability and be able to command a higher-than-usual rate if you're both an excellent wordsmith and skilled in the use of a print-design program like QuarkXPress or any of a number of Internet applications.

CONTRACT (AND RELATED) ISSUES

As for all writers, contracts can sometimes be particularly problematic for business writers. First off, there's the fact that too many writers who work for corporations and not-for-profits do so without a written contract. (The reasons you should never work without a written contract are spelled out in the section on contracts in Chapter 1, pages 12–17.) But having a contract does not, in itself, guarantee that you'll be treated fairly or provided with adequate protection. Lately, business-writing contracts tend to include a series of obnoxious clauses that can put you at legal risk and that place unfair and unreasonable strictures on your career. We'll deal again with some of these contract clauses in the "Rates and Practices" section, below, but it's important to describe them briefly here:

Indemnification clauses require you, the writer, to assume legal responsibility for "errors and omissions" in your work. This is gargantuanly unfair, since the work you do for a corporation or other organization will in all likelihood be produced as "work for hire" or the equivalent (and will not "belong" to you in any legal sense), because the client is supplying you with the information on which your work is based, and because your work will undoubtedly be checked, rechecked, and re-rechecked for accuracy and completeness by your bosses in the organization. The organization, not you, should assume full legal liability for the work.

For an explanation of work for hire, see pages 9–12.

Non-compete clauses restrict your ability to work for competitive firms within a given industry, generally for the period of the contract and for some specified time after the contract ends. There's a certain logic to the non-compete clause—no business wants you to be simultaneously lending assistance to a directly competitive firm and (perhaps) disclosing its plans and strategies to that other company—and some non-compete clauses are more or less acceptable. (In fact, you'll gain in professional stature if you're scrupulous about informing clients about any potential conflicts of interest.) The trouble is, some non-compete clauses are worded so comprehensively and/or extend the period during which you're prohibited from working for a competitor for such a long time that they would, if obeyed, unfairly restrain your ability to earn a living.

> *You'll gain in professional stature if you're scrupulous about informing clients about any potential conflicts of interest*

There's a third sort of clause you should also watch out for—a clause that would seem, on its face, to prohibit you from using for your own promotional purposes the materials you write for your client. Such "nondisclosure" clauses vaguely state that you may not "use" the written materials you produce—or not without the client's express permission. Again, the reason behind this kind of clause is understandable; it's the wording that's unfair. Under a work-for-hire or similar arrangement, the writing you produce will belong to the organization that hires you, and you cannot resell that work to another client or in any way republish it without permission. Fair enough. But you should *not* be restricted in your use of these materials *in your own portfolio.* These are your "clips," and your professional viability depends on your ability to present them to others as samples of your work. If you can't convince your client to eliminate this clause entirely, try to get the client to accept a rider to the contract that states that you may, without permission, use the materials you produce in the portfolio you show to other prospective employers.

It's essential that you recognize that contracts are almost always "boilerplate" documents devised by a firm's or agency's lawyers to provide that organization with a degree of protection equivalent to a four-foot-thick lead wall. (Some contracts are designed for other kinds of vendors and are simply inappropriate for freelance writers.) **Clients themselves, however, are often quite willing to negotiate specific contract points, and you should try to have clauses like those described above deleted from the contract or modified to your satisfaction.**

For tips on negotiating contracts, see pages 12–17.

These days, some corporate/not-for-profit writers are, like many tech writers, finding it difficult to secure work as independent contractors and are being forced to find work through agencies or to become employees of agencies (or "third-party employers") even when they've found jobs on their own. This unsatisfactory situation is discussed in detail in Chapter 1, pages 18–20. One strategy for maintaining your independence in an environment in which clients are increasingly reluctant to hire independent contractors is to self-incorporate, which may also give you the option of working as a "vendor" for some clients. The basics of self-incorporation—and some pointers about becoming a vendor—are also covered in Chapter 1, pages 20–22.

GRANT WRITING

Before turning to our discussion of prevailing rates and practices, we need to say a few words about grant writing for not-for-profit organizations, which differs in several ways from the other kinds of writing discussed in this chapter. For starters, many profession-al freelance grant writers—more so than other business writers—are *consultants* who not only write but also assist organizations in planning financial strategies. Because of this, it's unlikely that you'll make it very far in the grant-writing/development consultant game *unless* you've already held a fairly high-level staff posi-tion in a development office. Success as a grant writer depends on an in-depth knowledge of foundations and other funding sources in a given field. Furthermore, your prospective employers will want to see some concrete evidence that proposals you've worked on have actually won financial support. Various schools offer courses in grant writing, and these may be helpful, but there's no real substitute for the knowledge and experi-ence that working a development staff job can give you.

Success as a grant writer depends on an in-depth knowledge of foundations and other funding sources in a given field

Also, there's a peculiar tradition in the grant-writing world—one that, mercifully, appears to be waning but that you should still be wary of. This is the practice of paying grant writers on commission—that is, postponing some portion of the payment until the grant money rolls in (obviously, this part of the wage is paid only if the grant proposal is successful). This is *extremely* risky for the writer, since only a very small proportion of grants are ever funded—and, even when a proposal *is* funded, the money can be a long, long time in coming. Fortunately, many not-for-profit organizations have woken up to the fact that paying writers on commission is in nobody's interest. If a grant writer is working on commission, he or she may be tempt-ed to pursue a smaller grant (and to forego other, more distant but poten-tially more lucrative possibilities) merely because the yea-or-nay decision on that small grant will be made quickly or because a certain project seems a shoo-in to win it.

Not only should grant writers avoid working on commission, but they should always try to work for an agreed-on, acceptable hourly rate—*not* on a flat-fee, per-project basis. (It's also a sensible rule to have a minimum amount of time for which you must be paid—say, half a day—and not to accept jobs that pay less.) If you do decide to work for a flat fee, make sure that *all* your responsibilities are carefully spelled out in advance—and that you have the option of renegotiating the fee upward if the job outgrows the agreed-on terms.

Potential conflicts of interest are also probably a little sharper for grant writers than for other business/not-for-profit writers, since the pool of potential donors in any given field is usually small. Professional ethics would seem to demand that you think long and hard before accepting work from, say, three small museums that are likely to be competing for the same foundation money or for several AIDS social-service agencies that will be chasing after the same government and private grants. Again, it is important that you inform any clients of any conflicts, real or potential.

RATES AND PRACTICES

Unless otherwise noted, the data presented below are derived from a targeted survey of corporate and not-for-profit writers conducted in winter and spring of 2000.

Rates

As we've indicated, the field of corporate and not-for-profit communications encompasses a very broad and diverse range of project types. We wanted to determine the rates prevalent in the for-profit and not-for-profit markets for a variety of different kinds of writing. Table 6.1 (next page) indicates the range of rates reported for eight major types: advertising copy, annual reports, grant writing, manuals, marketing/promotional copy, newsletters, public relations, and video/film scripts. In each case, we've separated the responses into for-profit and not-for-profit categories. The only exceptions are ad copy, for which we received very few responses from writers for not-for-profit companies, and grant writing, which is restricted to not-for-profit organizations.

Contracts/Employment Modes

Whether you are signing on to write a newsletter for your local soup kitchen or an annual report for a pet supplies dot-com, you are entering a business deal. The terms of the agreement should be clearly spelled out before work begins or money exchanges hands. Too many writers still do not protect themselves by insisting on written contracts.

TABLE 6.1. **CORPORATE/NOT-FOR-PROFIT WRITING: HOURLY RATES**

Type	Sector	Low	Prevalent range	High	NWU recommends (at least)
Ad copy	For-profit	$20	$50–$80	$100	$60
Annual reports	For-profit	$25	$50–$100	$300	$60
	Not-for-profit	$20	$30–$50	$60	$40
Grant writing	Not-for-profit	$15	$25–$65	$120	$40
Manuals	For-profit	$20	$40–$80	$100	$60
	Not-for-profit	$15	$30–$50	$100	$40
Marketing/ promotional	For-profit	$20	$60–$100	$150	$60
	Not-for-profit	$15	$30–$60	$90	$40
Newsletters	For-profit	$15	$50–$75	$120	$60–$75
	Not-for-profit	$15	$30–$65	$90	$40
Public relations	For-profit	$15	$40–$80	$175	$60–$75
	Not-for-profit	$10	$30–$60	$90	$40
Video/film scripts	For-profit	$45	$50–$80	$125	$60
	Not-for-profit	$7.50	$30–$50	$100	$40

Source: Combined results from national survey of NWU-member business, instructional, technical, and electronic writers conducted in 1997 and the targeted survey of business/not-for-profit writers conducted for this *Guide* in winter/spring 2000. Data are supplemented by results from a survey of users of the NWU National Job Hotline conducted in summer 1999.

Twelve percent of writers responding to our survey said that they usually work without contracts. Although that figure may seem low, the picture is worsened by the fact that, when asked about specific jobs worked during the previous two years, many respondents reported that they did not know or did not remember the contract terms for those projects.

The great majority of surveyed writers reported that they find their jobs themselves and that they work directly for clients as independent contractors ("1099 contractors"). Most of these jobs are contracted on a work-for-hire or assign-all-rights basis. Table 6.2 shows percentages for the employment modes/contract types for the more than 300 separate jobs that our respondents together reported having worked during the previous two years.

TABLE 6.2. **EMPLOYMENT MODES**

	Percentage
Respondents worked directly for clients on a 1099 basis/work-for-hire contracts[a]	72.6%
Respondents worked directly for clients on a 1099 basis/did not know or recall contract terms	22.3%
Respondents found jobs themselves but were paid as 1099 contractors by an agency	3.1%
Respondents found jobs themselves but were paid as W-2 employees by an agency	0.5%
Respondents worked as vendors to clients ("corporation-to-corporation")[b]	1.5%

[a]Or the functional equivalent—for example, "assign all rights" contracts. Some contracts specified that the writer assigned all rights *if* work-for-hire provision turned out to be invalid.
[b]Writer did *not* pay him/herself a W2-type salary.

Sources of Work

Writers reported learning of work through a variety of sources, but, as Table 6.3 indicates, repeat business and referrals from existing clients seem by far the most important mechanisms.

Fee Structure

We asked corporate and nonprofit communications writers how they structure their fees. Their responses are summarized in Table 6.4.

TABLE 6.3. **SOURCES OF WORK**

Source	Percentage
Repeat business from existing clients	53%
Referrals from existing clients	23%
Personal networking	19%
Job fairs or trade shows	2%
Cold calls	1%
Personal brochures and mailings	1%
Posted job openings	1%

TABLE 6.4. **FEE STRUCTURE**

Structure	Percentage
Hourly	55%
Per project	36%
Per word	4.5%
Other	4.5%

The NWU considers an hourly fee structure the most equitable and advantageous for freelance communications writers. It is often difficult to estimate how much time you will need to complete a project. Unfortunately, most writers tend to underestimate and end up working much more (and earning much less) than they expect. With an hourly-fee contract, you avoid having to pay a penalty if the project takes longer than anticipated. Your clients are also less likely to drag their feet during the project if they are paying you by the hour.

In cases where you consistently write for the same client (putting out a monthly newsletter, for example, or maintaining an organization's website), it is much easier—and much better—to work by the hour and establish regular weekly or biweekly billing/payment cycles. This puts your relationship with your client on a more businesslike foundation than an endless series of separately billed, one-off projects. It also establishes you in your client's mind as its regular vendor of professional writing—just as the client has ongoing relations with other vendors, such as attorneys and accountants. Indeed, some public relations writers work on a *retainer* basis, agreeing to perform certain regular duties, as needed, on a monthly basis (but being paid the retainer even if no such work is required during a certain month). In retainer contracts, it's important to work out which kinds of work are and are not covered by the retainer. Work not covered by the retainer can be billed separately, on an hourly basis.

If you do charge on a per-project basis, try to build a maximum number of hours (a "ceiling" or "not-to-exceed" limit) into the contract and a provision for renegotiating should the project go over that maximum.

Timeliness of Payment

In freelance writing, getting a contract is often only half the battle; actually getting paid can be even more difficult. We asked freelance corporate and nonprofit communications writers how many weeks after invoice they get paid; results are shown in Table 6.5.

There is no justification for payment delays of more than 30 days. The ideal arrangement is to be paid within 10 working days, or two weeks, after submitting your invoice. If your attempts to negotiate a reasonable payment cycle fail, you might consider offering a discount—of, say, 2 percent of the invoice total—if you're paid within 10 business days. You can also build a penalty for late payment into your contract—for instance, adding 10 percent to the total for an invoice paid more than 30 days after billing date.

TABLE 6.5. **TIMING OF PAYMENTS**

	Weeks after invoice
Soonest	$1/2$
Prevalent Range	2–6
Longest	52

Expenses

How often are writers' expenses reimbursed by the client? Not often enough, as the information in Table 6.6 indicates.

A writer should never have to subsidize any part of his or her client's business. All reasonable expenses should be reimbursed. Make sure that your contract stipulates this and specifies the types of expenses considered reasonable and the maximum amount of reimbursement. It is also a good idea to have the client approve expenses before you lay out your own money. Remember that you must save all receipts and submit them to your client when billing for expenses.

TABLE 6.6. **EXPENSES REIMBURSED?**

Frequency	Percentage
Never	6%
Rarely	6%
Sometimes	29%
Frequently	18%
Always	41%

Bylines

As a corporate or nonprofit communications writer, you almost by definition have to remain in the background. The NWU believes, however, that you should receive byline credit for your work if you so desire. As Table 6.7 indicates, communications writers do not always get such credit.

Non-Compete Clauses

We asked writers whether their contracts contain non-compete clauses. As indicated by Table 6.8, this demand remains relatively rare, though we believe the practice is growing. The NWU believes that such clauses should be carefully worded so as not to interfere with a writer's ability to earn a living.

Indemnification

We also asked writers whether the contracts they sign require them to indemnify themselves against legal liability resulting from their work. Table 6.9 gives the results.

TABLE 6.7. **BYLINES RECEIVED?**

Frequency	Percentage
Never	18%
Rarely	11%
Sometimes	47%
Frequently	18%
Always	6%

TABLE 6.8. **REQUIRED TO SIGN NON-COMPETE CLAUSES?**

Frequency	Percentage
Never	59%
Rarely	18%
Sometimes	23%

TABLE 6.9. **REQUIRED TO PROVIDE INDEMNIFICATION?**

Frequency	Percentage
Never	31%
Rarely	19%
Sometimes	44%
Frequently	6%

The NWU believes that this practice is unfair. Writers should not have to bear the risk arising from work that they are doing under contract for an organization. **The NWU Media Perils insurance available to members provides protection against liability arising from errors and omissions–type claims. If you are sometimes required to sign contracts containing indemnification clauses, you should consider enrolling in this plan.**

Where the Grass Is Greener: Confessions of a Corporate Scribe

Keith Watson

I knew there was a gap between what journalists and corporate writers earned, but I saw the division as a quaint creekbed. On one side of the gulch lived journalists, who wore cutoff jeans as they mowed crabgrass and pulled up pigweed. On the other side were corporate types, who wore stiff clothes, treasured suburbia, and paid others to mow their lawns. Since they supposedly had to suck up to people in business suits, I accepted that corporate writers should get higher pay.

After I left journalism and crossed over, I realized that the gap was not a mere creekbed; it was a chasm. A steadily employed freelance business writer made five times what a freelance journalist earned in a year. And freelance business writers were treated with much greater respect. To show the disparities, here are some experiences from my career:

JOURNALISM

I was asked to write a 3,500-word feature on personal finance for a city magazine. The offer of $1,750 didn't seem insulting. However, considering that I was asked to cover six complex areas—banking, brokerage, real estate, accounting, insurance, and legal services—the pay was meager. I took the assignment to "break in" at this magazine; instead, the magazine did its best to break me. After six weeks of researching, writing, and rewriting, the piece was accepted orally and then killed two weeks later. A typed note told me I would receive only $467.50 (not enough to pay my rent). At the same time, I was trying to collect on a four-month-old, overdue invoice from a Texas magazine. The editor had been fired and the business manager wasn't returning my calls.

BUSINESS WRITING

I was called in to write a 20-minute speech for a vice president of marketing. I came in on a Tuesday morning and worked long hours for three intense days. On Friday morning, the executive delivered the speech and used only a few paragraphs of what I had written. But I billed the company $2,900 (rush rate) for my time and received the check within three weeks of invoice. The previous week, I had received a $4,200 check from a different firm for a 45-minute script I had written in about three weeks. The firm's managing partner also sent me a thank-you note.

So there you have it: less than $500 for six weeks of journalism work versus more than $7,000 for a month of commercial writing. The gap astounds and disgusts me. Education level and experience have virtually nothing to do with it. The gap is so wide that I don't know why any sane, experienced journalist beyond the age of 30 wouldn't cross the canyon and at least try doing commercial work. After all, magazines are running so many puff pieces and celebrity profiles that it's difficult to view the media as anything more than a commercial operation.

CORPORATE ASSIGNMENTS

When freelance writers think of commercial writing, they usually think of ad copywriting, technical writing, and public relations. Many journalists dread becoming "flacks." But corporate America has many writing needs, most of which have little to do with media relations. The assignments can be arcane and dull, but I usually write about topics that challenge me, and I get an insider's view of business.

Perhaps I've been lucky, but none of my corporate clients—who might have been portrayed in my Vietnam War–era youth as evil, greedy titans—has stiffed me. Unlike the so-called "liberal media," which often lack a sense of fair play, my clients don't understand the concept of a kill fee. My career switch may turn the stomachs of traditional union activists. But the media themselves, of course, are part of corporate America. And until journalists stop signing abusive contracts and working for peanuts, conditions in the publishing industry won't improve.

But back to the corporate market. An experienced journalist can make a good living as a freelance business writer. There's plenty of work—speeches, PowerPoint presentations, corporate website content, video scripts, letters, ghostwritten articles for trade journals—and the pay is often generous. But getting corporate work takes time, patience, and the right attitude. So here are some tips on making the transition:

ASSEMBLE A PORTFOLIO

To get your foot in the door, examine what you've written and how your skills might translate in the business sector. If you've written feature stories, you could write profiles for internal newsletters, website copy, or articles for corporate magazines distributed externally. If you've written about housing or architectural design, you could ask real estate firms if they need writing or editing help. But don't bring your poems or short stories to a marketing manager (unless he or she is a very good friend) and expect encouragement. Businesses aren't in business to subsidize your development as a creative writer.

TO JUMP-START YOUR CAREER, MAKE COLD CALLS

After I had moved from Houston to Chicago, I could no longer rely on word of mouth to get assignments. Forced to get new work or starve, I decided to make cold calls. The first call was difficult, but they got much easier. I don't remember anyone being terribly rude (certainly not as rude as some newspaper writers treat flacks). I suggest making five to ten calls successively, which takes only an hour or less. Do all the calling at once so that your spiel becomes second nature. Call marketing and public relations directors and say, "I'm a freelance writer. If you use freelancers, could I send you a few writing samples?" If the answer is yes, send a packet quickly, but don't expect an instant callback. It may be a year before you receive a return call.

HAVE FAITH

After you send out enough resumes and samples, someone will call you—even if you lack solid credentials. For example, a public relations manager for a hospital chain espied my resume and saw all the traveling I had done (Australia, Guatemala, Iceland, South Africa). She had lived abroad and wanted to meet me. Even though I had never done any healthcare writing, she assigned me a piece about traveler's diarrhea for her hospital magazine. The idea was far from glamorous, but it was a fun piece to research and write. She liked it and assigned me quarterly pieces in her company's full-color magazine. She also asked me to write an occasional press release and ad copy. We became good friends, and, with that work, I was able to obtain other corporate assignments.

CARE ABOUT YOUR CLIENTS

Many writers hope to make a quick buck off corporations so they can go home and write fiction. I have no problem with doing commercial work to support your serious writing. But I don't think you can succeed as a business writer unless you honestly care about helping clients with their writing needs. If you think of the work as easy money, your attitude is going to show, and it won't be appreciated. But if you get to know a big, arcane corporation well—its culture, its buzzwords—do good work, and are fun to work with, you may become overwhelmed with assignments. Repeat business is the key to financial stability.

DO PRO BONO WORK

A good number of corporate folks, unfortunately, lack imagination and fear the slightest risk. For example, if there isn't a press release in your portfolio, some people assume you're incapable of writing one. Never mind that you might have seen tens of thousands of releases and you could write them in your sleep. They need to hold one of yours in their hands. So, if you need to beef up your portfolio, do some pro bono press releases or a brochure for a charity. But make sure your volunteer work looks good. For example, I wrote an annual report for a public television station that won a national award from PBS. That gorgeously photographed and designed report earned me zero but helped me get a lucrative assignment to write an annual report for a law firm.

MIND YOUR MANNERS

Civility is a treasured value in corporate America, and a marketing director doesn't want to take a chance that an unknown writer will be less than polite to the higher-ups. Of course, there are dress codes as well. A bearded, long-haired fiction writer once asked me how he could get "some of that high-paying corporate work." Well, let's face facts: unless you're a respected creative director at an ad agency, you won't get away with exposed tattoos, multiple body piercings, and grungy hair. The upside of the corporate dress codes is that, particularly for men, dressing dull can be cheaper than dressing hip. I found a great used-clothing store in Chicago that stocked boring men's suits for $25 each. I have bought standard-issue black wingtips for $80 (or less). I refuse to pay good money for clothing that I don't want to wear. Once I started making money, I bought a couple of suits on sale for $300 each. Many companies now prefer "business casual," but do not confuse that with at-home freelancer casual.

CONSIDER A FULL-TIME POSITION

If you desperately need steady income, I would recommend pursuing a full-time job in a marketing/communications department. After my $467.50 debacle with the city magazine, I started looking for freelance corporate work but was asked by one firm to apply for a full-time job. Considering my years of experience, the salary offer was mediocre. I took the job, however, to learn the corporate ropes and get a steady paycheck. After a year and a half, I left the firm on good terms and took a good deal of freelance work with me. Oddly enough, the company was happy to pay me an hourly rate four times higher than what they had paid me to be on staff. Corporations tend to take in-house writers, whom they rarely promote, for granted, so I prefer to remain freelance.

As a child of the '60s, I never thought I'd "go corporate." But I got tired of editors passing up my story ideas, such as churches' slow response to the AIDS crisis or the seamy side of standup comedy shops. They wanted upbeat, noncontroversial pieces that created a cozy editorial environment to satisfy advertisers and intoxicate readers into consuming more, more, more. So, instead of doing meaningful articles with an iconoclastic bent, I found myself writing "service pieces" about how to choose a plastic surgeon and "advertorials" about real-estate developments. I didn't become a journalist for this.

I would never advise young writers, however, to pass up journalism in favor of high-paying work. When you're in your 20s, healthy, and single, who needs money? I am, in fact, puzzled by college students who aspire to work for a buttoned-down corporation. No one learns how to write well inside a big business.

The tragedy of the vast pay gap between journalists and corporate writers is that the quality of journalism suffers as mature writers leave the field. The quality has already declined because the industry loves to hire interns from wealthy families and freelancers with support from a spouse. Thus more and more articles are written by and geared toward upper-income readers.

I will occasionally write a magazine article for an editor-friend if no kill fee is involved, if payment is timely, and if the assignment interests me. But I no longer allow my labor to subsidize the production of profit-making magazines. Because of my switch to corporate work, I was able—at age 40—to start saving for retirement and put a down payment on a home. Sad to say, but these fundamentals of the American dream are beyond the reach of far too many freelance journalists.

CHAPTER 7

Instructional Writing

The workbook pages you toiled over in third grade were probably written by freelance writers. As were your high school biology textbook, the questions about *Julius Caesar* in your ninth-grade lit book, the grammar "tutorial" on the classroom computer, and ancillary materials, such as study guides, for your college courses. Vocational and adult education courses and ESL programs are among the many other places you will find materials created by freelance writers.

It is important to know about curriculum development, pedagogy, and the subject area

Most of these materials are published by a handful of major companies and their subsidiaries, but a few small educational publishers have yet to be gobbled up by the giants. Educational publishers often work through *development houses,* similar to the packagers trade publishers work with. (Corporations and not-for-profits also develop training and educational materials. However, they seldom "outsource" such projects, and when they do it is generally to companies, not individuals.)

Educational publishers think in terms of complete programs—a basal reading program for grades K through 8, for example—not single books. They hire freelancers to create specific components (student texts, workbooks, teachers' guides, tests, and so forth) or strands (all the third-grade vocabulary lessons, for example) of the program. These writers generally have a background in education, many being former teachers. Whether or not you have such experience, it is important to know about curriculum development, pedagogy, and the subject area (math, reading, social studies, specific job skills, and so forth).

The jargon is different for each segment of the market; that is, you need to know one vocabulary to talk to editors who develop adult education materials and another to impress el-hi (elementary and high school) editors. In el-hi publishing, you also need to be aware of the endless and ever-changing content restrictions imposed by the marketplace. For example, mentioning junk food, using brand names, and implying evolution (unless you're writing that segment of a science program) are taboo. You must also be able to write for students who read at specific grade levels. Once you get a job, you will receive detailed instructions and specifications about content and format. With all the rules and restrictions, completing the assignment is like solving a puzzle. This is not field for free spirits.

Instructional writers work either as independent contractors with work-for-hire contracts or as temporary employees. Independent contractors may be paid on a project, chapter, book, per-page, or hourly basis. Temporary employees are paid by the hour and may or may not receive benefits. Freelancers most often work on site for the length of the project, but they also receive freestanding assignments to be completed off site.

At the outset, project managers name the rate they will pay for a job as if it were nonnegotiable. But, of course, you should always consider all terms open to negotiation. To determine if a project, chapter, book, or per-page fee is fair, you need a clear sense of the scope of the job and the conditions you will be working under. Ask to see instructions, prototypes, and materials and try to get answers to these questions: How long is the book or chapter? How much text will appear on a typeset page? How complicated is the material? Will the project require research? Will you have a single contact person? Will you be expected to revise the first draft based on feedback from that person (or, worse, a committee)? With this information, you should be able to translate the fee into a rough hourly rate. The more experience you have doing a certain type of assignment the better your calculations will be.

To determine if a fee is fair, you need a clear sense of the scope of the job

Problems often result from unrealistic schedules, delayed and canceled projects, inadequate communications, changes in specifications, and cumbersome chains of command. Publishers often have inflexible deadlines and expect freelancers to meet the schedules regardless of unforeseeable obstacles. Writers contract to take on projects that are then postponed or canceled (as are their incomes), and they may struggle to get paid for time they put into work that had not yet been delivered. Writers may also be idle while waiting for information or feedback. They may need to revise because they were not kept informed about changes in the specifications. Editors may even ask for redos of material that had been completed before the specifications were changed.

Another cause of rewrites is built into the management structure. A manuscript that satisfies your editor may be sent back for revision by his or her boss, then by that person's boss, and so on. This problem is doubled when working for a developer since you need to satisfy the powers that be at two companies. **To protect yourself, try to modify the contract to include objective criteria for a "satisfactory" manuscript and to state that if specifications change then deadlines and fees will be adjusted accordingly. It also helps to keep a paper trail: write memos regarding the reasons for changes and delays and keep a project log.**

Educational publishing contracts contain many of the same terms that are found in those for technical and corporate writing (see Chapters 5 and 6). The prevalent rates, however, tend to be somewhat lower. Table 7.1 gives the hourly rates for different kinds of assignments reported by instructional writers responding to a 1997 NWU survey.

Pay may be relatively low and requirements exacting, but as long as there are schools, there will be a need for instructional writers. If the current political climate, with its emphasis on education, leads to increased government spending, it may lead to a boom for educational publishers, and some of the profits may even trickle down to the freelance writers on whom they depend.

TABLE 7.1. **INSTRUCTIONAL WRITING: HOURLY RATES**

Type of assignment	Low	Prevalent range	High
El-hi textbooks	$25	$30–$50	$60
College textbooks	$20	$20–$36	$36
Adult education textbooks	$20	$25–$50	$70
Courseware	$20	$40–$60	$75
Teaching aids	$15	$20–$50	$65
Video/film	$20	$50–$65	$85
Software	$20	$30–$60	$140
Multimedia	$20	$30–$60	$85
Lectures	$15	$25–$65	$100

Writing for Performance

Freelancers who write for the stage, the movies, radio, and television work under circumstances that are in some ways quite different from those that other kinds of freelance writers face. For one thing, these writers' work is primarily meant to be performed and viewed (or heard), not to be read. The kinds of contracts that writers of performance works encounter therefore differ from the contracts negotiated by book authors, freelance journalists, and other freelance writers. Film, TV, and radio scripts aren't generally published—or at least not in the ordinary sense of publication—and relatively few plays create so much interest outside the theatrical world that they are published by commercial book publishers. (When a play is published it is usually in an "actor's edition" produced by a licensing company, such as Samuel French, that oversees the granting of performance rights to amateur companies and the collection of royalties from such productions.)

There are differences between writing for the stage and writing for other performance media

There are also differences between writing for the stage and writing for other performance media—differences that, moreover, further distinguish each of these crafts from other types of freelance writing. For example, to a much greater degree than in other kinds of writing, scriptwriting for movies and, especially, television is often a collaborative enterprise, with several or even many writers contributing to the final product. Playwrights, unlike their writer-colleagues in the film and broadcast industries (and other freelance markets) *always* retain copyright in their work. And, unlike all other freelance writers, film, TV, and radio freelancers who achieve a certain, measurable level of experience become eligible for membership in a union, the Writers Guild of America (WGA), that actually engages in collective bargaining with movie studios, networks, and film, TV, and radio production companies.

Despite these important differences, however, freelance writers of works for performance—especially beginners—suffer many of the same kinds of injustices as other freelance writers. And, all too often, they make similar kinds of mistakes, unnecessarily relinquishing too many of the rights in their work for too little compensation or consenting to contractual agreements that give them too little creative control over their works' realization.

WRITING FOR FILM, TELEVISION, AND RADIO

For film and TV freelancers as for all other freelance writers, the absolutely basic rule of business is this: all the rights to your work are yours *until* you sign them away, so make sure that you don't give up your rights prematurely or for

Projects often have a very long life span, and profits can accrue over the long term

too little money. Those new to the movie- or TV-writing game sometimes don't understand that projects often have a very long life span—or more than one incarnation—and that profits can accrue over the long term. For example, a neophyte TV writer wrote a series of scripts for children's programs being produced for a local television station in the Northeast. The producers told her that the budget was extremely limited (which, in fact, it was at the time), and she settled for a contract that paid her $500 a script, period. Little did she dream that the series would end up being syndicated nationally, eventually earning big bucks for the producers but not a single additional dollar for all her labor, which was (of course) essential to the program's creation. The lesson? When negotiating a contract, anticipate a future that's more glorious than the present. There's no telling how far a project might ultimately go.

Similarly, if you're a new screenwriter who's produced a treatment or a full script, you've got to be careful not to get boxed into a deal that unfairly restricts what you can do with your material for too long a time or for too little money. There are plenty of self-important "producer"-types out there eager to convince you to let them option your material for small change—and then to pursue production possibilities with all the vigor of a squashed slug. The National Writers Union's Grievance and Contract Division has encountered cases in which would-be screenwriters have let year-long options on their scripts go for as little as $50, signing contracts that actually allow the other party to renew the option for second year for the same paltry fee. Sign a contract like that, and the dotted line will become a barbed-wire fence separating you from your prospects of earning a living from what you write.

Dean Paton contributed to this section.

Of course, there's not necessarily anything wrong with working cheap—especially when nobody else on a project is being adequately compensated for his or her labor. But, if you decide to work for little pay up front, make certain that the contract you sign guarantees that you'll receive a reasonable share of the proceeds if the project succeeds. "Success" doesn't just mean that a project ultimately turns a profit; it might mean, for example, that a poorly funded film project suddenly gets backing from a major studio—in which case you, the screenwriter, are entitled to a sizeable chunk of the production budget. You might want to know, for example, that 10 percent of a studio-produced feature film's production budget is typically earmarked for writing. Since completed scripts for such pictures generally incorporate several, or many, people's work, how that portion of the budget gets divvied up can in some cases be quite complicated, as can the determination of who gets screenwriting credit. Despite these complexities, the basic lesson's a simple one: the writer plays an essential role in a film's production and should be fairly compensated—if not up front then later on, when some money rolls in.

Ten percent of a studio-produced feature film's production budget is typically earmarked for writing

You're not being "greedy" if you insist that a contract be written in a way that ensures that you'll benefit from a project's success. If everyone involved in an independent film—director, actors, costume designer, key grip—is working for next to nothing, you'll probably have to partake in the poverty, at least while the movie's being made. But it's incumbent on you to understand something about prevailing film-industry rules so that you're not left out in the event your little independent movie becomes the next *Blair Witch Project.* For example, it's a principle of moviemaking that early investors earn a rate of return that's higher than those who provide funding at a later stage of production. If you've written the initial script for a film, you're right there at the project's inception, and you should benefit from a similar principle—with the money you are *not* paid counting as an "investment" in the production. If you work for $10,000 in a capacity where the standard minimum is $30,000, the $20,000 you're not earning now should be treated, contractually, as an investment; a sensible contract might stipulate that, when and if the project makes money, you'll be paid that twenty grand *plus* a percentage of gross that's equivalent to that made by an early investor.

In other words, knowing what you, as a writer, are due means becoming familiar with some basic industry standards. Fortunately, the movie and television industry—unlike, say, the book-publishing industry—has real minimum standards regulating the terms and conditions under which contract writers work and stipulating how much they must be paid depending on the exact nature of their contribution to a project. These standards are negotiated (and renegotiated every few years) by the WGA and the (literally) thousands of entertainment-industry companies that are signatories to WGA contracts. (The WGA, by the way, is actually two affiliated unions, the Writers Guild of America, East and the Writers Guild of America, West; members belong to one or the other depending on which side of the Mississippi they reside.)

> *The movie and television industry has real minimum standards regulating the terms and conditions under which contract writers work*

The industry minimum standards are all set out in excruciatingly fine detail in the current WGA contract. The most recent of these agreements is the *1995 Writers Guild of America Theatrical and Television Basic Agreement* (with an addendum of amendments adopted in 1998), a redoubtable 400-page document that you can find in the library or buy directly from the WGA. (The cost, including postage, is about $22.) To order it, or to find out about the rather complicated requirements for membership in the WGA, access the WGA, West's website, at www.wga.org or the WGA, East's website, at www.wgaeast.org.

Eligibility for WGA membership is determined by a "credit" (or point) system in which you have to have done certain amounts of certain kinds of work within a certain time frame in order to join. Once you've accrued the requisite credentials, chances are you'll join the WGA—and benefit from the substantial clout it wields in the entertainment industry. Until you've accumulated that experience, however, you should join the National Writers Union, where you'll have access to the NWU's basic contract advice as well as all the other benefits NWU membership provides.

Do take care, though. Screenwriting contracts are often arcane and can be mind-breakingly complicated. **The entertainment company that hires you will, without doubt, have hired an attorney to prepare the contract, and—unless you're working with an experienced agent—you should fight fire with fire by finding an entertainment lawyer of your own to examine any contract you're offered before you sign it.** (Newcomers should take note that it's getting harder and harder to find an agent willing to work with you unless you've already got a produced project under your belt. When you most need an agent—when you've yet to get that first script produced—most don't seem to want to touch you.)

Hiring an attorney is, of course, an expensive proposition, but no amateur can match the degree of expertise that an experienced entertainment lawyer will bring to this task. Deciding not to spend the money on an attorney's fee now may mean that you'll end up losing *much more* in the long run.

A note to radio writers: Many freelancers who write for radio are independent producers. That is, they not only write their material but actually create their own spots—taping, interviewing, editing, doing all the voiceover and sound-effects work—which they then sell to networks (like NPR) and stations that buy freelancers' work. Since 1984, independent radio producers have had their own professional organization, whose appropriate acronym, AIR, stands for the Association of Independents in Radio. For information on AIR's mission, membership requirements, and benefits, visit its website, at www.airmedia.org. Though not officially affiliated with the NWU, AIR participates in the NWU's group health-insurance plan.

PLAYWRITING

Beginning playwrights—and even many playwrights who've had a moderate amount of work produced—face a quandary that's not unknown to book authors. If you're an unknown, it can be very difficult to get an agent, but, if you don't have an agent and are doing it on your own, navigating the morass of contracts and contractual language can be very perilous indeed. Actually, playwrights may feel this dilemma even a little more sharply than writers of books, since the number of agents who handle playwrights is miniscule as compared to the number of literary agents generally.

Help, however, is available, through the New York City–based Dramatists Guild of America, which represents some 6,000 playwrights (and theatrical lyricists and composers) nationwide. Though the Guild isn't a union—it cannot engage in collective bargaining, does not act in a dispute-resolution capacity, and in general shies away from taking collective action on behalf of its members—its mission includes "promoting and protecting . . . the interests of authors in their works, including their rights of property, artistic integrity and economic compensation, and the conditions under which those works are created and presented." Prerequisites for membership in the Guild are minimal. You can join the Guild as an associate member even if you've never had a play produced (you must, however, have written a dramatic work), which means that even newcomers to the profession can avail themselves of the Guild's model contracts, contract advice, and other member benefits.

Chris Wilson, executive director of the Dramatists Guild, says that beginning playwrights make "every conceivable" kind of mistake when trying to get their work produced, and in an interview for this *Guide* he pointed to three kinds of errors that he says are woefully prevalent. Inexperienced playwrights, he said, often give the producer who will mount their play's premier production too high a percentage of their subsidiary rights—guaranteeing the producer undeserved participation in the take from later stage productions or movie deals. A related (and equally common) mistake involves giving people other than the producer (e.g., a dramaturge, a director) a share in the subrights. Third, playwrights are often pressured by directors into signing agreements that give the director the right of first refusal to direct planned productions or that tie a play's production to that director's being hired to direct it. According to Wilson, playwrights often don't see that giving a particular director such powers can reduce the chance that a play will actually get produced. The Guild offers advice on avoiding such arrangements—and on negotiating contract provisions that will reduce such agreements' unfairness when playwrights find they have little choice but to relinquish some rights or some control.

Inexperienced playwrights often give the producer too high a percentage of their subsidiary rights

Production contracts—and the royalties a playwright is likely to realize—differ according to the venue in which a play is being produced. Except for Broadway theaters (which abide by Guild-approved production contracts) and some LORT (League of Regional Theaters) venues with which the Guild has comparable arrangements, there are no standard royalties schedules. Typically, though, royalties for non-Broadway venues range between 5 and 7 percent of box office receipts. (Broadway percentages are actually somewhat lower.) In the absence of standard royalties arrangements, the Guild strongly advises that playwrights abide by the following two rules when negotiating their cut: *always* try to make sure that royalties are determined by box office receipts, not profit (that is, royalties should be a cut of the gross, not the net), and *always* insist on being paid something for a production in which anyone else is being paid.

Playwrights have traditionally wielded a great deal of control over the creative aspects of their plays' production—including, for example, the right of approval over choice of director and casting decisions. The Dramatists Guild is dedicated to upholding those rights. In this vein, the Guild advises playwrights not to enter into agreements that deprive them of the sole right to approve any changes to a script made during production or that restrict their ability to participate in decisions regarding even such matters as costume design and advertising.

For more information on the Dramatists Guild of America's membership requirements and activities, visit the Guild's website, at www.dramaguild.com.

The Literary Market

At first glance, the term *market* might seem a misnomer when applied to the publication of poetry, short fiction, and literary nonfiction in the United States. Sure, there remains a handful of general-interest magazines that publish poems, short stories, and literary essays—*The New Yorker, The Atlantic Monthly,* and *Harper's* are among the best known—and that pay reasonably well for the work they publish. And the number of such outlets has actually expanded—very slightly—over the past few years, with the advent of online general-interest magazines such as Salon. Nevertheless, the total number of venues for literary work that have substantial readerships and that pay somewhat decently is miniscule.

The number of venues for literary work that pay decently is miniscule

The major market for poems, short stories, and belles-lettres is provided by literary magazines. There are thousands of these publications, ranging from prestigious, beautifully produced reviews such as *Grand Street* and *The Paris Review* to desktop-published magazines put out by individuals on their home computers (augmented, recently, by a growing number of online literary magazines that do not have print editions). The circulations of even the most prestigious print literary magazines are, however, very limited, and literary magazines in general pay very little or—more likely—not at all for the work they publish.

Despite the paucity of compensation, however, the world of literary journals *is* a market, with real implications for writers' economic lives. Publication in a well-regarded literary magazine isn't just a mark of professional respectability—a sign that you've achieved a certain level of craft. It can also be a prerequisite to furthering your career: to publication in yet other journals, to being invited to give readings of your work, to winning grants and awards, to book deals, and to teaching positions. Though it is obviously much else besides, your relationship with a literary magazine is also a *business* relationship, and someone who writes for the literary market has as much right to fair treatment as any other writer.

PAYMENT

You probably did not go into writing poetry or short stories for the money. In fact, writers seriously committed to making it in these genres must be prepared to support themselves by other means. That doesn't mean, however, that you shouldn't be paid for your work, nor that you have no right to expect timely payment in those cases where payment is offered.

Frequency and Rates

To get some idea of how often poets are paid for publication in literary reviews, we took a look at *Poet's Market 2000*: of the 1,187 poetry-publishing magazines listed there, a mere 205, or about 17 percent, pay. And in a targeted survey of poets and short story writers conducted for this *Guide,* respondents were asked how often they were paid for literary work published during the preceding five years. Results appear in Table 9.1.

Don't let the comparatively high number answering "sometimes" give you a false sense of optimism, however. When respondents were asked about specific poems and short stories published during that five-year period, it turned out that they were paid for their published work in only one-third of the cases. Payment, where there was any, was generally very small. For short stories, it ranged from $5 to $200. For poems, the range was from $35 to $400. Interestingly, the higher rates, for both short stories and poetry, were *all* for work published online.

The fact that the chance of your getting paid by a literary magazine is slender does not mean, however, that these publications should not be

TABLE 9.1. **FREQUENCY OF PAY**

Response	Percentage
Never	14%
Rarely	29%
Sometimes	43%
Frequently	14%
Always	0%

expected to pay. A distinction has to be made between the truly "little" magazines, which are run on budgets that might be described as frayed shoestrings, and well-established publications. Journals such as *Descant, The New England Review, Ploughshares, Poetry, The Southern Review,* and others are supported by universities or foundations. They therefore do not rely on sales to cover their operating costs and usually make an attempt to pay writers. You should research the market before you submit work to literary magazines, and demand to be paid by well-established publications.

Timeliness

A problem that all freelance writers encounter is that publishers often take too long a time to pay. When publishers hold onto money owed you for months, they are essentially forcing you to provide an interest-free loan.

When publishers hold onto money owed you for months, they are forcing you to provide an interest-free loan

For writers who publish in literary magazines this is both less and more of a problem than for other writers. Since the amount of money involved tends to be nominal, it's doubtful that you'll be waiting for the check to arrive so that you can pay your rent. On the other hand, you are unlikely to see any money at all for over a year after submission, since, as a rule, literary magazines that pay do so on publication—which might be six months after acceptance, which in turn could well be six months or more after you submit your work for consideration.

Worse, it is not uncommon for magazines to delay payment after publication. Respondents to the *Guide*'s survey of literary writers reported delays in payment of up to 12 months. There is no justification for this.

Ideally, if a magazine commits to publishing your writing, the editors should pay you within 30 days of accepting the work. Widespread implementation of the payment-on-acceptance principle, however, will involve a thoroughgoing change in the culture of literary publishing.

Free Copies

Though cash payment is the exception in the world of literary magazines, such periodicals do commonly "pay" writers by giving them free copies of the issue in which their work appears. Respondents to the *Guide*'s survey reported receiving, on average, between one and four contributor's copies. **At minimum, try to negotiate for at least two free copies of the issue in which your work appears, regardless of whether you have been paid for the work or not.**

SUBMISSIONS

The majority of literary magazines work with skeletal staffs. That, combined with the fact that many such publications are inundated with submissions, means that literary magazines can be inordinately slow in responding to writers—and this, in fact, has traditionally been one of the major complaints voiced by writers who publish in such venues. The situation does appear to be improving, however. Though respondents to the *Guide*'s survey did report response delays of up to ten months, the prevalent range now seems to be within one to three months after submission. **The NWU believes that there is no justification for a publisher to take longer than three months to respond.**

The ethics and efficacy of *multiple submissions* (simultaneously submitting a piece of work to more than one periodical) have long been debated within the literary community. Publications used to frown on the practice, but most now realize that there's nothing they can do to police it, and editors admit that policies against multiple submissions are unfair to writers eager to see their work in print. Writers themselves have argued over the wisdom of making multiple submissions, some insisting that a scattershot approach—sending work to as many magazines as possible—improves the odds for publication, others saying that it makes much more sense to research the market carefully and to submit pieces of work, one at a time, to the magazines you feel are most likely to accept them. The *Guide*'s survey discerned no pattern concerning the number of literary writers who make multiple submissions, with about equal numbers declaring that they do it always, frequently, sometimes, rarely, and never.

If you do make multiple submissions, you should keep careful track of which pieces you send to which publications. In the event a piece is accepted by any of them, you should immediately inform the others, withdrawing that work from their consideration. This isn't just a matter of courtesy (though it is that); your reputation will suffer if an editor has to change publication plans because you neglected to inform her that a piece she wants has already been accepted by someone else.

PUBLICATION

Waiting for a response to your submission is only the beginning. After your work is accepted, you will have to wait even longer to see it in print. The problem, in part, is that most literary magazines are published relatively infrequently: quarterly, semiannually, or even annually. We asked respondents to the *Guide*'s survey about waiting time between acceptance and publication. Results are shown in Table 9.2.

Although literary magazines work under real constraints, they should make every effort to notify the author of the projected publication date, and publication should occur within one year of acceptance. **Further, if the date is unacceptably distant, the author should have the right to withdraw the work and submit it to other publications.**

TABLE 9.2. **TIME OF PUBLICATION (IN MONTHS AFTER ACCEPTANCE)**

Range	Months
Min/Max	1/13
Average	6
Prevalent range	2–12

COPYRIGHT

In submitting your work for publication, whether paid or unpaid, you are offering the publisher a limited grant of rights to publish the work, usually first North American print rights. Some publishers, however, try to gain control of the copyright to the work. Without exception, this practice is unacceptable.

Copyright is your claim to ownership of the work and the assurance of your continued ability to reproduce the work and derive income from it. If you sign over the copyright to a publisher, you'll have to get the publisher's permission to reprint the work or use it in any other way.

The *Guide*'s survey asked poets and fiction writers how often they retain copyright of their published work. To our surprise, respondents reported that they had retained copyright 96 percent of the time for work published in literary magazines over the preceding five years. This number—much higher than obtained by the survey conducted for the original edition of the *Guide,* in 1995—is encouraging.

Electronic Republication

Much less encouraging, however, is the fact that writers are seeing their work republished electronically without their permission and (of course) without compensation. The Web has spawned a culture that is heedless of copyright and intellectual property. All writers, but especially poets, are facing a situation in which they have less and less control over where their work appears and in which they must increasingly suffer the injustice of people using their work without permission and without compensation. Fifty-seven percent of respondents to the *Guide*'s survey said that they had discovered that work of theirs had been republished electronically without permission. One oft-published poet reported being aware of 200 instances in which his work had been published on the Web without his authorization! Needless to say, this is a *big* problem that, like so many of the copyright problems the Web has engendered, promises only to grow larger. If your work is published without your authorization, you have a legitimate grievance against the publisher, and—if you're an NWU member—you should consult a grievance officer.

> *One poet reported 200 instances in which his work had been published on the Web without his authorization*

↗ For more on the Grievance and Contract Division, see Chapter 14, "The Grievance Process," page 241.

LITERARY COMPETITIONS

Success in the literary world—especially for poets—is increasingly contingent on winning competitions. Writers need to watch out for fake competitions—bad-faith, moneymaking enterprises in which every entrant is declared a "winner" and then pressured to buy a book in which all submissions are published. But there are hundreds of legitimate competitions sponsored by literary magazines, small presses, university presses, writers' societies, and other organizations. The best guides to these contests are *Grants and Awards Available to American Writers,* published every other year by PEN American Center (the most recent edition was issued in July 2000), and *Poets & Writers* magazine, a bimonthly publication that lists submission guidelines for competitions whose deadlines are approaching and that, in each issue, announces recent competition winners.

There are problems, however, with the ways in which even many legitimate competitions are run. For one thing, they are expensive to enter. Competitions for book-length poetry manuscripts, for example, typically charge an entry fee of $20. Since the publication of poetry books in the United States is increasingly tied to competitions, and since competition is fierce (with prestigious contests typically receiving upwards of 1,500 entries), poets intent on seeing their manuscript published may spend hundreds of dollars a year, year after year, on competition fees without any guarantee that their investment will pay off. That so many poets feel the necessity to do this is understandable, since it's virtually impossible to land a creative-writing teaching job at a college or university without having had a book published.

Second, many competitions do not announce ahead of time who the contest judge will be. Opinion is divided about whether or not the well-known writers who serve as competition judges generally tend to select work that resembles their own, but many writers feel that knowing who will judge a contest is a crucial piece of information for them to have when making the decision whether to spend the money to enter a particular contest.

Third, poetry-book contests typically promise the winner the publication of her manuscript and a cash prize. (The size of such awards varies greatly, ranging from $500 up to $5,000 or more.) What isn't said is that such "prizes" usually serve as de facto advances against royalties. In other

Poets may spend hundreds of dollars a year on competition fees

words, the winning poet receives the prize and is presented with a book contract that gives her no royalties whatsoever on her book's first print run. (Since very few such books ever have a second printing, this means that the poet is unlikely ever to receive any proceeds from the sale of the book.) That many poets, who don't expect to make money from their work, aren't bothered by this doesn't stop it from being an ethically dubious practice on the part of competition sponsors. **The NWU believes that cash prizes, which in many cases are derived from entry fees, should be distinct from royalties and that competition-winning writers are entitled to a fair share of the profit from their books.**

Other problems with competitions are akin to those that writers encounter with literary magazines. Some competitions delay payment of the cash prize to the winner or break it into installments paid over many months' time. Sometimes, winners find that it takes a year or longer for their book to make it into print. Additionally, some competition sponsors (e.g., small literary magazines) may not have arrangements in place with distributors, meaning that "published" books are not really available for purchase anywhere, not even from the big online booksellers.

Some book-competition sponsors treat their award winners very well—for example, by distributing prizewinning books to all entrants or to all members of the sponsoring organization, by holding awards ceremonies and underwriting book tours, by advertising the winning books and making sure that review copies are sent out, and by nominating books for post-publication prizes. Some (eventually) publish the work, (eventually) give the writer a check, and that's that.

Unfortunately, there's no easy way to find out ahead of time how you will be treated should you win a given competition. Perhaps if enough writers ask enough questions persistently enough, competition sponsors can be edged toward fuller disclosure of how their contests are run and what benefits award winners can actually expect to receive.

The Way a Cluster of Words Breaks Through

Emma Morgan

On a day in May 1993, my closest friend and I wedged our borrowed Coleman stove between our luggage, a large cooler of provisions, and a heavy box of books in the hatch of my 1985 Toyota Tercel. Destination, Miami. I was 27, and we were going on my first "real" book tour.

My first collection of poetry, *Gooseflesh,* had been released a month earlier, by Clothespin Fever Press in San Diego. Since reading a *Poets & Writers* article by Maxine Kumin a few years earlier, which detailed Kumin's own book tour adventures, I had decided that this was the ultimate romantic fantasy, and I aspired to it. So, when my publisher invited me to sign books at the American Booksellers Association convention but said she could only afford the convention itself and not the travel (I live in Massachusetts, the ABA convention was in Miami Beach), I knew just what to do.

My best friend and I met weekly over maps and breakfast at the local diner for several months running. Between rendezvous, I put together makeshift press kits and made contacts with numerous women's and alternative bookstores on the eastern seaboard. Book tours, of course, were not part of the Clothespin Fever Press marketing budget, so I had to fundraise. A small, targeted direct mailing, plus a book party (my first solo reading, in a local bookstore that had supported my work for years, followed by a potluck and live music in a friend's rented house), yielded close to $1,000, and that was all it took.

Connecting the dots between women's bookstores, we traced a feminist constellation through the Bible Belt. We stayed in cheesy motels, bookstore owners' homes, campsites, and friends' apartments. We ate anything that required no more cooking than boiled water, picked up antibiotics in Roanoke, and lost our alternator somewhere along the Blue Ridge. Between readings, we went hiking, sightseeing, and beaching on Assateague Island among the wild ponies.

Sometimes we got depressed—or broke. And boy was I glad to get to Miami, where I wasn't the only Jew in town! Mostly, we had a grand time. For me, there was the excitement of seeing window displays of my books in towns I'd never been to, getting introduced by old friends to new audiences, meeting famous writers and favorite publishers at the ABA, and selling books, selling books, selling books.

But the real treasures were contained in a fistful of moments that ultimately constitute the greatest rewards of a career in poetry. Here's one. I had come full circle (ellipse, really) to the bookstore in Jamaica Plain, Massachusetts, where I had first conceived of the book I was now celebrating. When my first published poem appeared in print (and that Maxine Kumin article was newly out), I booked a mini-tour for the editor of the anthology and several contributors who lived close enough to participate in the three Massachusetts readings. Crone's Harvest was our third stop.

This had been the first time I'd spent such concentrated time with other published poets—some with whole books to sell—and, to my complete shock, people kept expressing disappointment that I had no books for them to purchase. At Crone's Harvest, someone had actually asked from the audience where she could get my book. This experience permanently shifted my whole perception of myself as writer. I went to work almost immediately on compiling a manuscript, and my book was accepted for publication a few months later. All because those women had believed that this book existed and had wanted it.

Now I was back in Crone's Harvest with that book in hand, and a woman came rushing up to me at the end of my reading, saying, "You're the one who wrote the poem!" The poem? She explained that she hadn't planned on attending my reading. She was a painter and just happened to be shopping in the store, rushing to get out before the reading began. And then she heard "the poem" and thought, "Oh, my God, . . . the poem, . . . that must be the woman who wrote the poem!" "The poem," still one of my personal favorites, is one she had clipped from a Boston-based gay and lesbian weekly some years before. She'd had it blown up to poster size and had hung it over her easel so that she could read it aloud every day for inspiration. There is no higher accolade for a poet. She grabbed my arm and pulled me to a shelf in the store that displayed greeting cards with photographs of her paintings. She let me choose one. Of course, I hung it over my typewriter.

Crone's Harvest filed for Chapter 11 within a year of that event. And Clothespin Fever Press went bankrupt a year later. The climate was changing for small literary presses and independent bookstores around the country, and women's (read: feminist and/or lesbian) businesses (along with certain other alternative independents) were hardest hit. Inland was the only "major" independent distributor connecting these presses and bookstores to one another, and it was foundering. But it's not only lesbian and other minority poets who suffered—and continue to suffer—in the age of corporate conglomerate publishing. It's all poets, since the reality is that most poetry today is published by small literary presses that, in turn, rely on independent booksellers.

A career in poetry has never been a lucrative venture—not for the professional, not for the widely published, and not for the famous few. So don't bother doing it for the money. Not only is writing poetry for money not a real possibility in today's America, but it makes for lousy poetry.

The only reason to choose a career in poetry is that it chooses you. A poet writes, simply put, because she *has to*. I don't mean, because it's good therapy. It isn't. Rather, we write because we lust insatiably for that elusive turn of phrase, that combination of words and analogies that will turn ordinary language into sensory experience, break sound barriers, and jimmy open long-locked doors in the reader's mind and heart.

Does this completely impractical excuse for a career mean we can afford to ignore the business aspects of our craft? On the contrary. A poet must be as concerned as any writer about copyright protections, fair pay, and so on. But a poet protects copyright not because of its potential monetary value (even when she hopes it will have some), but so that she can retain artistic control over how her work is used. And, though "fair pay" is a non sequitur when pay is all but nonexistent, a poet must constantly challenge the cultural "norms" that insist this is either acceptable or inevitable.

Unless you are one of the handful of famous living poets, the avenues for publishing your work are narrow—and were so well before the mega-mergers began—especially if you care about the quality of the poems that will keep yours company on publication day. A literary periodical will receive hundreds, if not thousands, of prospective poems each month; a thematic anthology editor is deluged with poetry on a daily basis; and national glossies, if they print poetry at all, will publish one or two poems an issue from the many hundreds the editor receives. In "po-biz" (as Maxine Kumin has called it), a personalized rejection letter is considered an achievement to celebrate.

Then there are those pesky "no simultaneous submissions" clauses. Most periodicals no longer expect to get an exclusive look at a small batch of poems, but they will try. Since response time from literary venues runs anywhere from three to nine months, heeding the simultaneous submissions rule would mean sending out each poem a mere two, perhaps three, times a year! Ignore the rule, and you risk hurting your reputation with editors, unless you're careful to withdraw your poem from the desks of potential competitors immediately upon receiving an acceptance letter.

Once you find your way in, most anthologies and literary journals don't pay . . . well, not in money, anyway. A copy or two of the issue or anthology in which your work appears is standard. An outfit that's more flush might offer you a whole subscription. Those journals that are funded through universities or are otherwise endowed will pay to the tune of, say, $20 per poem.

Poetry books are no big money-makers, either. Since the operative cultural mythology is that "no one reads poetry anymore" and therefore that "poetry doesn't sell," few publishers are willing to "take the risk." The small literary presses that do publish poetry often haven't the funds to pay an advance. My own first book started with a print run of 500 copies—not unusual. I sold the first hundred out of my own backpack in a matter of weeks and had practically exhausted the whole run by the end of my Bible Belt tour. I got a second run at 1,000 copies, as I was now a "Clothespin Fever Press bestseller," but I never saw a dollar in royalties, because I'd signed a contract that promised royalties only after costs were met (then I was to receive 15 percent), and Clothespin closed up shop before that day arrived. I did make plenty of pocket change, buying up my own books at 60 percent of retail, and selling them anywhere and everywhere—even making enough to buy out the inventory at remainder prices in the end, but never enough to call it compensation for my labor.

In addition to writing without pay, poets generally perform their work for free. It's expected. Granted, readings are the prime way to sell books, but the profits are mostly (if not entirely, as in my case) shared between the publisher and the retail outlet where the reading is held. This may not sound egregious, unless you consider that the writing itself is not compensated, and that a good poetry reading is a carefully rehearsed performance. Which other performers are expected to volunteer their skills? Even in the unusual event that no cover charge is asked of the audience, a musician can expect an honorarium. The exception to the no-pay-for-readings rule is the university campus, where I've been offered anything from $50 to $400. One hint: reading in venues other than bookstores means high sales profits, as long as you are willing to schlepp your own stock.

My second book, *A Stillness Built of Motion: Living with Tourette's,* began as a self-publishing venture. The poems were timely, my vision was clear, and I knew my market well. Meanwhile, I was getting strong-armed by a so-called feminist press concerning an anthology I was editing under contract (that's what got me in the National Writers Union!), and I was ready to experience some control over my creative enterprise. The trajectory from vision to publication of a beautiful arts-edition chapbook was less than four months. And it was I who collected the bulk, if not all, of the profits when my books sold.

In a month's time, I was in the black, and in three, I'd garnered enough in profits for a second printing. My inventory waned to 20 percent by the end of a year, and my profits reached 125 percent. Keep in mind that 125 percent of a negligible amount doesn't add up to much, but it covered union dues and gasoline, tires and the like, and, on a poet's budget, it was a veritable windfall! I didn't save any money to reinvest this time, but just as I contemplated going out of print, my book was discovered by a new press on the west coast that needed a title with a proven track record.

Now I was in the union, and my local contract adviser helped me draft what amounted to a nonexclusive, one-print-run-only co-publishing agreement. The other publisher underwrote the project, and it was published under his imprint, but I retained control over production and design (which I coordinated on a work-for-hire basis). I got a 25-percent royalty beginning with book one and the option to buy copies at 50 percent of retail. With a nonexclusive, I could market the chapbook elsewhere, should I choose to, either as itself or as part of a full-length manuscript. Much of my earnings came from my time on the production end, but I did sell books and cashed a quarterly royalty check, which paid for many a lunch and sometimes even dinner.

The rewards of a life in poetry are many, but financial sustenance is not one of them. It's those sound barriers . . . and the way a cluster of words breaks through. Like the time I read before a conference of neuropsychiatrists—the folks who treat people with Tourette's syndrome—taking aim at the minds of those to whom people like myself must, of necessity, entrust the kind of power that can make or break a person's chances at dignity and self-realization. Or the time a classmate at Vermont College's Adult Degree Program—a documentary painter for the U.S. military—bought my first book, hot off the press, just before he was called up for active duty in Somalia. When he returned to school, he told me that he had carried my book with him throughout his service, that his own artwork and my poetry were what got him through—my Jewish, explicitly lesbian poems. He said the other guys would pester him about his reading habit in the barracks and ask to know what was in those pages that so compelled him. "Oh," he'd say shyly, "it's just something personal . . . something that helps me get by."

CHAPTER 10

Academic Writing

Some people might wonder why a book on freelance writing includes a section on academic writers. True, many academics do not see writing as their primary professional pursuit or identity, and certainly writing is not a major income source for most academics. But it is also true that college and university teachers produce a large proportion of all published writing and that publishing is crucial for most academic careers.

College and university teachers produce a large proportion of all published writing

In recent years, as the tenure system has broken down and more and more scholars have found themselves trapped in poorly paid adjunct positions, the indignities suffered by academic writers have become all the more onerous. Adjunct faculty, many of whom work for wages of $3,000 or less per course, have a greater need to augment their income through their writing than do professors in full-time, permanent positions. But this chapter isn't addressed only to miserably paid adjuncts. The NWU firmly believes that all academic writers need and deserve the same equitable standards and practices that freelance writers are fighting for in other markets.

PUBLISH OR PERISH

It is a fact of academic life that to succeed you have to publish. At every stage of an academic career, one's productivity as an author is an important gauge of achievement. Whether you are looking for a first job, trying to change jobs, being reviewed for tenure, or up for a salary increase, your publication list plays a critical role in the decision.

In order to find out just how deeply ingrained the need to publish is in academic writers' psyches, a targeted survey conducted for this edition of the *Guide* asked a group of academic writers how important the ability to pub-

Ken Wachsberger contributed to this chapter.

lish in the academic press is to their professional success. The results, shown in Table 10.1, indicate that academic writing is indeed crucial.

This "publish or perish" climate makes academic writers particularly vulnerable to inequitable treatment by publishers. Since an academic's livelihood depends on his or her ability to publish, most academic writers would choose to accept an unfair publishing deal rather than run the risk of alienating the publisher by negotiating for better conditions. Indeed, many academic writers do not seem to be aware that they *can* negotiate. It is important for all writers to realize that the terms initially offered by publishers are not set in stone, and that in most instances discussion—and contract changes—are possible.

TABLE 10.1. **IMPORTANCE OF PUBLISHING TO ACADEMIC CAREER**

Degree	Percentage
Extremely important	59%
Very important	23%
Important	18%
Not important	0%

PAYMENT

In an effort to get a sense of economic conditions in the academic marketplace, we asked survey respondents to indicate their annual income derived from writing. The figures that appear in Table 10.2 are telling.

TABLE 10.2. **ANNUAL INCOME DERIVED FROM WRITING**

income	Percentage
$0–$999	38%
$1,000–$2,999	12%
$3,000–$4,999	12%
$5,000 or more	38%

Clearly, the publish-or-perish mentality of many academic writers affects the level of financial remuneration they receive—and expect to receive—for published work, even though many of them are not on the tenure track and can never expect to gain tenure. Advances for scholarly books (when they are given at all) are usually considerably smaller than for nonfiction trade books. The smaller advances are partly justified by the comparatively small print runs that most scholarly books receive. (Our survey respondents reported initial print runs ranging from 300 to 5,500 copies, with 2,000–3,000 copies the prevalent range.) But royalty percentages are also typically smaller for academic books than for trade books, and, in fact, academic-book contracts sometimes stipulate that the author will receive no royalties at all on the first 500 or 1,000 or 1,500 copies sold. There is no sound basis for this sort of discrepancy, especially since academic book publishers often have a built-in customer base, coupled with a policy of setting high cover prices, that facilitates their reaching break-even on their books. Put simply, academic writers tend to get the short end of the stick because publishers know that academics are likely to accept any conditions as long as their work is printed, and often don't know better anyhow.

The situation is just as troubling if one looks at professional journals. It is, for example, practically unheard of for academic journals to pay authors. One often hears, of course, that contributors to journals are not paid because academic-journal publishing is not a profit-making business. That argument begins to sound disingenuous, however, when one sees academic journals being gobbled up by the dozens by large publishing concerns. (Elsevier Publishing, for example, now owns more than a thousand journals.) If there's no money in it, why are some big publishing houses eager to add more academic journals to their lists?

Can conditions for academic writers be improved? The National Writers Union believes they can. By arming ourselves with information and standing up for our rights, all writers, including academics, can begin to develop consistent, equitable standards in publishing.

COPYRIGHT

The most insidious trend in academic publishing is the seizure of copyright. Responses to our survey indicate that book publishers and, especially, academic journals frequently pressure authors to sign over the copyright to the publisher (see Tables 10.3 and 10.4).

TABLE 10.3. **RETAINING COPYRIGHT FOR BOOKS**[a]

Response	Percentage
Yes	64%
No	29%
Respondent did not know	7%

[a] Respondents were asked whether or not they had retained copyright for the most recent book they had published with a university or other academic press during the last five years.

TABLE 10.4. **RETAINING COPYRIGHT FOR ARTICLES**

Response	Percentage[a]
Yes	28%
No	67%
Respondent did not know	5%

[a] Percentages are based on total articles published by survey respondents during the preceding five years.

It would be an understatement to say that these statistics are alarming, particularly in the case of the academic journals. Your copyright is your claim to authorship—and thus ownership. By registering copyright in someone else's name, you essentially give up ownership of your work.

A typical grab for copyright on the part of a publisher is likely to be worded something like this:

> Copyright to the work will be taken out in the name of the Press. This does not mean that the Press owns the material, but simply that the copyright is in the Press's name.
>
> The Author will grant the Press the full and exclusive right during the term of the copyright to publish or allow others to publish the work in all forms and in all languages throughout the world.

This is an expert piece of obfuscation—or, to put it more bluntly, a con job. **What the language in these two paragraphs is trying to do is to blur the distinction between copyright and publishing rights.**

Copyright guarantees the author of a work the legal ownership of that work. **It is patently untrue, therefore, to say that the holder of the copyright does not own the copyrighted material.**

For more information on copyright, see pages 5–9.

Publishing rights are the conditions under which the copyright holder authorizes the publisher to print and sell the work. By including a grant of publishing rights, the publisher in the above example is attempting to reinforce the impression that the author would remain the owner of the work after signing the copyright over to the publisher. This is simply not true, and the second clause is irrelevant.

To pacify authors, a publisher trying to seize the copyright will often include in the contract a clause such as this:

> The Author may publish his/her work after informing the Press of the planned publication. No payment will be required, but reference should be given to the original publication.

In other words, you will essentially have to get the publisher's permission to reprint your work in the future. (You will not—small mercy—have to pay for it. Surprisingly, many academic writers are taken in by this "generosity" on the part of publishers.)

In recent years, publishers have attempted to justify their copyright grabs by claiming that they need to control copyright so that they can quickly utilize emerging technologies. While it is true that the new electronic media are evolving rapidly, publishers can in fact quickly exploit these new technologies without actually owning copyright. An author retaining copyright in her work can simply lease these rights, either on her own or through the NWU's Publication Rights Clearinghouse. (Information about registering your work with the PRC can be found at the NWU's website, www.nwu.org.)

Publishers are not the only ones guilty of taking advantage of academic writers by seizing their copyrights. Some colleges and universities require their faculty to register copyright of published work in the name of the institution. The rationale for this is that the work was produced while the author was an employee of the college/university and therefore belongs to the institution. Schools will sometimes make this claim regardless of whether or not you were actually on the job when the work was produced—in effect, laying claim to your entire life, on a 24/7 basis.

The seizure of copyright—whether by publishers or by colleges and universities—is an exploitative practice, for which there is no justification. It subverts the principles on which U.S. copyright law is founded, and it robs writers of the products of their intellectual labor. **Beware of copyright clauses in your contracts and negotiate hard to retain your copyright.**

CONTRACTS

A surprisingly high proportion of academic writers enter into agreements with publishers without a written contract. Written contracts are in fact critical for all types of writing—not just books but also journal articles and contributions to multi-author anthologies and reference books.

There is no reason not to have a contract with your publisher. Contracts define relationships. Should a disagreement arise, having a written contract makes it easier to sort matters out. Most important, a contract specifies the rights that you are granting to the publisher. Despite the myth that there is no money in academic publishing, electronic rights can actually be quite lucrative, especially for reprint use in databases and coursepacks. Thus, even if your work is an unpaid journal article, retaining the electronic rights may ultimately generate some income.

Despite the myth that there is no money in academic publishing, electronic rights can actually be quite lucrative

In considering contracts, it is vital to remember that they are written with the publisher's—not your—interests in mind, and that they are meant to be seen as starting points for negotiations, not take-it-or-leave-it propositions. Virtually all publishing contracts are largely boilerplate. By its nature, boilerplate is designed to be changed. **You should never, therefore, just sign. Negotiate.**

ACADEMIC JOURNALS

The academic-journal market has some distinctive characteristics and poses some special problems. As we have noted, written contracts are important for all types of work, but contributors to academic journals seem to find it particularly hard to obtain contracts. As a group, our survey respondents reported that they did not have written contracts for 57 percent of the articles they'd published in academic journals during the past five years. This state of affairs is not unavoidable—a publisher may well agree to sign a contract if you insist. We suggest using the NWU Standard Journalism Contract as a model when proposing a contract or evaluating a contract that a journal publisher gives you. Pay special attention to allocation of rights, even if the article itself is unpaid.

The NWU Standard Journalism Contract appears on page 100.

Pay rates are not an issue for many academic writers for the simple reason that most academic journals do not pay. Just under half of our survey respondents had at some point been paid for articles in academic journals, showing that pay unfortunately remains the exception, not the rule. Overall, only 36 percent of the articles reported were written for pay.

Contributor's Copies and Reprints

In lieu of pay, many journals compensate their authors solely with contributor's copies of the issues in which their work appears and sometimes with reprints of the article as well. Our survey respondents had generally received anywhere from zero to five contributor's copies for articles published during the previous five years. The NWU recommends that authors receive no fewer than two copies. Reprints (in quantities up to 25) were received much less frequently. In the old days, academic journals produced reprints and distributed them to their contributors as a matter of course, but, with the advent of high-quality photocopies, many journals no longer order reprints. They are useful additions to a dossier, however, and authors should certainly inquire about their availability.

Waiting

A common complaint among academic writers is the amount of time it takes publications to respond to submitted material and then to publish work they accept. Academic writers are certainly not alone in this. Journalists, book authors, and—especially—poets and fiction writers who publish in literary magazines have similar problems and express the same frustration.

The days after sending an article to a publication for review can be the longest in a writer's life. Will the article be judged to be well researched and written? Is it significant enough? Is it original? Under such emotional pressure, a week can seem an eternity. And it usually takes publications a lot longer than a week to respond to submitted articles.

Table 10.5 shows what our survey revealed about waiting times for responses from academic journals.

Even after your article has been accepted, you are not really home free. Many publications have large backlogs of material and therefore take months—sometimes even a year or longer—to print the articles they accept

TABLE 10.5. **WAITING TIME FOR RESPONSE**

	Months
Min/Max reported	1/10
Prevalent range	3–6

(see Table 10.6). This can be a particularly significant problem for an academic applying for a new job or awaiting a tenure review, because some colleges and universities do not recognize a publication credit until the work has actually appeared in print. Some journal editors are sensitive to this plight and will make an effort to publish your article prior to an important date. They won't know unless you tell them, though, so be sure to inform your editor if you have a tenure review coming up.

TABLE 10.6. **WAITING TIME UNTIL PUBLICATION**

	Months after acceptance
Min/Max	1.5/24
Prevalent range	2–9

Simultaneous Submission

When asked about submitting articles to more than one journal at the same time, one academic writer answered succinctly: "Major sin." Journals either strongly discourage or prohibit the practice outright. Almost all (92 percent) of our survey respondents indicated that they do not make simultaneous submissions.

Time-sensitive articles are a possible exception to this rule. If your article pertains to current events and must be published before too much time has passed, journal editors will sometimes be understanding. Make sure, however, to explain why you are making a simultaneous submission and to withdraw the article promptly from other journals if it is accepted.

ACADEMIC BOOKS

Book publishers often treat academic writers quite differently from other authors. Many of the basic economic and contractual issues involved will, however, be familiar to all book authors. We therefore suggest that academic writers use the guidelines provided in the "Building a Better Book Contract" section of chapter 2 of this *Guide* as well as the *National Writers Union Guide to Book Contracts* to evaluate book deals. In addition, they should contact the national office to request the services of a volunteer contract adviser, who has been trained in the subtleties of print and electronic book contracts.

For more information on book contracts, see pages 37–52.

Royalties

In trade publishing, royalties are generally a percentage of the list price of a book. The results of our survey indicate that, in academic publishing, royalties are more often based on the publisher's net (see Table 10.7).

This is a significant difference that often slips past authors unnoticed. Publishers sell books to retailers at a large discount, usually in the range of 40 to 60 percent, so a 15 percent royalty based on the publisher's net generates only about half as much income as the "same" royalty based on list price. **Make sure you know what your royalties are based on, and fight for full list price–based royalties.**

TABLE 10.7. **BASIS FOR ROYALTIES**

Basis	Percentage
Based on list price	30%
Based on publisher's net	60%
Respondent did not know	10%

Multi-Author Works

Contributors to multi-author anthologies and reference books seem particularly ill-treated in the academic market. As shown in Table 10.8, our survey found that contributors to multi-author works regularly work without written contracts.

In addition, contributors to multi-author works who *do* have contracts often work under exploitative work-for-hire conditions that strip them of copyright to their work. Reference book work-for-hire contracts often grant the con-

TABLE 10.8. **CONTRACTS FOR MULTI-AUTHOR WORKS?**

Response	Percentage
Yes	42%
No	50%
Respondent did not know	8%

tributor a paltry "honorarium" for his or her article (typically 10 cents a word) but do not provide for any additional compensation if the article is republished in a subsequent edition or in a "spinoff" print or electronic product.

The NWU firmly opposes these practices. We believe that all authors need the protection of a written contract, should retain copyright in their work, and deserve additional compensation when their work is republished.

Advances

Just under a third of our survey respondents reported receiving advances for their books, while others were paid solely in royalties. Those who received advances for books published during the previous five years reported that advances ranged from $350 to $3,500.

Market Conditions

A couple of factors have combined in recent years to make the academic book market particularly difficult for scholarly-book authors. First, as commercial houses' interest in publishing serious general-interest nonfiction has evaporated, university and other academic presses have picked up the slack. In some ways, this is a positive thing—it means that a good number of serious general-interest nonfiction books are still being published! But, as academic presses publish more trade books, they are reducing the number of scholarly monographs on their lists. Second, the emergence of print-on-demand technology means that publishers can dramatically reduce their initial print runs and reprint additional books as needed. Thus many academic writers are finding it more difficult to get their books published, and when they do find a publisher, the print run is often smaller than they expect.

As academic presses publish more trade books, they are reducing the number of scholarly monographs on their lists

Conditions in the academic market are not all bad, however. Most academic presses provide a relatively high degree of editorial care, and also tend to be less pressured and deadline-oriented than their trade counterparts. Perhaps these considerations account for the fact that many academic writers say they feel well-treated by their publishers, despite the various problems that we have discussed.

ONLINE INSTRUCTION

The explosion of interest in online education (or "distance learning") in the last few years has created pressing new concerns for academic writers, many of whom have become involved in developing online courses and curricula. Universities and corporations eager to cash in on this boom have been moving quickly to commodify, distribute, and sell the instructional materials associated with online courses, including lectures, exams, and other courseware.

Historically, universities have acknowledged that faculty, as the authors of courses, own their lectures and other course materials and hence hold copyright to them. With the advent of online instruction, this is changing. Before they can sell potentially lucrative licenses to distribute and market their online educational products, colleges and universities need to control the rights to these materials. Thus many universities are now routinely attempting to seize copyright to all online materials created by their faculty.

Many universities are now routinely attempting to seize copyright to all online materials created by their faculty

The NWU, along with a number of faculty professional organizations, believes that this practice is unfair and possibly illegal under U.S. copyright law. Academic writers who develop online courses deserve to retain the copyright to their work, and should beware of any attempt to seize copyright on the part of their college or university.

Before you agree to teach a course on line, find out what your school's policy is regarding copyright of online course materials. If your teaching contract contains no language about copyright, the copyright will belong to you—but play it safe and attach an addendum to the contract, or write a letter to your department's chair, stating that you hold copyright to the course materials you write and that they cannot be republished or sold without your permission. If your school has instituted a policy of seizing copyright for online course materials, you may want to join with other faculty in fighting this abusive practice. Find out what your local faculty union already is doing to rectify this policy. If your school's faculty do not belong to a national teachers' union—organize to unionize.

HOW THE NWU CAN HELP

As we have seen, academic writers labor under a number of adverse conditions, ranging from low or nonexistent pay to attempts to seize their intellectual property to long waiting periods before publication. The NWU believes that academics, like other writers, should receive equal, fair treatment from publishers. There are a number of ways in which the NWU is working toward this goal.

Through this *Guide* and other publications such as the *NWU Guide to Book Contracts,* the union endeavors to arm writers with the information they need to fight for their rights. NWU contract advisers are available to assist union members in negotiating their publishing contracts, and the union's grievance officers stand ready to help members who have been mistreated by their publishers. Perhaps most important, the NWU strives to organize writers to work collectively toward establishing equitable standards and practices in the academic market as in all other freelance writing markets.

Reviewing Book Reviewing

Marie Shear

Do you want to grow up to be a book critic? Me neither. But new writers, as well as veterans who want to change or expand the scope of their work, may find book reviewing worthwhile.

Book reviews let you reveal your first-rate mind, extensive knowledge, and deft pen. Reviewing sharpens your writing skill and ability to edit your own work. As you delete deadwood, enliven the remaining words, and check logic, clarity, and tone, your proficiency grows; that proficiency can improve whatever else you write, even corporate memos at your day job. And reviews can enhance your professional reputation.

My reviews, which often deal with media, language, and women, and occasionally with topics as dissimilar as Danny Kaye and Clarence Thomas, began appearing in 1979. Here are some pros and cons and do's and don'ts, along with a bit of pontification about ethics and pitfalls, based on 20 years' experience as a widely unheralded book critic.

For openers, when space is tight because an editor has allotted you only 200 or 300 words, you learn to write on a postage stamp. Forced to focus, you summarize a book's content and flavor with terse fidelity and become highly selective in choosing which of your critical comments to include. Almost everything must be left out, for lack of room. So you edit early, while reading the book and making notes, mentally deleting giant chunks of material before starting to write.

Obviously, compression is less of a problem in longer reviews. These can be much richer in analysis, reflection, allusion, and interpretation. A book can be compared to others in its genre and put into the pertinent context—such as popular culture, domestic violence, a major news event, or the population explosion of grunions in East Overshoe. The reviewer can also discuss issues that the author may have addressed or ignored. Still, prune extraneous copy with care; longer should not mean looser.

© 2000 by Marie Shear

Nor is a long review an excuse to treat the book like a boarding pass for a flight on Ego Airlines. Self-indulgent critics devote disproportionate space to overblown, overgrown maundering, until the book nearly vanishes. That's unfair to authors. The percentages of exposition, context, and evaluation should be sound.

The longer the review, the more copy I draft and the later I cut it to fit. More space requires more mental sifting and revisions, to decide what to leave out after gazing, gimlet-eyed, at each page. (I say "page" because I've returned to drafting in longhand, on paper or cards. Physically shaping words with a pen or pencil helps me shape my thoughts better than undifferentiated fingertip tapping on a keyboard. It's sort of like carving soap. Other writers will prefer other methods.)

Some advice for reviewers is self-evident. Critics should like to read, should respect authors in general, and should approach a new book in a receptive frame of mind, remembering that it's much harder to write one than to review it. Ideally, the critic should already know something about the author's topic from previous reading or experiences, although ignorance can be useful when it's coupled with curiosity and intelligence.

If you've got an axe to grind, don't write the review. Tell the editor about any connections or clashes between you and the author as soon as the assignment is offered. The editor may decide that coziness or animus compromises, or might appear to compromise, your review and thereby embarrass the publication. You may lose the gig but gain the editor's respect.

Write spirited copy, then edit judiciously to eliminate any showboating. An inviting lead, lively core, and pointed finish will draw and hold your readers. But skip the cheap shots. Books, like foxes, are living creatures. Don't saddle up and race after one, baying and hallooing for sheer sport. If a book is malevolent or its prose is indefensibly poor, say so. Then allow time, as a separate step during revisions, solely to reexamine your astringent passages and scrutinize the parts of the book that prompted them. I excoriated one book for its heartless analysis of a controversial issue. Before submitting the manuscript, I went back over the book, my notes, and my copy several times before concluding that scathing criticism was warranted. Some well-known critics apparently skip this step.

Even if the review is a rave, check its voice. Try to read the copy as if you'd never seen if before, perhaps after setting it aside for a week so that you can look at it afresh. Does the tone suit the book? Are you being jocose on a somber topic or pedantic where the author is antic? Are your unexpected turns of phrase welcome seasoning, like drops of pepper sauce that spark a salad, or are they labored and obscure? Be pithy but not snide, crisp but not cryptic. Critics who fancy whimsy should use it sparingly, lest it induce diabetes in readers.

Use the appropriate vocabulary. Do not write for a clique; that just annoys readers who aren't part of it. If most of your readers are doctors who specialize in sports medicine, you needn't define "anterior cruciate ligament." But use jargon as warily as whimsy. Write what I call Scholarspeak and the ghosts of Strunk and White will stalk your dreams.

As Ira Gershwin wrote, "Don't be a woman if you can." Many ostensibly civilized periodicals favor male authors, critics, and pundits. *The New York Review of Books,* for a random example, listed 17 contributors in the table of contents for its January 20, 2000 issue; only two of them were women. Lots of publications share this chromosomal problem: they spell "exxclusion" with two Xs. (We ourselves need not cite the usual suspects. Handy reference books, like Rosalie Maggio's *New Beacon Book of Quotations by Women,* published by Beacon Press in 1996, let writers swiftly find authorities without exacerbating the testosterone glut or missing a deadline.)

Check all quotations and facts meticulously, and keep a record of each source. This record will list the pages of the book you quoted from and the passages that substantiate your verdict that the book is poignant, turgid, hilarious, or ungrammatical. An editor or fact-checker at the publication may ask you to support your opinions. List, and file, sources for anything outside the book that your copy refers to, as well. Don't trust to memory. In a 1985 review, I inaccurately identified states that had failed to ratify the Equal Rights Amendment; having recalled my error with perfect consistency year after year, I mistook certitude for accuracy.

Chastened, I now check spellings, names, and quotations, as well as things I think I recall. I often find one or more errors, like a missing initial in the author's name or a misplaced ellipsis. Critics invite ridicule when we err, even when mistakes under our bylines originated elsewhere. Lesley Stahl's own network, CBS, misspelled her name when I phoned to check. A newspaper changed an accurate reference, "Pete Hamill," to "Peter" without checking with me. Yet I'm the one who looked dumb. Fact-checking is time consuming and deeply boring. But unless you want to feel as if you've swallowed a cupful of worms, avoid misteaks.

Once published, reviews are helpful for professional promotion. Circulate copies to past, present, and prospective editors, clients, and employers. You may want newspaper or magazine assignments or clients in a field you're already familiar with, either because you usually write about it or because you want to start writing about your experience in horticulture, homemaking, child care, law, bus driving, or clerical work. The business writer specializing in widgets, whose review of *Widgets in Song and Story* is published, may get an article assignment from a trade magazine as a result or may improve her or his standing with a current employer or client.

If you seek assignments in a different field, reviews can show prospective editors or clients that you're the right person for a project by proving that you're knowledgeable in the new area. Your marketing expertise in writing newsletters and brochures about widgets can interest a fresh group of potential clients—like pet stores, breeders, and national associations of cat lovers—when your generic pitch letter describing your marketing credentials is accompanied by your recently published review of *The Maine Coon Cat: Beast or Puddytat?*

Publishing reviews on widely varied topics can be helpful. When I enclose clips about politics, advertising, assisted suicide, and tobacco, my cover letter needn't brag that I'm versatile. The clips make the point.

As a professional courtesy, send the review to the publicity director of the company that published the book. Unless you hated it, send a separate copy to the author. Send copies to people or organizations the review mentions, even in passing; to people who may find it useful in their own work; and to members of your individual "network." Published reviews also freshen, lengthen, and diversify the portfolio you show when seeking more profitable work.

Before the word "profitable" makes your heart sing, notice the bad news about book reviewing: (1) no pay; (2) low pay (about what Asian women get for making athletic shoes); and (3) people purring that the review is so trenchant that they'd *love* you to write for their publication or organization—for free.

A publication that pays little or nothing may, however, provide something of value if you negotiate in advance. It may run complimentary ads for your professional services or your other published work. It may provide a free subscription or extend the one you paid for. It may supply a batch of free copies of the issue containing the review. Journals that make offprints may make extras without charge, or at a discount, when you request them early enough. If you decide to photocopy the review instead, don't reduce the type size to save money on copying or postage. Your promotional mailings will be competing with all the other reading matter inundating your recipients. Unless you're sending your work to bald eagles, small type will put you at a competitive disadvantage.

Book reviewing, then, increases your proficiency at writing and editing; demonstrates your professionalism to editors; builds your portfolio; enhances your credentials in your current field and establishes your expertise in new areas; helps you troll for more assignments and clients; and gets your opinions onto the public record. Besides, you get to keep the book. The comparative freedom to say your say may please you, too. Someone who usually writes annual reports that are rewritten by a committee of 15 people may relish the chance to use words like "slathered," "nuzzling," or "gasbag" in a review. That pleasure won't buy groceries or health insurance. But it can help stave off brain rot.

Finally, if you manage to earn a living as a book critic, tell me how.

The Politics of Writing

CHAPTER

Censorship: A View From the Trenches

Joan E. Bertin
National Coalition Against Censorship

Attacks on free expression have become persistent front-page news. The 1989 political assault on the National Endowment for the Arts for supporting the work of Robert Mapplethorpe and Andres Serrano foreshadowed a

One would think that free speech would be more popular today

decade in which "family values" conservatives, well-heeled religious right organizations, "communitarians," and politicians of nearly all political stripes joined in maligning First Amendment values. Political demagoguery fueled constant attacks by political leaders and advocacy groups on art, literature, film, and anything else they considered blasphemous, pornographic, or otherwise subversive of "traditional values" in libraries, public exhibit spaces, funding programs, humanities courses, theaters, and even the curricular and research work of university scholars. The simplistic appeal of "not-with-my-tax-money" rhetoric and of blaming the arts and entertainment for social ills encountered little effective rebuttal.

One would think that free speech would be more popular. During the 20th century, First Amendment protections were extended to an increasingly diverse group of speakers and ideas, and promoted numerous large social movements that depended on the right to advocate controversial ideas. Organized labor; civil rights, feminist, and lesbian/gay rights activists; sex educators and advocates of reproductive rights; members of religious minorities, including the Amish, followers of Santería, and atheists—all were able to deliver their message thanks to the First Amendment. The press, publishers, entertainers, whistle-blowers, open-government groups, and countless writers, readers, artists, museumgoers, Web surfers, researchers, and others benefited.

Hardly anyone has the stomach to counter bad speech with more speech

It's ironic, then, that the expansion of First Amendment protections has not greatly enhanced appreciation for the value of free expression. Concerns about hate speech have made some question their support for freedom of speech. Those whose livelihood depends on free expression, especially in the entertainment industry and in the arts, often seem reluctant to defend it. Hardly anyone has the stomach to counter bad speech with more speech.

Instead, there is now widespread tolerance for, and acceptance of, the impulse to suppress unwelcome ideas. In some intellectual circles, the notion that hurtful or offensive speech is assaultive has more currency than a principled defense of free expression. Issues like human rights, economic justice, and the environment have assumed greater urgency compared to traditional civil liberties, and scholars now often opine there is too much focus on individual rights and too much irresponsible speech.

In sum, censorship is advocated these days not only by right-wing "family values" types, but by some political and social liberals, radicals, and feminists who argue that the First Amendment primarily serves to advance racist or sexist values or the speech of large corporations and propertied white males. Granted, most censorship battles continue to originate from right-wing political, social, and religious groups, which have been vigilant and well-organized in their attacks on sexual content of almost any kind and on any material perceived to be subversive of religion, traditional families, or authority. Assaults from the left do not match these, but have significance far beyond their actual numbers, in the withdrawal of moral legitimacy for the cause of free expression

A final irony is that, in the parts of the world where there is little or no protection for free speech, it is increasingly seen as a critical component of human rights. Only in the United States, which enjoys perhaps the most sweeping protection for this freedom, is it so often taken for granted and treated so shabbily.

From efforts to ban J. K. Rowling's popular Harry Potter books in grade schools, to campaigns urging that virtually all sexual content on the Internet should be filtered from computer terminals in public libraries, free expression is caught in the cross fire of an ongoing culture war. No medium, form of expression, or idea is exempt, as the following examples reveal.

ART CENSORSHIP

The most dramatic instance of art censorship in the recent past was the 1999 effort by New York City mayor Rudolph Giuliani to shut down the Brooklyn Museum of Art because of his religiously based objections to *Sensation,* an exhibit of young British artists from the collection of Charles Saatchi. The event was remarkable in part because of where it occurred, in the epicenter of art and culture.

The facts of the incident were well publicized. In brief, while protests against the exhibition's first mounting, at the Royal Academy in London in 1997, had focused on other parts of the installation, par-

Free expression is caught in the cross fire of an ongoing culture war

ticularly Damien Hirst's formaldehyde-filled tanks containing animal carcasses and Marcus Harvey's portrait—made of hundreds of tiny hand prints—of British child-murderer Myra Hindley, in New York it was a work with a religious theme that drew official ire. Chris Ofili, a British artist of Nigerian descent, created a painting of the *Holy Virgin Mary* using African themes, images, and materials, including dried, painted elephant dung. Calling the painting "sick stuff" that was insulting and offensive to his Roman Catholic faith, Mayor Giuliani not only blasted the artist and the museum but attempted to withhold funds for the museum's operating expenses and instituted legal proceedings to evict the museum from the city-owned building it occupies. The museum filed a legal action of its own, claiming that the mayor's actions violated the First Amendment. (This position was upheld by a federal trial judge; while on appeal, the case was settled favorably to the museum.)

An important theme underlying objections to the *Sensation* exhibit was the claim that expression perceived to be critical of religion constitutes a form of "discrimination" on the basis of religion. The same sort of argument had been made a year earlier, in 1998, by the Catholic League for Religious and Civil Rights in protesting the production of a Terrence McNally play, *Corpus Christi,* because its main, Christ-like character was gay. The Catholic League called the play blasphemous and sought to have public funding withdrawn from the Manhattan Theatre Club, claiming that public sponsorship of art critical or subversive of religion is discriminatory. The argument draws on analyses, made by legal scholars in race and sex discrimination theory, that condemn biased expression and justify its suppression.

While efforts like these have so far largely been legally unsuccessful, the blurring of the distinction between discriminatory *actions* and hateful words, ideas, or images has created widespread confusion about the reach of the First Amendment and its relationship with civil rights laws and policies. The importance of the distinction is perhaps most obvious in the disputes over *Sensation* and *Corpus Christi.* If suppression of "objectionable" views were permissible on the ground that "offensive" speech does the *same kind of harm* as a discriminatory act (like refusing to hire an otherwise qualified person because of his or her religion), society's ability to hear, discuss, and consider important ideas—an essential goal of the First Amendment—would be severely compromised. (This is not to deny that words and ideas have power and can influence actions both for good and evil; hence the injunction that the cure for bad speech is "more speech, not enforced silence.")

The blurring of the distinction between discriminatory actions and hateful words has created widespread confusion

The attempted censorship of the *Sensation* exhibit has had interesting and inconsistent consequences. On the one hand, the noisy public debate made people take notice of both the issues and the art. Like *Corpus Christi,* which sold out after the public protests against it, this exhibit drew thousands of viewers to Brooklyn, some to see what the fuss was all about and others to express support for the museum and for artistic freedom. After the events in New York, however, Australia's National Gallery, in Canberra, canceled its plans to host the exhibit. Most sobering, it has become extremely doubtful that any publicly funded arts organization will sponsor anything that is potentially controversial without careful thought to the possible repercussions, at least so long as there is political capital to be made from censorship.

MEDIA VIOLENCE

A decade of increasingly political attacks on Hollywood culminated in 1999 with a public campaign called "An Appeal to Hollywood." Capitalizing on public outrage over two Colorado teenagers who gunned down teachers and classmates before committing suicide, the "Appeal to Hollywood" condemned popular culture as "toxic." It asserted that "overwhelming evidence" links violent entertainment to "the horrifying new crimes we see emerging among our young" and cautioned that "allowing children unsupervised access to today's media is the moral equivalent of letting them go play on the freeway."[1]

Framed as an effort to encourage voluntary reform, the Appeal nonetheless implicitly threatened government censorship if the industry failed to regulate itself. Even as the Appeal was being promoted on the Internet and in full-page ads in major national newspapers, Senators who endorsed the Appeal also proposed federal legislation to impose labeling requirements and age restrictions for violent entertainment (film, video games, music, etc.). The proposal, ostensibly for "voluntary" industry action, was hardly voluntary, since it would require government approval of industry efforts and impose criminal penalties.

The Appeal drew endorsements from across the political spectrum—presumably from many who deplore the low quality of some popular entertainment but have not fully considered the implications of letting the government decide what kind of violent entertainment is acceptable, and for whom. Proliferating legislative proposals targeting video games, rock concerts, popular music, and the like indicate that this issue is not likely to disappear any time soon.

DANGEROUS IDEAS

If only censorship efforts were confined to electronic media! A few of the more memorable examples of censorship of print media from the past couple of years include efforts to suppress J. K. Rowling's Harry Potter books, Judy Blume's *Blubber, Seventeen* magazine, and, of course, Mark Twain's *Huckleberry Finn.*

The most recent authoritative compilation[2] identifies nearly a hundred recently banned or challenged books but states that "approximately 85% of the challenges to library materials receive no media attention and remain unreported." The books targeted by would-be censors range from *The*

---

1. As if getting hit by a car were the same as getting "hit" by an idea or a picture! Among other things, the "Appeal to Hollywood" ignored the fact that the most horrifying violence in the world today—e.g., ethnic warfare in places like Kosovo, Rwanda, and East Timor—has no possible relationship to media violence. Members of the Free Expression Network, including the National Coalition Against Censorship, countered these and other assertions in a statement entitled "An Appeal to Reason," available on line at www.freeexpression.org or from NCAC, at www.ncac.org.

2. Robert P. Doyle, *Banned Books 1999 Resource Guide: Free People Read Freely,* published by the American Library Association.

Stupids Die, by Harry Allard and James Marshall (because "children shouldn't refer to anyone as 'stupid'") to *Anne Frank: The Diary of a Young Girl* ("two parents charged that the book was pornographic") and everything in between: *Little House on the Prairie, Native Son, Beloved, Of Mice and Men, The Bell Jar, Deliverance, The House of the Spirits, I Know Why the Caged Bird Sings, The Martian Chronicles, The Handmaid's Tale, One Hundred Years of Solitude, The Drowning of Stephan Jones, Heather Has Two Mommies,* and many more. Included on the list were two notable nonfiction books: Elaine Nicpon Mariels' *Human Anatomy and Physiology,* published by Scott

Protests against the Harry Potter books have raised censorship of children's literature to a whole new level

Foresman/Addison Wesley, and *What's Happening to My Body? Book for Girls: A Growing-Up Guide for Parents and Daughters.*

Protests against the Harry Potter books have raised (or lowered!) censorship of children's literature to a whole new level. The complaint is that the fantasy series, which relates the adventures of Harry Potter, a student at the Hogwarts School of Witchcraft and Wizardry, is antireligious and encourages belief in witchcraft and Satanism. Challenges were reported in at least eight states during October 1999 alone, according to the Office for Intellectual Freedom of the American Library Association. The OIF-ALA observed that "it has been confounding to many educators that after a decade of despair over a generation lost to video games and television . . . the very books that have lured huge numbers of elementary school children to reading are being denounced as dangerous."

The frequency of book challenges in schools is attributable at least in part to the failure of the federal courts. Faced with First Amendment claims of both students and teachers, the Supreme Court has tended to subordinate free expression and elevate the discretion of school administrators. The consequences can be troubling: for example, gifted teachers with proven track records have been disciplined and even fired for using controversial materials.

An often overlooked lesson of these cases, however, is that courts will generally uphold the exercise of discretion by school officials regardless of how that discretion is exercised. Thus, when school officials exercise their discretion in a manner that *respects* free expression, the courts will also uphold their right to do so. In a recent decision by the U.S. Court of the Appeals for the Ninth Circuit, the court upheld inclusion of *Huckleberry Finn* and William Faulkner's story "A Rose for Emily" in a high school English curriculum, rejecting a challenge by parents claiming that use of such materials constituted a form of racial discrimination.

SUBVERSIVE SCIENCE

Kansas educational officials recently decided to remove the study of evolution from the required high school science curriculum. In Kentucky, school science guidelines no longer use the word "evolution," but have substituted the phrase "changes over time." One is tempted, like Katha Pollitt writing in *The Nation,* to say "Go ahead! Be like that! Handicap your kids for life. Let the 'secular humanists' have all the good colleges and get all the good jobs." As Pollitt observed, however, this latest skirmish in the seemingly unending war over teaching creationism in the public schools wasn't something parents or students sought, but the result of a successful "political maneuver by Christian conservative politicians." What is perhaps most shocking, however, is the uniform support by presidential candidates for the proposition that the "decision to teach evolution should be left to local school boards." Where, Pollitt asks, are the "soldiers in the science and education wars who profess to uphold standards and truth . . . ? [Where are] the ferocious defenders of the scientific method?"

If so few are standing up for teaching high school students about evolution, it should come as no surprise that other material is missing from the science curriculum, too. Sex education has perhaps suffered even more than science in schools around the country as a result of a small provision in the 1996 federal legislation overhauling the nation's welfare laws.[3] Little noticed or debated at the time, the provision allocates federal funds to teach "abstinence education." The statutory language makes it clear that the purpose is to undermine, if not replace, comprehensive sex education and to preclude discussion of same-sex and extramarital relationships, contraception, and abortion. In December 1999, the *New York Times* reported that one-third of all school districts in the country teach "an abstinence-only curriculum that permits discussion of contraception only in its failures." Fewer than half offer students information about how to obtain birth control, and only about a third mention abortion or sexual orientation as part of the curriculum.

---

3. The Personal Responsibility and Work Reconciliation Act of 1996 (42 U.S.C. §710, et seq. [1996]), is better known for its provisions imposing limits on receipt of public assistance and "ending welfare as we know it."

No discussion of the effects of censorship on scientific inquiry and knowledge would be complete without mentioning Congressional Resolution #107. The saga began in 1998, when the American Psychological Association's peer-reviewed professional journal, *Psychological Bulletin,* published a meta-analysis evaluating research on the long-term psychological consequences of child sexual abuse. The study, according to social psychologist Carol Tavris, found "no overall link between childhood sexual abuse and later emotional disorders." Given the study's explanation that the term "child sexual abuse" refers to a wide range of behaviors, including "the repeated rape of a 5-year-old girl by her father and the willing sexual involvement of a mature 15-year-old adolescent boy with an unrelated adult," as well as "sexual interactions involving . . . no contact (e.g. exhibitionism)," it should come as no surprise that not all these events have the same lasting negative psychological consequences.

The study received little public attention until it was picked up by Dr. Laura Schlessinger, the radio talk-show host, and congressional allies of the National Association for the Research and Therapy of Homosexuality, a group that promotes the idea that homosexuality is a mental disorder. Touting the study as the "emancipation proclamation of pedophiles," members of Congress attacked both the study itself and the APA for publishing it. Displaying what Tavris called "a stunning display of scientific illiteracy and moral posturing," Congress unanimously passed a resolution condemning the study as "severely flawed" and encouraging "competent investigations"—presumably only those whose results members of Congress approve.

CYBER-CENSORSHIP

It will come as no surprise that cyberspace has also been the target of censors who fear that children will gain access to all manner of dangerous ideas, information, and images. Countless measures have been proposed in Congress and state legislatures to "protect" minors from receiving "indecent" or "harmful" material on the Internet or from accessing "pornography" and other "dangerous" material on school and library computers. The most important of these, the Communications Decency Act, was held unconstitutional by the Supreme Court's 1997 decision in *Reno v. ACLU,* which has limited the ability to censor the Internet if not the impulse to do so.

The CDA prohibited use of the Internet to display "indecent" material or make it "available" to minors. In finding that the statute violated the First Amendment, the Court established that content on the Internet is entitled to the highest level of First Amendment protection. The Court rejected the argument that the Internet, like radio and television, should be subject to greater government regulation of content and enjoy less First Amendment protection than printed matter. Further, the Court held that it is impermissible to restrict the rights of adults in order to protect minors. Quoting from an earlier case, the Court noted that "the level of discourse reaching a mailbox simply cannot be limited to that which would be suitable for a sandbox."

Cyberspace has also been the target of censors who fear that children will gain access to dangerous ideas

Based on this decision, lower federal courts have rejected other federal and state efforts to regulate the Internet to "protect" minors. In *Mainstream Loudoun v. Board of Trustees of the Loudoun County Library,* a Virginia federal court rejected efforts to install filters on all computer terminals in a public library to keep minors from accessing pornography. Other decisions have invalidated state law restrictions on use of the Internet to transmit sexually explicit material to minors.

These court victories have hardly quieted the debate over Internet filtering, however. Fueled by hyperbolic claims about pedophiles stalking children on line, "family values" organizations continue to pursue a vigorous campaign for filtering in libraries. One particularly aggressive example is the American Family Association and the Family Research Council's concerted effort to force ballot initiatives in Michigan calling for the withdrawal of funding from a library if it fails to install filters. One town faced with such a situation, Hudsonville, Michigan, discontinued Internet access in its library rather than be caught in the cross fire between its First Amendment obligations and advocates of filters. As of this writing, voters have defeated one such proposal, but that is not likely to settle the debate.

CHILD PORNOGRAPHY

In 1996, Congress enacted the Child Pornography Prevention Act. Hardly the first federal effort to restrict sexual images involving children, the CPPA marks a new direction in the law of child pornography. The Supreme Court had previously sanctioned restrictions on child pornography, notwithstanding the First Amendment implications, because of the importance of protecting *actual* children from exploitation inherent in the creation of sexually explicit materials. On the same theory, the Court permitted penalties for adult possession of such material, reasoning that the state's interest in destroying the market for sexual materials involving *actual* children justified a departure from the general rule protecting the First Amendment rights of adults to sexually explicit but non-obscene material.

Unlike earlier laws, the CPPA prohibits the creation, possession, use, and distribution of sexually explicit materials (including "lascivious display of the genitals") that *appear* to involve minors, *even if no minor is actually involved.* The statute provides no exceptions, even for works with artistic, historical, educational, or scientific value.

Thus, the recent movie version of *Lolita,* even though filmed with an adult "body double," could be deemed "child pornography" simply because it *appears* to involve a minor in *simulated* sexual activity. Of course that's what *Lolita* is about—a man's sexual obsession with a pubescent girl. The law is so broadly drawn that it could arguably apply to works of art such as Balthus's painting *The Guitar Lesson,* to some renditions of *Romeo and Juliet,* to photographs of tribal puberty rites, to some sex education materials, and to graphic depictions of incest and child sexual abuse—even if made for the purpose of opposing these abuses.

The CPPA reflects a significant shift, from a focus on protecting minors from exploitation to a focus on penalizing the *viewer* of such materials. No longer satisfied with protecting actual children, Congress has taken aim at materials produced *without* exploiting or even using children. The theory is that such images encourage pedophilia and provide materials that can be used to seduce minors. But there is no evidence that viewing certain kinds of images causes the commission of sexual crimes against children. It makes as much sense to say that belief in religion causes violence, because violent acts are depicted (and justified) in the Bible and some violent criminals cite the Bible as their inspiration. This overreaction to child nudity, moreover, emboldens local prosecutors, who, with some regularity, file charges of "child pornography" against parents and grandparents for taking snapshots of their children nude, as occurred recently in Ohio.

The rights of minors are poorly defined, and so they have become the focus of most censorship campaigns

NEW YORK'S CIVICS LESSON

In sum, it is neither the best nor the worst of times for free expression in the United States. As noted at the outset, many gains have been achieved in the past century. With the exception of child pornography and "obscenity," adults enjoy access to a wide variety of materials. Political speech is rarely targeted overtly, although it is still subject to more subtle forms of attack. The rights of minors are poorly defined, and so they have become the focus of most censorship campaigns, a development that corresponds with the emphasis on "family values" and parents' rights.

In an especially ironic turn of events, aggressive censorship in New York City may have done more to advance an appreciation for free expression than advocates alone could have ever accomplished, by teaching the whole city a civics lesson about the meaning of the First Amendment.

The effort to censor the *Sensation* exhibit at the Brooklyn Museum of Art was only one in a series of high-visibility efforts by City Hall to suppress speech that city officials didn't like. The mayor and top aides closed crime scenes to the press, restricted demonstrators' access to City Hall steps, threatened protesting taxi drivers with arrest, denied permits to the organizers of the Million Youth March, and barred city employees from speaking to the press. Thanks in part to this repressive campaign, a wide range of organizations and individuals whose expressive rights had been infringed came forward in 1999 to defend the right of the Ku Klux Klan to hold a peaceful demonstration. It took a city government with the worst First Amendment record in memory to bring together civil rights organizations and immigrant taxi drivers to support the Klan's right to march, knowing that their own ability to speak out also hung in the balance.

Including All Our Voices

As this *Guide* makes clear, all writers—within particular genres and across genres—face similar problems in getting their work published, protecting their rights, and earning a living from their writing. The NWU recognizes, however, that writers who belong to underrepresented groups—writers of color, writers with disability, queer writers, and others—often have a more difficult time succeeding, professionally, than do their white, able-bodied, straight, "mainstream" colleagues.

The reasons for this difference—cultural, political, psychological, economic—are complex and systemic. Solving the special problems confronted by minority writers and making sure that all writers are able to pursue their careers on an even playing field aren't easy tasks, but they're ones that the NWU, through its National Diversity Committee, has committed itself to. In this chapter, three writers address current publishing industry conditions as they bear on writers of color, writers with disability, and lesbian/gay/bisexual/transgender writers.

Reading, Writing, and Race
by Yleana Martinez

Why should the book publishing industry pay heed to the changing face of American society? The most obvious reason, of course, is economic. Never before has this country experienced such a sustained wave of financial prosperity. Many people have a lot more money to spend, and publishers stand to make a lot of money by cultivating communities of readers that they, in the past, have largely ignored. Authors like Gish Jen, Isabel Allende, and Walter Mosley have exploded the myth that there is no audience for nonwhite writers. The enormous success of artists of color in other areas of the entertainment world affirms that consumers like and support them. Books, the original form of personal, portable entertainment, are no exception.

In 1994, the federal Equal Employment Opportunity Commission released statistics showing that whites accounted for 87.2 percent of the publishing-industry workforce. That same year, Harold Hodgkinson, director of the Center for Demographic Policy of the Institute for Educational Leadership, told the American Association of Publishers, "It is an interesting challenge for industries like your own, which is dominated by old, white, rich people, to figure out how to develop new markets."

The image of publishing houses as elite, untouchable bastions contains more than a grain of truth

But, given the scarcity of editors, agents, and marketers who truly understand the trends, moods, and buying habits of these burgeoning markets, even the most well-meaning effort to reach out to them may fail. Worse, when people of color are excluded from the decision-making process, such endeavors can result in biased offerings—material that can be perceived as condescending to the tastes and intelligence of minority readers. (In this essay, I focus on major book publishers, but a parallel dynamic occurs at most newspapers, magazines, and literary publications.)

The National Writers Union was formed to protect the working conditions and economic interests of all writers. The problems faced by writers in all genres—fiction, nonfiction, journalism, technical writing, business writing, poetry—are myriad, but writers of color in every sector of the industry experience these problems in ways that distinguish them from their mainstream (i.e., white) colleagues.

The image of publishing houses as elite, untouchable bastions contains—as do almost all stereotypes—more than a grain of truth. Until the last half of the 20th century, women were rare on the publishing scene. These days, one is much more likely to encounter female executives, but the number of people of color in book publishing remains exceedingly low, and it's almost impossible to find a person of color in a top-level position at a commercial publishing house.

Disproportionately low representation in publishing can easily lead to reliance on a handful of authors of color. Latino authors often complain that their work is difficult to sell unless it is set in a barrio or written in the vein of "magic realism." The Mexican-American author Sandra Cisneros has said that a publisher once "proudly" told her she was the only Latina on their list. "As if that is a great honor," Cisneros said. "But you need to ask yourself, 'Why am I the only one?'"

Asian writers have their own set of prejudices to contend with. And the problems can differ greatly according to which Asian culture one hails from. Chinese Americans account for 24 percent of the United States' Asian population, but they are more heavily represented in the literary marketplace than, for example, Filipino Americans, who represent 21 percent of Asian Americans but who are virtually nonexistent on the mainstream publishing scene. Must Asians always write about the "old country" or about being "caught between two cultures" to be taken seriously by publishers? Some believe this is the case. "I hope that twenty-five years from now, we'll achieve the kind of standing that Jewish American writers have, that is, that we'll just be judged as writers," says Gish Jen. "What we don't want is to be lumped together, ghettoized."

African-American novelist Terry McMillan faced such a "ghettoizing" attitude when an editor told her that naming a character Zora sounded too "preppy." Her response? "I said, 'Look, she's not barefoot and pregnant, living in the projects and getting her ass kicked. I cannot apologize because some of us have been to college, okay?'"

McMillan's rise to the top of the bestseller lists did not happen overnight, as some might believe. Her tireless efforts at self-promotion—lugging books across the country in the trunk of her car so that she could sell them to black reading clubs, at church get-togethers, and at other stops on the minority circuit—are, she believes, what led the marketing divisions to notice and, eventually, to back her. When the big-bucks promotion machine kicked into gear, McMillan's appeal to readers of all kinds—not to mention the money she racked in—stunned the trade.

The paucity of people of color in the publishing world multiplies the hindrances faced by minority writers

All writers struggle to get meaningful support from agents, editors, and publicists. But the paucity of people of color in the publishing world multiplies the hindrances faced by minority writers. Blacks, Latinos, Asians, and Native Americans are generally absent from the sphere of high-stakes publishing. They just don't get invited to the cocktail parties, readings, or other events where lucrative publishing deals are often conceived. The obstacles to networking, lack of "insider" status, and limited gateways for minority writers ultimately deny the reading public a diversity of perspectives.

To be sure, minorities have begun to infiltrate the system. But there are still too few key players able to transform manuscripts into press runs or to get less well-connected (but no less worthy) writers of color onto bookstore shelves. "Often white editors and publishers don't understand the talent in the black community, and if it weren't for black agents communicating that culture to a very white culture, there would be a lot fewer black books," says Adrienne Ingrum, associate publisher of *Black Issues Book Review.* Ingrum adds, "No way would there be a boom in black books without a black literary agenda."

The NWU is committed to leveling the playing field for all writers

The prospects for black writers may be better in some markets than in others. According to Robert Fleming, author of *The African American Writer's Handbook,* the market is currently hot in particular genres: quirky romances, high-tech science fiction, disaster thrillers, and "tales of the young and confused."

The NWU is committed to leveling the playing field for all writers, an agenda that includes exposing the economic racism that exists in publishing. The union has succeeded in bringing diversity issues to the forefront of its organizing efforts on behalf of all the writers—journalists, book authors, poets, and business and technical writers—it represents. Other strategies aimed at improving working conditions for underrepresented writers include these:

* Actively recruiting from these groups so that their voices are heard at the bargaining table

* Building coalitions and working partnerships with other writers' organizations on a variety of issues that affect writers of color and other marginalized groups (events and groups with which the NWU has worked include OutWrite, Indigenous Peoples' Day events, First Amendment Supporters of Mumia Abu-Jamal, and others)

* Developing and providing lists of agents and publishers (white and non-white) who have a proven track record of working with writers of color

* Urging editors of anthologies to seek material from non-mainstream sources

* Initiating programs to introduce more writers of color into the field of technical writing

Bringing more people of color into decision-making roles in the publishing industry—and expanding the possibilities for publication of writers of color—will be no easy feat. The industry's employment practices, based on an apprenticeship system that relies heavily on interns and that pays entry-level employees pathetically low wages, are deeply entrenched. Unless applicants have additional income support, like family money, those who wish to enter the profession are at an immediate disadvantage. Most major publishing houses are located in cities like New York, where the cost of living is very high. Industry insiders acknowledge that, because of this, many minorities are kept out of the loop from the very start.

Relatively few colleges and universities have publishing programs, and, even where these exist, participation by minorities is generally small. (Two exceptions are Howard University's Book Publishing Institute, in Washington, D.C., and the Publishing Certificate Program at the City College of the City University of New York.) Moreover, given the small number of mentors available to help them navigate their career development paths, minority graduates of such programs who enter the field are likely to drop out.

On the writing side, there are too few agents and acquisitions editors who actively seek writers of color. Many still believe there is no mass market for such work. That belief, however, is self-fulfilling prophecy, for when publishers are not meaningfully connected to communities of color, the return on their marketing plans will be disappointing. No smart business invests in a product it doesn't know how to sell. The shame, though, is that there *is* a market out there—and legions of talented creators ready and able to satisfy that market's demands. Ultimately, the big book publishers will have to figure this out, or get left behind.

Writers with Disability

by Tommye-K. Mayer

Disability as a minority is distinct from other minorities in one critical way. It is the only one you can join against your will. That said, if you're lucky you'll live long enough to join—to be disabled. Writers relying on computer keyboards often succumb to the disabler of the Information Age, repetitive strain injury (RSI). It isn't inconceivable that the concerns of writers with disability might become pertinent even to you. I hope not, while at the same time I do hope you live long.

Let's say you're a person with disability and you've decided to become a writer. When you picture it, you're working alone and writing at home. Perfect. Maybe the disability makes it hard to get yourself elsewhere on a regular schedule. Or maybe you don't feel comfortable putting yourself in a group of strangers, even long enough for those strangers to become colleagues.

You imagine you'll write about things that interest you: hobbies, knowledge you've acquired over the years, human interactions you've observed or participated in, and commentary on topics in the news. It sounds like a great plan. People often remark how well you write. So why not go for it?

HOW WOULD A WRITING CAREER WORK FOR A WRITER WITH DISABILITY?

As you consider a writing career, the thought crosses your mind, "Do editors I would work with by phone, fax, or over the Internet need to know? Do they need to know about my disability"? If no one knew you have disability, could there be problems with your being treated "differently?" Could there be issues with discrimination, perhaps, over what you'd be seen as qualified to write about?

I've wondered, and I've heard plenty of stories, stories on both sides of the answer. Some say that, once the editors learn of a disability, the range of stories assigned shrinks like cotton in hot water. Others claim their editors know and it doesn't make any difference. In fact, sometimes the impossible is assigned, as if to see how a gymp would cover it. In short, the jury may be out forever because the answer seems to depend on the editor.

As writers, our work is directly related to and influenced by our observations, by our experiences, and by everything that makes us who we are: where we've been, what we've seen, whom we know, what we haven't seen and don't know, and how it all happened or didn't happen. What a writer writes about, what interests him or her, comes from that sum total of the whos, whats, whens, wheres, hows, and whys of our lives and experience. All of our experience.

There's no doubt in my mind that disability is one factor coloring who you and I have become. It's one factor, just as is each of our major life experiences, as well as our physical characteristics of tallness, shortness, voice tone, bone structure, hair color and type, and so forth. Just like the rest of our packaging, the disability has shaded, but only shaded, the you that is *you*. It has helped frame how you see the world as a writer, what you observe, experience, and find interesting. I look at my disability the same way I look at all those other factors that define me—gender, age, ethnicity, sexual preference, race, birth order, marital status, and economic status (and changes over time).

GETTING STARTED AND DOING THE WRITING

Often, at the beginning of a writing career, you're encouraged to write about what you know. A writer who gardens might choose to break in by submitting articles about gardening. If this writer also happens to have disability, at some point she or he might ponder "letting slip" that fact by sharing creative methods enabling the gardening despite the disability. For example, what if that disability involves hand dexterity? Perhaps insights about tools that make gardening more enjoyable and more doable would be valid for able-bodied gardeners, too. Wouldn't that experience and information be important to otherwise able-bodied gardening enthusiasts who suffer from arthritis, as well as to gardeners with a temporary hand injury?

There's a risk of falling victim to an editor's tendency to pigeonhole a writer

What if the gardener-writer uses a wheelchair? Wouldn't insights about how to arrange the garden, or to access the plants, or about particular tools be helpful for gardeners suffering a back injury or other injury that makes gardening while standing impossible for longer than they'd like to be away from their gardens?

One might think.

Sometimes it seems no matter how valid the argument that writers with disability are perfect instructors for others who are temporarily incapacitated, as well as for those who are newly disabled, there's a risk of falling victim to an editor's tendency to pigeonhole a writer. The risk that a reference to disability will cause an editor to question placement of your article might be a valid concern.

Your piece on gardening, which tangentially mentions disability, might be rerouted from the front of the magazine to a special section or sidebar for disability issues. It might be killed altogether, with the explanation that readers don't want to be confronted with disability.

Should you worry about becoming known as a writer with disability, lest you be dismissed as capable of writing only about disability? This is a concern because such dismissal greatly limits the markets open to your work. If you're trying to earn a living with your writing, the wider the audience to buy and read what you write, the better.

What if you want to write about "what you know"—disability?

For some reason, mainstream (read well-paying) markets tend to prefer disability stories that fall into the inspirational supergymp-overcoming-the-unbearable-against-all-odds category. While these are probably important pieces for the world to read, it's awfully hard to write inspirationally about yourself, unless the story is done humorously. Outside disability circles, humor can be hard. People don't seem to laugh much at, or about, disability.

Mainstream markets prefer disability stories that fall into the inspirational category

This seems to leave few options: to write supportive pieces about adapting to, or living with, disability for the disability media (read less well-paying); academic papers for medical journals; or articles for healthcare association publications and support group newsletters (read typically non-paying).

So what's a gymp who wants to write to do? An "end-around"? It's my favorite football play, a go-for-broke tactic. That's what I chose to do.

While peddling my book proposal for *One-Handed in a Two-Handed World* (the step-by-step guide to managing just about everything with the use of one hand) to more carefully selected publishers than I care to recall, I heard over and over what an important, functional, and—yes—inspirational book it was. I then heard, "It isn't for us." One editor did respond, "I love it!" But 18 months later this editor confessed, "While it's an important and inspirational book, marketing can't imagine where bookstores would shelve it."

An imagination problem or a discrimination issue? I decided not to get bogged down in righteousness. Instead, I examined the market once again.

Hundreds of thousands of stroke survivors live on one-handed. As people live faster and harder, thousands survive accidents each year after an arm or hand is amputated. Millions of able-bodied people struggle to manage for months using one hand due to RSI, broken bones, strains, sprains, tennis elbow, and arthritis.

In this era of managed healthcare, these temporarily one-handed people are left alone to manage at home and at work once the acute care has been rendered. The potential market was huge, and I was the expert who could help all these people manage to get on with life while able to use only one hand. *One-Handed in a Two-Handed World* was the book I wish had been there for me when I first needed it, and it needed to be there for others.

I then looked into ways to do it. How did a bunch of 8½ x 11" sheets of paper become a book? How could I package words on paper to look like the bound volumes stacked on shelves in bookstores across the country?

It isn't impossible. I'm doing it. Do know that publishing your work your-self is by no means the easy way out. When you publish independently, you take on everything: the production, the distribution, the marketing, the enthusiasm, and the bookkeeping as well as the writing.

If you plan carefully, if you put in a lot of effort, if you really want it, your work can get past marketing departments that "can't imagine where book-stores would shelve it." *One-Handed in a Two-Handed World*, now in its sec-ond edition, is even used as a text by occupational therapy students in half a dozen colleges and universities in the United States and Canada.

CONSIDERATIONS WHEN WRITING WITH DISABILITY

Social Security and Medicare/Medicaid. Before you take the plunge, there is yet another matter that writers with disability who are currently supported with Social Security benefits need to consider. While Social Security benefits are enough money to live just below the poverty line, this is hardly a secure living. Nonetheless, as the rules are currently written (some changes may be forth-coming), if you earn enough money to be considered "gainfully employed" (now about $700 a month if you receive SSI, $200 a month if you receive SSDI), you jeopardize not only your Social Security benefits but also your Medicare and, if you qualify for Medicaid, your Medicaid healthcare coverage, too.

Just having a disability probably means you have a physical or mental impairment requiring medical attention. Often, health insurance plans avail-able on the open market won't cover conditions diagnosed or treated before your enrollment, known as pre-existing conditions, without charging a much higher premium. So, as things currently stand, if you earn as little as $700 a month with your writing, you jeopardize not only your subsistence-level Social Security income but also the health insurance that sustains your very existence. Now that's a Catch-22.

The trick to succeeding in moving from Social Security to self-support, despite your disability, is to consistently earn enough to replace your Social Security benefits plus enough to buy health insurance that will cover medical expenses related to your pre-existing condition (your disability). Hopefully you already know that writing doesn't often produce high tax-bracket incomes. For every John Grisham and Jacqueline Susann, thousands of writ-ers are struggling to make ends meet.

So how do you juggle everything—the writing about what you know because of (or perhaps despite) your disability, the potential for pigeonholing, and the risk of losing your Social Security income and healthcare benefits? I think while Social Security is at least minimally supporting you, it's important to focus on honing your skills as a writer. Read, write, join writing groups, volunteer, develop areas of expertise, and practice. When you're ready, if you decide writing is something you've just got to do, then you have to believe in your ability and give it your best shot. And maybe, just maybe by then, the Social Security system as it applies to people with disability will have been adjusted so that moving from support to self-sufficiency doesn't require a terrifying leap into an abyss without health insurance.

AFTER YOU'VE TAKEN THE LEAP

What if you pitch an idea to an editor, get the go-ahead, and then your MS, your CFS, your RSI, your whatever acts up or your medications react? What if your disability sabotages you and you're unable to fulfill the contract you've obligated yourself to? Some disabilities don't vary much, so this may not be an issue. For others, however, it's a real concern—an ethical issue for sure, but also a potential liability. You need to be sure to examine the fine print of any contract you sign so—with the help of a National Writers Union contract adviser—so that you know the ramifications should the unthinkable occur.

We're Here, We're Queer, and They've Sort of Gotten Used to It

by James Waller

The publishing-industry realities faced by lesbian/gay/bisexual/transgender writers have changed dramatically over the past decade—in some cases for the better, in some for the worse, and in some cases for better *and* for worse. Let's take a look at a couple of those "glass is half empty/glass is half full" scenarios first.

The rise of the superstores and the advent of online bookselling mean that LGBT-oriented literature and nonfiction are now available virtually everywhere. By the same token, these systemic changes in the bookselling business have forced the closing of many independent bookstores—including some of the gay, lesbian, and women's bookstores that were so centrally important to the movement's consolidation and growth. For those lesbian/gay bookshops

---

© 2000 by James Waller

that manage to hang on, diminishing profit margins and an increasingly disloyal customer base make life very tough indeed. The long-term effects of this trend on the careers and pocketbooks of queer authors are unclear: as gay bookstore-owner and literary agent Norman Laurila points out, lesbian/gay bookstores have heretofore always been the primary venue for selling queer books. If they disappear, what happens to queer literature?

LGBT-oriented literature and nonfiction are now available everywhere

Similarly, the proliferation of queer websites means that queer news is available everywhere virtually. You no longer have to live in a town that has a lesbian/gay community paper to access queer news easily. Queer websites give queer freelance journalists a greater number of venues in which to publish their work. But, once again, there's a downside: the Internet has made it all that much easier for ethically lax publishers to steal queer writers' work by republishing it online without permission and without compensation.

THE (MOSTLY) BAD NEWS: BOOKS

From the late 1980s through the mid-1990s there was a boom—or maybe it should be called a "boomlet"—in major commercial book publishers' interest in gay men's fiction and nonfiction. (Lesbian fiction and nonfiction didn't fare so well, though for a very few authors the picture did brighten briefly.) Gay novelist and journalist Jameson Currier links this blossoming of mainstream publishing's interest in gay topics to the surge in the mainstream media's coverage of lesbian and gay life at the time of the 25th anniversary of the Stonewall riots. For whatever reason, the gay market was "hot," and gay authors—and a few lesbian writers—were suddenly able to sell their books on proposal (something that had rarely if ever been possible before) and, in a number of cases, to command sizable advances.

But the boomlet went bust. According to Norman Laurila, the publishers signing those books generally didn't bother to consider the books' limited crossover potential or even the quality of what they were publishing. In half a dozen cases, Laurila says, commercial houses gave away quarter-million-dollar advances for books that stood little chance of selling more than 20,000 copies. The publishers forgot some basic principles of arithmetic, and they got burned. The ironic and sad effect of that foreshortened Golden Age has been to make it more unlikely that a major commercial house will take the risk of signing a book with queer content or will give a queer author even a livable (much less a sweetheart) deal.

That about-face, however, doesn't mean that there aren't plenty of publishers—smaller commercial houses, small presses, university presses, gay and lesbian presses—still eager to publish books with queer content. It does mean that the career prospects of queer book authors aren't so sunny as they seemed a mere half-decade ago. Even some relatively successful queer authors are being forced to take their projects to smaller publishers and to settle for smaller advances, smaller print-runs, weaker distribution, and threadbare promotional budgets. Women have it even tougher than men. Lesbian novelist and playwright Sarah Schulman points out that there are virtually no literary agents willing to handle books with what she calls "primary lesbian content" (as opposed to a novel with a minor character who's a lesbian, say, or a nonfiction book one of whose chapters covers lesbian issues), and she says that editors—even out lesbian editors—at the big commercial houses typically steer clear of such books.

Even some relatively successful queer authors are being forced to take their projects to smaller publishers

Some of the problems faced by queer book authors are undoubtedly the result of old bigotry in new and subtler guise. Schulman claims that mainstream periodicals maintain an unspoken—but nevertheless strictly enforced—quota-system regarding the number of lesbian and gay books that get reviewed. They typically assign gay writers to review gay books, reinforcing the notion that queer writing is "niche" literature. Editors at commercial houses—queer or straight—refuse to entertain the possibility that a book with queer (especially lesbian) content might escape its niche and demonstrate real crossover appeal. Fiction issued by lesbian and gay presses isn't taken seriously by the literary establishment. Queer writers have trouble breaking through a perception-barrier that separates "American writers" (whose work, it's presumed, might be of interest to any common reader) from those who are "merely" lesbian or gay writers (whose work, it's presumed, is of interest only to a parochial audience). Funding agencies—especially the big private foundations—don't support queer-themed projects. And so on. There are a few queer authors whose careers are exceptions to these rules, of course, but the fact that one can so quickly rattle off the list of their names shows just how rare they are.

THE (MOSTLY) GOOD NEWS: JOURNALISM

For queer freelance journalists things aren't nearly so grim. Many, many mainstream periodicals now frequently cover queer stories, hire queer writers to write them, and accord them the same editorial treatment that they give the other stories they cover. As longtime gay freelance reporter Duncan Osborne puts it, "Now, lesbian and gay content is unexceptional. It's sort of expected." It's not just the *Village Voice* that's regularly running stories about lesbians, gay men, bisexuals, transgender people and their lives, it's the *L.A. Times*. *The New Yorker* carries gay-themed cartoons. *Metropolitan Home* features gay couples' apartments. We're here, we're queer, and the print media have (to a great extent) gotten used to it.

Moreover, the lesbian/gay media are in many respects flourishing. During the past decade, glossies like *Out* and *Genre* managed to overcome one of the gay press's major hurdles by attracting major mainstream advertisers to their pages. There appear to be more lesbian/gay community papers than ever: nearly every sizable American city has one, and several cities have more than one. The "bar rag"—that mainstay of gay saloons, with its badly lit photos of local drag entertainers, febrile reviews of movies and shows, lurid classifieds, and questionable editorial standards—shows no signs of obsolescence. The past decade saw the inauguration of a lesbian/gay TV magazine, *In the Life,* on PBS. And of course there's that expanding crop of queer websites—sites like planetout.com and gay.com.

The lesbian/gay media are in many respects flourishing

But merely saying that the queer media are alive—and lively—doesn't convey the complexity of the situation facing queer writers. First, the lesbian press—as a distinct entity—is much less robust in terms of the number and variety of periodicals than it was during its heyday in the 1970s and 1980s. Like lesbian book authors, lesbian freelance journalists have fewer outlets for their work and a generally tougher row to hoe than their gay male colleagues. Though the national gay magazines all run lesbian-oriented news, features, reviews, and columns, there's nothing like parity with the amount of gay male–oriented editorial content they carry. Moreover, *all* writers for the lesbian/gay press must endure comparatively (sometimes abysmally) low pay scales. Like the alternative media in general, lesbian/gay outlets are often tenuously funded: not only do they pay little, but those little checks can be a long time in coming. Interestingly, word has it that the glossies—with their relatively lavish budgets—are sometimes bigger offenders when it comes to paying writers on time than are their down-at-heels community-newspaper cousins.

Too, community newspapers sometimes deal with writers' work in a less-than-professional manner. Jameson Currier tells a horror tale about writing a story for one such newspaper and seeing it reprinted—without his permission and without his being paid—in a number of other lesbian/gay papers around the country. At least those reprints kept his byline. When he later found the same story republished on a website, no writing credit was given. As all freelance journalists know, it's hard to stomach such unethical and illegal re-uses. But seeing one's rights as a writer abused in this way by "community" organs—publications with a "progressive" political agenda and that one would therefore expect to care about how people are treated—can be particularly aggravating.

Seeing one's rights abused by "progressive" publications can be particularly aggravating

Duncan Osborne descries another troubling trend—one he connects with a decline in journalistic standards generally. He says that over a decade as a freelance reporter, he's seen lesbian/gay journalism become less hard-hitting, less investigative in nature: "I get this impression," he says, "that people are content to do less and are much more interested in creating a story that has some entertainment value." Osborne worries that the Internet exacerbates this trend. Like many other magazine-format websites, queer websites are heavy on entertainment- and consumer-related features, short on hard news, and almost entirely lacking in in-depth, investigative reporting.

FUTURE TENSE

Just what the future holds is—no surprises here—hard to say. If the easy accessibility of queer news on the Internet has the effect of driving print publications out of business, queer freelance journalists a few years hence may find that they have fewer, not more, outlets for their writing—and outlets that, in general, eschew in-depth reporting or any writing that doesn't toe the consumerist line.

When asked what advice he'd give lesbian and gay book authors who are just starting out, Laurila says, "Well, I would give up the fallacy that you don't want to be considered a 'gay writer' or a 'lesbian writer' because you have dreams of a crossover market. Unless you're extraordinarily lucky and find an editor at a major house who loves your work and will put some time and energy behind it, you really need the book-buying support of the gay and lesbian community."

Interestingly, Schulman—who paints a pretty disheartening picture of the situation facing lesbian book authors today—is more sanguine about the future. "It will change eventually," she says. "I think that agents have to just keep getting inundated with openly lesbian material. And if editors who are outside the gay niche are constantly presented with gay material, they'll get used to it. I feel it is inevitable: there will be a day when a book with primary lesbian content will be seen as an 'American novel.' It has to happen."

PART

3

About the National Writers Union

The National Writers Union: A History

by Alec Dubro

"You can't organize freelance writers," they said. "They're too isolated, too individualistic. They don't want a union." Nearly 20 years later, 6,000-plus National Writers Union members have proved them wrong. Of course, whenever a new group tries to organize a union, someone always comes up with a reason why it won't work.

In October 1981, we decided to make our own space

In 1935, both labor and management told Heywood Broun that you could not organize newspaper reporters, because they were too individualistic. But Broun, who began the Newspaper Guild that year, noted, "The snobbishness of the white-collar groups is on the whole exaggerated. A very considerable proportion of white-collar workers are ready now to join the parade of organization if only space is assigned to them."

But no space was ever assigned to us. American labor law defines free-lancers as "independent contractors." As such, we are not protected by the National Labor Relations Act and are therefore prohibited from bargaining collectively. So, in October 1981, we decided to make our own space.

There had been other attempts to organize. In 1921, 350 writers formed the Authors League. But its book and magazine wing, the Authors Guild, quickly abandoned collective bargaining. In the early 1930s, the Communist Party promoted a Writers Union, which had one goal: to create a public-works project for out-of-work writers. When Franklin Roosevelt's Federal Writers Project hired 6,000 writers, that union faded.

© 2000 by Alec Dubro. Particular thanks to Elliot Negin and Nancy DuVergne Smith for their scholarly articles on the formation of the union, and to John Dinges, Bruce Hartford, Suzanne Gordon, and others for their recollections.

After Broun's successful effort to organize newspaper writers in the 1930s, screen, TV, and radio writers were also organized—into the Writers Guild of America and the American Federation of Television and Radio Artists. But freelance print writers continued to go it alone until the 1980s.

Matters finally came to a head during that decade for two major reasons: the right-wing threat to freedom of expression and the explosive growth of media conglomerates, which enriched owners but not writers.

In 1979 the Authors Guild released a study that determined that writers working a minimum of 20 hours a week averaged $4,775 a year. While that figure was contested by publishers, no one disputed that magazine fees were plummeting. In 1960, *Reader's Digest* paid $2,000 for a feature article; in 1980 the magazine paid $2,850. In real dollars, that was a 49 percent drop.

So the desire of writers to spend a little of their time and money to pressure for industry-wide changes was not surprising. What was surprising was that we acted on that desire.

HOW IT BEGAN

The timing was not great, I will admit. Ronald Reagan had just fired the striking air traffic controllers; union membership was dropping nationwide; media coverage of labor was nonexistent; employers were hiring union-busters.

Still, in early 1981, small groups of writers in Boston and New York formed the Organizing Committee for a National Writers Union (OCNWU). Their immediate goal was to place the issue of a union on the agenda of the American Writers Congress, which was meeting in New York City that year. Although the congress's organizers were dubious, they agreed.

Anticipating a small caucus, congress organizers reserved a room for about 50. When hundreds showed up, the meeting had to be moved to Town Hall. The packed house rose in wild applause over the idea of forming a union, and, when the congress was over, activists had gathered more than 500 names and a little purse of donations. Some months later a similar congress was held in San Francisco, with a similar large turnout and conclusion. So it began.

At the first national meeting, held in Princeton, New Jersey, in May 1982, it was apparent that the union had a built-in conflict. There were those who favored strong local chapters and those who wanted a centralized organization concentrating on New York and the publishing industry. In writing the constitution, John Dinges, the union's first secretary for organization, worked out a compromise that gave the union a strong national directorate as well as local autonomy.

Under its first president, novelist Barbara Raskin, OCNWU worked out a structure. The union is run by its delegates, elected proportionally from the locals. The delegates, who meet each year, nominate a National Executive Board (NEB), including a president, secretary-treasurer, and numerous vice presidents. The NEB oversees the work of the paid national staff and steers the goals made at the Delegates Assembly.

Organizers reserved a room for about 50. Hundreds showed up.

In the fall of 1982, the OCNWU met again, this time in Brooklyn, New York, to ratify the constitution. From then on, we were the National Writers Union. We elected feminist writer Andrea Eagan as the first president, and we started organizing.

CHAMPAGNE GOALS ON A NEAR-BEER BUDGET

From the start, the Writers Union faced a difficult problem: How do you organize people whose annual income from their work is frequently far less than that of a minimum-wage job? Simply holding together any organization is costly, and organizing is very costly. We supplemented our dues the old-fashioned way: we begged.

During our first years, the union received money and in-kind donations from other unions: the Communications Workers of America, International Ladies' Garment Workers Union, United Food & Commercial Workers, United Steelworkers of America, Hotel Workers & Restaurant Workers Union, and others.

Perhaps most important, District 65 of the United Auto Workers in New York donated office space and free copying. For six years, the Writers Union operated out of an overheated 10-by-20-foot office at 13 Astor Place in lower Manhattan. It wasn't pretty, but it did the job.

We had vowed to rely on the work of members themselves, but they couldn't do all the work of processing memberships, answering phones, or printing and mailing documents. We managed, somehow, to hold it together with part-timers and volunteer help until 1986, when the union hired Kim Fellner, who had been communications director of the Screen Actors Guild, as our first full-time executive director.

Meanwhile, the union idea was taking root across the country. Locals formed and prospered in Boston, the San Francisco Bay area, Washington, and Chicago. Others arose in Baltimore, Oklahoma, and Philadelphia, only to struggle and fail. Areas where writers abound, like Los Angeles, did not organize for several years; other areas, with smaller numbers of freelance writers (like Minneapolis–St. Paul and Santa Cruz, California), built locals and held on.

With support from the locals, the national office was able to provide backup when we went for our first collective-bargaining contracts at *Mother Jones* and *The Nation.* In 1984, the union proved itself able to fight hostile publishers when it took on *The Rebel,* a news magazine owned by Larry Flynt that had stiffed freelancers out of more than $50,000. We got the money. Since then, the total of reclaimed fees has risen to more than $1.3 million.

In 1984, the union proved able to fight hostile publishers

By our second annual delegates assembly, held in Cambridge, Massachusetts, in 1985, we had 1,300 members. And we had handled grievances and contracts, provided support, and, perhaps best of all, built a strong, cohesive group that actually liked to work together.

UAW AFFILIATION

But it was also apparent that we faced severe limitations on growth if we did not get some help. When I was elected president in 1987, I wanted to see the NWU affiliate with a larger union, not only because we needed resources but, even more important, because we needed to be more firmly inside the house of labor.

In every other industrialized country, freelance writers are organized by a journalists union. According to many European writers/union activists, free-lancers have little chance of prevailing on their own. "We need the journal-ists union, even if there are strains between staff writers and freelancers," said one.

We began a series of committees, searches, board meetings, and assem-blies. We met with the Newspaper Guild, Writers Guild of America, and two major industrial unions: the Communications Workers of America and District 65 of the United Auto Workers.

I left office in 1990, and Jonathan Tasini took over the job. The affiliation debate continued, but, in the end, conflict strengthened members' resolve to accomplish it.

Then, at the July 1991 Delegates Assembly, the delegates overwhelming-ly approved affiliation with the UAW. The subsequent membership vote came in at 70 percent in favor, 30 percent opposed. In January 1992, we became United Auto Workers Local 1981 (the date of the American Writers Congress at which the NWU originated).

CLASS STRUGGLE IN CYBERSPACE

With greater organizing resources, and the UAW backing us, the union decid-ed to venture into new areas.

While issues involving the computerization and the consolidation of media ownership had earlier been discussed in the union, it was not until 1991 that we applied for a grant to study computer databases. What we found confirmed our worst fears: major publications were reselling articles to companies such as Lexis-Nexis, Dialog, and others without compensating writers.

In 1993, President Tasini and Secretary-Treasurer Bruce Hartford, a computer-industry technical writer, drafted a white paper entitled *Electronic Publishing Issues.* At the 1993 Delegates Assembly we established a standing New Technologies Committee. At the same time, we sanctioned support for a lawsuit brought by a group of union members—including Tasini—against the *New York Times*, the Times-Mirror Corporation, Lexis-Nexis, and other publishers. They had been routinely reselling freelance articles through computerized databases without authorization and without paying writers for the reuse.

The lawsuit was part of a broad strategy to make writers players in the evolving battles over technology

The lawsuit was only part of a broad strategy to make writers players in the evolving legal and legislative battles over technology. As Tasini and Hartford wrote, "If we remain silent on the sidelines, the rules, practices, and customs of the new electronic marketplaces will be determined entirely by publishers and vendors for their benefit and not ours."

As it turned out, the lawsuit came to symbolize much of the union's resistance to increasing publishing industry demands for additional republication rights. Over the course of six years, the suit had its ups and downs, reaching a low point in August 1997, when U.S. District judge Sonia Sotomayor ruled against the plaintiffs. Then, in September 1999, it hit a high point when the Court of Appeals reversed Sotomayor and ruled that the reuse of freelance work on databases and CD-ROMs without the authors' express permission constitutes copyright infringement. In short, the union has prevailed over the *New York Times,* Time-Warner, Times-Mirror, and other massive media conglomerates . . . for now.

During this period, the union also launched a number of other remedies aimed at curbing the increasing appetite of publishers. We negotiated with the Copyright Clearance Center to provide royalties for writers whose works have been photocopied, and we backed temporary workers at Microsoft in their fight to retain overtime pay. But perhaps the most innovative approach was the Publication Rights Clearinghouse.

The PRC grew out of an agreement with a database that resold articles by fax to researchers. The firm agreed to pay writers registered with the PRC approximately one dollar for each copy of each of their articles sold; these fees would be collected by the PRC and then distributed to the writers. The union reasoned that other companies that engage in resale—whether by fax, online, or hard copy—might be willing to comply with copyright law and also pay into the fund. At the end of the century, though, it was still an uphill battle.

TRADITIONAL CONCERNS

Not all union action was related to new information technologies. Despite predictions of its demise, the book was doing very well thanks to the growth of superstores, Oprah's Book Club, and a general increase in literacy. But book writers were still suffering. In response, the union undertook a highly successful project to create a network of book contract advisers, similar to the union's grievance officers. Under the guidance of Vice President for External Organizing Phil Mattera, local-designated advisers were trained and made available to any paid-up union member.

Also during the mid-1990s, the union recognized that an increasing number of members were not writing primarily for publications but for private industry, government, and not-for-profits. A caucus was formed, eventually becoming the BITE (short for Business, Instructional, Technical, and Electronic) Division. As in the union's other divisions—Book and Journalism—BITE writers shared information on trade practices, exchanged tips, campaigned against industry abuses, and fought for necessary legislative changes. Out of this work emerged the union's successful Job Hotline, which helps find paying work for members in all genres.

The union received a boost in membership by offering, and constantly refining, its health insurance plan. Then, in 1998, it also began a most unusual form of insurance, called Media Perils. This group policy is basically libel insurance—an increasingly necessary protection for freelance journalists and book writers (indeed, for anyone who ventures an opinion in print).

In 1994, one delegate to the annual assembly noted that the attendees looked "more like the Writers Union of Iceland than of America." Minorities were woefully underrepresented in the union and its leadership. Recognizing that being truly representative meant including *all* writers, the union launched a diversity campaign whose goal is to address issues related to the union membership and underrepresentation of writers based on cultural, ethnic, racial, religious, sexual/gender orientation, and disability factors. By 1999, diversity concerns were very much on the table at the Delegates Assembly, and debates over how best to institute diversity policy played a large role in that year's Executive Board elections.

The union also engaged in some traditional solidarity work by urging the independent Graphic Artists Guild to affiliate with labor, specifically with the UAW. After a lengthy internal search and campaign, the New York–based Guild (membership: 3,100 as of early 2000) voted overwhelmingly to join us in the UAW. Long an ally of ours, the Guild now helps us form a substantial corner in the UAW composed of freelance media workers.

THE NEW CENTURY

Nineteen ninety-nine was a contentious year for the union. For the first time in more than a decade, a dissident slate ran for the presidency and board offices. Issues ranged from the length of presidential tenure to the direction in which the union should go. Challenger Miryam Williamson ultimately made a respectable showing, but Jonathan Tasini was returned to office with 56 percent of the vote. Voters picked and chose among candidates from both slates, proving the writers, like all American voters, are increasingly independent of "party" lines.

At the start of a new century, the union continues to add members, to look for new ways to protect its membership, and to advance the labor movement. As President Tasini has said, "We have to be the leading organization for writers in the United States, the one that takes the risks." It's not a foregone conclusion that we will prevail, but it is a certainty that we'll continue to fight—sometimes among ourselves, but always for the greater good.

CHAPTER 14

The Grievance Process

by the NWU Grievance and Contract Division

Among the most important services that the National Writers Union offers its members are contract advice and assistance in pursuing grievances. These are the jobs of the union's Grievance and Contract Division (GCD).

When we tell writers what our division does, the typical response is, "I don't have any grievances. I've been writing for *Magazine X* for five years. I get along well with the editor, and they always pay me."

But often, if the conversation goes on, a different,

Too often we tend to tip the balance in the publishers' favor

less rosy picture emerges: "They *are* a bit late paying me this month. They usually pay after 60 days, but now they're a month late. And they've been putting my articles on the Web, which I really don't mind, but I recently saw one of my articles for sale by a major online information reseller."

This writer has several grievances—and very serious ones at that. The NWU advises writers that, except for book manuscripts, they should be paid within 30 days of submission. Unless this writer's contract states otherwise, this publisher is always late with payment—this month, particularly so. And unless the writer's contract specifically states that she has given the publisher all rights or specific rights for electronic republication and resale to a database, the publisher has wrongly appropriated these rights without payment.

Too often, when we writers weigh our good relationships with editors at particular publications against our right to be treated fairly, we tend to tip the balance in the publishers' favor—letting them get away with practices that are unethical and, in some cases, illegal. It shouldn't be this way. Our work is essential to the publication process. Without us, publishers do not have products. Not only should publishers treat us as if we're valuable to them, but *we* should act as if we're valuable to them, too.

Let's get back to our writer who has multiple grievances. They are for nonpayment and infringement of rights—both for publishing the story on the

Web and for selling rights to a third party without permission or compensation. What steps should the writer take? And what steps should you take if you find yourself in a similar situation?

First, make sure your NWU membership is up to date. (We cannot assist nonmembers or lapsed members.) Almost every NWU local has at least one grievance officer (GO). Check your local's newsletter to see if the GO's name and contact information appear there. If not, contact either of the NWU's national offices and someone will put you in touch with a GO.

Before beginning the grievance process, think about what you want to achieve

Be prepared to give the GO copies of all documentation—including the contract and any relevant correspondence—pertaining to your grievance. Also, before beginning the grievance process, you should think about what it is you want to achieve. Do you want to be paid? Do you want your article removed from the Web? Do you want a current royalty statement? Many times, writers aren't sure what they want, or they change their minds as the process goes on. It will be very difficult for a GO to work with you if you don't have a clear idea of what you expect the process to yield.

You will have to fill out a very brief form authorizing the GO to assist you. The GO will help you write a demand letter, which will lay out your demand to the publisher and give the publisher a date by which the situation must be resolved. If this deadline passes, the GO will take over, writing letters and/or making phone calls to the publisher, contacting other organizations, publicizing the grievance, and taking other actions designed to persuade and pressure the publisher into settling. If, in the end, the publisher isn't responsive or won't budge from an unacceptable position, the GO may have to suggest that you take legal action.

It is important that you follow the GO's advice, which is based on the collective experience of many GOs over the years. Remember, too, that if your own GO is ever unsure about how to proceed, he or she has a large network of other union GOs to turn to for advice.

Some grievances are unavoidable: disputes occur; clients don't pay. But some grievances can be avoided by making sure your contracts contain clear language. It helps if you have a clear understanding of your task. Don't let an editor get away with saying, "You know what I want." Make sure that what the editor wants is spelled out—and that you agree to the contract terms. Also, before you take on an assignment, check the publisher's reputation. An NWU contract adviser (CA) can check our internal database to see if there have been problems with the publisher in the past. The CA can also assist you in advance of your taking any journalism or work-for-hire assignment or before you sign any book contract so that you can negotiate an agreement designed to head off grievances before they occur.

Although you may be terrified when you begin the grievance procedure, remember that most grievances are winnable. In the second half of 1999, our GOs helped writers win 74 percent of all grievances closed during that period. That's a great track record.

GRIEVANCES—FACTS AND EXAMPLES

More than half of all grievances are for nonpayment. The rest involve copyright infringement, unintelligible or nonexistent royalty statements, contract disputes or breaches, lack of communication, inappropriate editing, and any number of other kinds of disagreements that can arise in the business relationship between writer and publisher.

Let's look at a few examples.

A writer complains that she was assigned a story, given a due date and word count, told how much she'd be paid, and informed that the publication pays on acceptance. She submitted the story on time. Now, more than a year later, it still sits on the editor's desk. The editor, who also owns and publishes the small magazine, apologizes, says she's swamped, and promises that she'll get to it.

This writer has a grievance. In fact, she has multiple grievances. She needs to know whether the story is accepted. If it is, she should be paid immediately. If she no longer wants the magazine to publish it, she should let the editor know that she maintains the rights to that story—that is, if she has not contractually signed them away. But even if she has signed the rights away, if no money has changed hands, the contract has been breached and so the rights should revert to the writer. Now the writer, with guidance from a GO, must decide exactly what she wants to happen.

In another case, a writer submitted a story in December. The contract said that the publisher would pay on acceptance. The story was published in March. By June, the writer still had not been paid. The publisher pleaded poverty and promised to pay a portion of the money within two weeks and the rest when he had it. The two weeks went by, but the money still didn't materialize. By the time the writer contacted a GO, even more time had passed. When the GO contacted the publisher about this nonpayment grievance, the publisher gave the same story about not having the funds. On the GO's advice, the writer eventually went to small claims court and won. The court froze the publisher's bank account, and the writer was paid. Another writer stiffed by the same publisher did the same thing and was also paid.

Unfortunately, five other writers in the same boat were unwilling or unable to go to court. The publication closed, and those writers lost out.

Another writer signed a book contract with a print and electronic publisher giving the publisher all rights in all formats forever. A year after submission, there was no activity indicating that the book would ever be published. After discussion with a GO, the writer decided she wanted back all rights to the book. The publisher indicated his lack of interest in going forward with publication and said he would return the manuscript and all the rights.

Another writer wrote a newspaper feature that was a personal account of events in her life. In editing, the piece was changed to such an extent that the events were no longer recognizable. The writer asked that the piece be restored to its original format or that her byline be removed. Through negotiation between the writer and the publisher, based on guidance from a GO, the problem was amicably solved.

Another writer worked for years on a book for a university press. Her editor gave her suggestions for changes, which the writer made. But then the editor seemed to lose interest. When the writer asked about the status of the project, the editor sent her a letter terminating the contract and asking her to return the advance she had been paid. The writer fought this with a GO's help, and the publisher relented, agreeing to accept repayment when the writer sold the book to another publisher.

A famous writer wrote an article for a specialty magazine owned by a major publishing conglomerate. After the article was published, the editor, who was sympathetic, informed the writer that the magazine was not paying its contributors and suggested that the writer consider taking action against the publisher. Within days of a letter from a GO, the writer received a check.

A HIGH SUCCESS RATE

The moral of these stories? Although the GCD doesn't win all grievances, our level of success is high. Between the inception of the grievance procedure and January 2000, we won about $1.3 million for our writers. That's $1.3 million that may not have been paid without our help. We won $50,000 in the last six months of 1999 alone, and nearly $40,000 in the first five months of 2000.

We don't give legal advice, and we can't act as a grievant's attorney. But we can give our members good practical advice aimed at forcing publishers to fulfill their contractual responsibilities, and we can intercede on our members' behalf, increasing the pressure and producing results.

So next time you *think* you have a grievance, make sure your NWU membership is current, and then contact a GO. He or she will know what to do next.

National Writers Union Membership Benefits

For more information about any of the benefits below—and on the National Writers Union's current campaigns and other activities—visit the NWU website, at www.nwu.org.

Organizing and Education
The NWU's Journalism, Book, and BITE (Business/Instructional/Technical/Electronic) Divisions are improving conditions for all writers through innovative organizing and invaluable professional development seminars.

Contract Advice and Grievance Resolution
The NWU's nationwide network of contract advisers assists members in understanding and negotiating publishing contracts of all types. Assistance is also available for negotiating author-agent agreements. NWU grievance officers have recovered more than $1.3 million for writers from publishers through individual and group grievance claims. Grievance officers also assist members in the resolution of non-monetary disputes.

Health Insurance
The NWU makes group health insurance at competitive rates available to virtually all NWU members. Our group policy has minimal restrictions for pre-existing conditions. For more information, contact our benefits administrator, Customer Service Solutions (CSS), at (800) 258-3669.

Libel Insurance
The NWU provides access to a unique Media Perils Insurance group policy covering libel, invasion of privacy, and other legal claims relating to the content of what you write.

Job Hotline

Employers nationwide utilize the National Writers Union Job Hotline. The Hotline lists a variety of jobs in many writing genres. For more information, visit the NWU's website.

Publication Rights Clearinghouse

The Publication Rights Clearinghouse (PRC) gets members paid for the reuse of their work. Through it, NWU members are receiving royalties for fax-document delivery rights, republication on electronic databases, and academic-reuse permissions.

Publications and Model Contracts

The NWU's *Guide to Book Contracts* provides advice on and model language for all major clauses of a book publishing contract. Model contracts developed by the NWU include the Standard Journalism Contract, the Standard Webzine Contract, and the Preferred Literary Agent Agreement. The NWU is constantly preparing and making available a variety of other useful and topical publications. In addition, the union publishes *American Writer*, a quarterly magazine for members.

Databases

NWU members have access to useful databases offering realistic perspectives based on the experience of union members; these include the MagazineRates Database and the NWU Agent Database (listing hundreds of agents and evaluations by NWU members).

Events

NWU locals regularly host seminars, panels, and parties. Members also have the opportunity to exchange experiences and expertise through a national electronic listserv, NWU-CHAT.

Press Pass and Members Discounts

The Union certifies members as working journalists and issues press credentials. NWU members get reduced prices for NWU-sponsored professional seminars, PRC enrollment, and NWU publications. Discounts are available for car rentals and an international courier service.

Contributors

Jay Anning (designer) is an award-winning art director who has designed scores of books—especially illustrated books—for major publishing houses.

Joan E. Bertin is executive director of the National Coalition Against Censorship, an alliance of 48 national not-for-profit organizations, including labor, professional, religious, educational, artistic, and civil rights groups, committed to defending freedom of thought, inquiry, and expression. She frequently speaks and writes on legal and policy issues and is the author of more than 30 chapters and articles in professional books and journals.

Mike Bradley is a technical writer and former carpenter, teacher, editor, and other things. He's a veteran of the anti–Vietnam War movement and the feminist men's movement, for which he coauthored a strange little book called *Unbecoming Men.* He joined the National Writers Union because he was proud of his father's work in BSEIU and because it was a writers' organization that managers wouldn't join. He's an NWU contract adviser specializing in work-for-hire contracts.

Cate T. Corcoran writes about business, technology, culture, and media. Her work has appeared in the *Wall Street Journal, Wired,* the *San Jose Mercury News,* Salon, and many other online and print publications. She serves as the journalism chair for the National Writers Union and teaches classes about the business side of freelancing. She lives in San Francisco.

Denell Downum has worked in the editorial departments of Doubleday and Hyperion. She is currently a graduate student in English at the Graduate Center of the City University of New York.

Alec Dubro held numerous leadership positions in the National Writers Union, including national president (1987–1980). He sold his first article to *Rolling Stone* in 1968, and it's been pretty much downhill since then. Today, he lives in relative obscurity on Washington's Capitol Hill, writes for labor unions and nonprofits, and spends most of his free time hiding in the crawlspace. He appears regularly on the Nostalgia Channel's *Survivors of the Sixties.*

Betsy Feist is a freelance writer and editor of instructional materials and business communications. Her knowledge about RSI and ergonomics comes from personal experience, research, and workshops, including a 40-hour training program at the UAW Health and Safety Training Institute. She was a "worker consultant" on *Repetitive Strain Injuries: A Training Workbook for Office Workers* (Labor Institute, 1997) and wrote about carpal tunnel syndrome for *The Family Encyclopedia of Disease* (W. H. Freeman, 1998).

Bruce Hartford is Secretary-Treasurer of the National Writers Union (a volunteer position). Since 1981 he has made his living as a freelance technical writer in Silicon Valley. He is coauthor of *Breaking into Technical Writing,* published by the NWU Technical Writers Trade Group.

JoAnn Kawell is a nonfiction book author and the NWU's National Contract Adviser for Electronic Book Rights.

Susan Lee, EA, CFP, specializes in tax and financial services for writers and other freelancers in New York City.

Judith Levine is a book author and freelance journalist and a contract adviser and grievance officer for the National writers Union. Recently, she's been a columnist on oxygen.com and a frequent contributor to nerve.com. Her latest book, *Harmful to Minors: How Sexual Protectionism Hurts Children,* is slated for publication by the University of Minnesota Press in 2001.

David Lida is the author of *Travel Advisory* (William Morrow), a collection of short stories set in contemporary Mexico. His journalism has appeared in the *New York Times, Forward, Interview,* and the *Village Voice,* among other publications.

Yleana Martinez writes from Cambridge, Massachusetts. She has been a member of the NWU's Boston local since 1991 and is active in the union's National Diversity Committee.

Philip Mattera has been the NWU's National Book Grievance Officer and a national book contract adviser for more than a decade. He is the author of four books on economics, business, and labor, and he does research on corporations for community organizations and labor unions.

Tommye-Karen Mayer is a longtime member of the National Writers Union and the author/publisher of the internationally acclaimed and distributed *One-Handed in a Two-Handed World.* Described as a step-by-step guide to managing just about everything with the use of one hand, the book is endorsed by Dr. C. Everett Koop, Senator Bob Dole, former Veterans Administration chairman Senator Max Cleland (D-Ga.), and Patricia Neal. Mayer's articles and essays are published in *Topics in Stroke Rehabilitation, The Stroke Connection, Home Office Computing, Shooting Commercials,* the *Boston Globe, Boston Tab, North Shore Sunday, Marblehead Magazine,* and *Regional Review.* Mayer is an alumna of Wheaton College (Norton, Mass.), with a *cum laude* B.A. in sociology. She is also a nineteen-year survivor of a nearly fatal cerebral hemorrhage.

Activist, artist, and sometimes puppeteer, **Emma Morgan** lives and writes in Northampton, Massachusetts. She is the author of the poetry collections *Gooseflesh* (Clothespin Fever Press, 1993) and *A Stillness Built of Motion: Living with Tourette's* (Echolalia Press, 1996). Her work appears in anthologies, such as Kenny Fries's *Staring Back: The Disability Experience from the Inside Out* (Plume, 1997). Morgan has served as chair of the NWU's National Diversity Committee and is a member of the Boston local.

Todd Pitock formerly served as the chairperson of the National Writers Union's Journalism Division.

Catherine Revland has published 24 trade books, many of them in collaboration. She recently sold her first screenplay, *Joe Hill,* coauthored with Art Gatti.

Marcia Savin began her writing life as a playwright and by writing feature articles on the theater. Her short play "Just a Song at Twilight" is collected in *New Plays for Mature Adults* (Coach House Press). She now writes children's fiction. *Will Lithuania Comstock Please Come to the Courtesy Phone?* (Bridgewater Books) was her second book. She lives in Brooklyn and has two children and two grandchildren.

Marie Shear is a writer and editor by trade, a satirist and musical-theater lover by temperament, and a feminist by necessity. Her work has appeared in more than 40 publications. She has written and edited for publishers, nonprofits, business, and government and has received an award from the International Association of Business Communicators. A member of the National Writers Union since 1984, she lives in Brooklyn. When she grows up, she wants to be a syndicated columnist and social critic.

Jonathan Tasini is the president of the National Writers Union. He has written about labor and economics for numerous magazines and newspapers. He is also the author of *They Get Cake, We Eat Crumbs: The Real Story Behind Today's Unfair Economy,* available at www.workinglife.org.

Ray Tennenbaum has written about sports for all the golf magazines as well as for *Newsday, Wired, The Weekly Forward,* Yahoo!, *Internet Life,* and many other publications and websites.

Ken Wachsberger is the founder and first cochair of the National Writers Union's Academic Writers Organizing Caucus, as well as a book contract adviser specializing in academic publishing contracts, the NWU's Central Region vice president, and cochair of the Southeast Michigan Local. He is a freelance editor and the managing editor of several international academic journals. He is also the author or editor of numerous books. He teaches writing at Eastern Michigan University in Ypsilanti.

James Waller is a sometime journalist, sometime PR flack, sometime writing teacher, and sometime editor who lives in Brooklyn, New York. His work has appeared in *Out* and *Poets & Writers,* among other publications. He is secretary-treasurer of the Arch and Bruce Brown Foundation, which funds lesbian- and gay-themed arts projects.

Keith Watson worked as a small-town news editor in Minnesota and big-city TV critic in Texas before going freelance in 1985. He turned to business writing in 1990 and now works as a change management consultant. (Translation: "I write communications helping employees understand changes happening in their companies.") His small corporation, First Word, Ltd., is based in Chicago.

Index